NO HURLING AT
THE DAIRY DOOR

Dedicated to the memory of my parents

NO HURLING AT
THE DAIRY DOOR

Billy Rackard

BLACKWATER PRESS

Editors
Rosemary Dawson
Margaret Hawkins

Design & Layout
Paula Byrne

Cover Illustration
Joanne Clements

Historical Research
Joanne Clements

ISBN
0 86121 893 0

Produced and printed in Ireland by
Blackwater Press, 7/8 Broomhill Business Park, Tallaght, Dublin 24

British Library Cataloguing-in-Publication Data
A catalogue record is available from the British Library.

The author would like to thank all those who contributed photographs and other
material for use in this book.

CONTENTS

CHAPTER ONE

It was a bracing spring morning in the year 1895. The Wexford-Dublin train came to a halt at Enniscorthy station. As it did so, its brakes screeched as steel rubbed fiercely against steel. Steam hissed from the train's underbelly and the people waiting on the platform took a step or so backwards.

One of the passengers, Bob, an auburn, curly-haired youth, looked sad and apprehensive as he stood there. It was a big step for him, leaving his father's farm to go to Dublin and try his hand at the bar trade. With a heavy heart, he placed his few belongings on the rack overhead. As the train started to move, the door was suddenly yanked open and an excited young couple almost fell into the carriage. Putting their suitcases to one side, they proceeded to lean out the window, waving goodbye to their friends. Eventually, they sat down, still holding hands and exchanging furtive glances with their shy travelling companion.

Little did that trio realise the hand that fate was to play in their future. The happy couple were James and Esther Doran who were setting off on their honeymoon. They were not to know then that their companion on the train that day, Bob Rackard, was to marry their first born child, Anastasia, twenty-three years later. Bob and Anastasia were to have nine children, five boys and four girls. I was their youngest boy.

The young Bob Rackard became a popular and reliable barman, working in several different city hostelries and finally raising sufficient collateral to make a strong bid for a public house in Blackrock. The year was 1904. Many years later, whenever we travelled to Dublin with him, he would always go through Blackrock. Slowing the car to almost a crawl, he would point at the pub. "See there," he would say. "I don't know who your mother would have been or what you would have looked like, but if I had bid £10 more for that pub that is where you would have grown up."

He always said the same thing. Every time we approached Blackrock we would exchange knowing winks as the pub came in sight. Bob Rackard could have bid the extra £10 but there was a little voice inside him telling him to stop. He knew that just a few miles from where he was born back in County Wexford, a good property more suitable to his needs was coming up for sale. It was a fine old pub with a grocery business and approximately 120 acres of land. It was being sold by the Hickey family and was the original homestead of the 1798 hero, the famous John Kelly alias The Boy from Killanne.

The young Rackard a born stockman, had a deep love of the land. He was also a good judge of horses, a talent he was to put to good use and substantial financial gain through buying and selling, especially what were known as 'troopers' – a type of horse that was in big demand at that period. A few minutes was all he needed with a horse to tell you its defects.

He quickly went to work, was an immediate success at both business and farming and inside a short period, carried out extensive refurbishments to the old house which included a new slate roof. Prior to this, the house was deemed, by some, to be the longest thatched dwelling in the county. With the success of the business, he quickly added other parcels of land to his already considerable acreage.

For someone with a modest education and living in such a remote area, he surprised a lot of his friends by his intuition and daring in speculating successfully on the stock market. In the early thirties, he was to invest again. This time he purchased another pub with a farm attached, about three miles away in the neighbouring townland of Caim, a property which is now owned by my brother John.

His financial success was to offer him a good lifestyle. Enjoying his batchelor status to the full, he was the proud owner of a splendid motor car, which in those days was a real public declaration of financial well-being. Had his future wife, who was only about seven years old when he took over Killanne, remained where she was born in Glenglass, she and her family would have become customers in his new shop. But fate again intervened. Her mother, my grandmother, the former Esther Ann Keating, inherited a substantial house and farm in the neighbouring parish of Davidstown. Consequently, the first time that Bob set eyes on Anastasia, he was thirty-five and she eighteen. I often heard it said that my mother and her sister Molly were two of the finest girls ever to leave the parish of Davidstown. They stood an imposing five feet, eleven inches, with beautiful dark hair and each endowed with a good figure. In addition, they had a full secondary school education in the Loreto Convent, Gorey. There was no doubt but they were fancied by a lot of young men.

He meets his match

It was the autumn of 1914. Bob's two sisters, who were helping him to keep house, decided they should give a party. "Ask whoever you like!", encouraged their brother in an expansive mood. "What about those Doran girls over in Moneyhore?" suggested one. "A bit young", said Bob, "but ask them anyway."

When the party was in full swing, his sister tapped him on the shoulder. "Bob," she said, "I want you to meet Statia Doran." He turned about and there stood one of the most striking young women he had ever set eyes upon. "Statia Doran!" he repeated. She stood three inches above him and he couldn't take his eyes off her. "And you're only eighteen. . . ?"

As the party progressed, it was noted that the teenage girl and the older man were having cosy intermittent chats. As the evening came to a close and people were taking their leave, Bob was covered in confusion. "Hey Statia," he blurted, "you hurry up and get older!" His two sisters rounded on him. "For God's sake, Bob, what's come over you?" they chorused. The footloose and fancy-free bachelor was completely thrown. He was tiring of his bachelorhood and for the first time he had seen what he wanted most in his life and unusually for him, he just did not know how to handle it.

The next years were to be tortuous ones for him. At his age, how could he make a play for a strictly reared and convent educated eighteen-year-old? "Impossible," he thought, yet he kept hankering back to those delightful conversations he had had with her at the party. The only antidote to his agony was to totally immerse himself in the running of his business and farm.

CHAPTER TWO

It was the summer of 1915, nearly twelve months since Bob Rackard had first seen Statia. He was reading the newspaper in the garden, when, around came his friend Mike O'Brien. Mike was a man you trust and a man with a sense of humour. The sun was dropping into a western sky, silhouetting the contours of the Blackstair mountains behind him.

"It's you, Mike," he welcomed, "come on in and I'll get you a whiskey." He produced a bottle of seasoned Irish whiskey. Both men liked a drink and could hold their own if necessary with the strongest tipplers. After the first one, Mike began to chortle. "What's so funny?" Bob asked. Mike stood up. "Bob," he said, "you're a gambling man. I want to have a bet with you." "A bet?" echoed Bob. "Look" says Mike, "I'll have an even pound with you that you'll be picking the fraughans on the mountain next Sunday." "Me picking fraughans next Sunday? It's twenty years since I did that and I got bloody soaked. That's only for teenagers," he blurted. "You're out of your bloody mind, that's all. I'll take the bet." He slapped a pound on the table. "Cover that."

Bob couldn't help but notice the confidence on Mike's face as he produced his pound. He knew his friend wasn't a bluffer and this thought undermined his confidence. "Mike, you sod, you have some inside information!" Mike was smiling like the proverbial coal scuttle. "That's right," he retorted. "I'm told they never miss it." His grin got even better. "And it's usually just the girls on their own . . ."

"You bloody auld codger," hissed Bob, "but remember that bet isn't won or lost until next Sunday evening." "Fair enough," said Mike.

During the week, Bob ruminated over his options. He would sacrifice everything to catch up again with those Doran girls. This impulse was matched only by his desire to wipe that smirk off O'Brien's face.

During that period there were three events in the year which brought the people of the parish of Killane and surrounding district together. These events offered an opportunity for socialising – meeting old friends as well as making new ones. These occasions were the pattern in Killanne; Mountain or Fraughan Sunday and the local flapper race meeting. Fraughan Sunday, which appealed more to the energetic younger generation, consisted of the picking of dark little berries which grew on close-knit low-lying shrubs, and were to be found in abundance amongst the heather-mottled shoulders of the Blackstair mountains. Locals were known to make Fraughan jam and pie. Likewise, at one stage there was an outlet for them at a depot in Enniscorthy, where the fruit was dispatched again and used in the process of manufacturing dye.

It was 2.30 p.m. on Fraughan Sunday afternoon, and Bob Rackard had come to terms with the situation. He was driving from his home in Killanne, passing through the village of Rathnure about two miles away, and was now heading towards the far end of the parish where he would turn right up into Coolbawn, making it possible to travel with the pony and trap on a track angled along the side of the mountain onto the plateau which was the assembly point for the Fraughan pickers. Another three quarters of an hour's climb on foot would bring you to the summit, where a huge tide of heather intermingled with the fruitbearing shrub. Somewhere in the area he had hoped to meet up with the girls. The pony dug in his heels as he met the rising ground, lowered his head, straining into his collar like a good one. He had bought this pony recently. Now he knew for certain that he had a genuine animal and a good mover, all of which the vendor had told him. This thought pleased him and was having a soothing effect on his irascible mood. However, there was still the niggling thought, that even if he didn't attain his goal, he would still lose his bet, something which he knew his friend would never let him live down.

"What the heck!", he consoled himself, 'It's a lovely day and I'll enjoy the air and the view. To his surprise, the plateau was quite alive with activity. The few traders who made their way up had set their stalls and were bellowing vociferous advertisements about the mouth-watering delicacies they had to offer. Higgledy-piggledy about the place were donkeys and carts plus horses and ponies of all shapes and sizes; some bearing traps, more between the shafts of the simple flat-spring cart. Bicycles were dotted about, with an odd pair here and there giving the appearance of a pair of drunks as they propped each other upright. He tied the pony securely and started at a brisk pace up the scrubby hillside, his gaze continuously on the lookout for a pair of taller than average dark-haired girls.

As his gaze raked the hillside, now and then looking back down, his thoughts were diverted by the sheer splendour and exhilaration of the view down below. He could detect the Wexford coastline to the South, especially the havens of the Saltee islands; the greater Saltee remembered by historians as the place where Bagnel Harvey and Coleclough were captured after the 1798 rebellion. He saw Bree hill, Vinegar hill, Oulart hill, Forth mountain, and Carrigbyrne hill, (another fraughan-picking hill).

His mind wandered back in time to the rebellion of '98 when the insurgents lit fires on these high vantage points to pass on a quick message. It was almost twenty years since he was last here. It was a bright warm day and it was doing him good. Climbing higher, he looked back again, a warm breeze pulling at his face. Small light banks of clouds followed by bright patches of blue, swept across the valleys and hills way down below doing their best to rouse the endless patchwork of fields slumbering in the sun right across the baronies of Wexford. He was now approaching the summit.

He had exchanged greetings with many. Some acted with surprise at the sight of him, and others poked fun.

"Hey Bob, didn't know you were a fraughan picker." shouted a middle-aged man.

Climbing higher and higher onto the blue rocky plateau of the Blackstairs, passing a spot a couple of hundred yards to his right where a German fighter plane was to crash with full loss of crew members during the last world war. He picked his steps across the enormous rocky brow of the mountain top. He wasn't disappointed. There beneath lay the counties of Carlow and Kilkenny – a gargantuan sprawl of fertile fields stretching as far as the eye could see, and away to the left the silvery outline of the River Barrow as it snaked its path through Graiguenamanagh into picturesque St. Mullins on its way to meet up with its sister river the Nore, on their mutual journey to New Ross and Waterford.

As he looked down, he remembered reading in some history book that the Cistercian monks of Duiske Abbey in Graiguenamanagh, had crossed over this very mountain, bringing the message of God to the Wexford side. In the process, they were to found a new monastery in the townland from which it gets its name – Monksgrange.

He was so absorbed that for a short while he forgot his raison d'être. Bob Rackard was not a man to stand and stare, but as the warm bright sunshine flooded up and across the mountain top, a gentle wind lapped at his trouser legs, adding further pleasure to the senses. He stood enthralled and fascinated by the vast panorama. He had been working late the previous night and felt a little tired. He stretched out on the spring grass topped turf, pulling his hat over his eyes. He felt drowsy and in minutes he was fast asleep. When he finally looked at his watch, he was surprised to know he had been in this somnolent condition for over an hour. He leapt quickly to his feet, he brushed himself down, and hurried down the mountain side, his eyes scanning left and right in the hope of seeing the girls. There weren't many people to be seen.

Arriving back at the assembly plateau, he could see most people had left, there were just a few carts and an odd bike still there. He untied the pony, hopped in, and began the descent at a steady trot. He was feeling beaten. Driving at speed down a rugged path demands skill from both animal and driver. The more he drove this pony the more he liked him, a judicious pull on his mouth was all that was needed. The pony responded instantly, dropping his backside into the breeching, which were the only brakes available on the hazardous downhill journey. Again the joy of driving such a well-trained and honest animal was helping his mood. He made the descent to the boreen that would bring him eventually onto the main road, which was approximately three miles from Killanne and his home. About a half-mile on this road, there was a V-junction, where you turned left for Killanne, and right towards the parish of Davidstown. There were two similar ponies and traps, pelting along about two hundred yards ahead. His pony was pulling hard which was a mixture of wanting to get back home and to catch up with the others, he thought. His mind was a sort of blank as he was closing on the pair in front, but at the V junction, they both went right. He kept straight on. For about thirty yards, he could see across the low fence of the V junction. There were two people in the trap in front and they were waving at him. Two girls. He stood up to look closer, it was

them alright. He quickly waved back, but in seconds they were gone
out of sight.

Pattern at Killanne

Killanne is located at one end of the parish of Rathnure, where the
Catholic church, school and graveyard are. The original Catholic
church, the Church of St. Anne (hence 'Killanne') stood in the present
graveyard. There are no traces of it to be seen. The remaining rubble
was used in the building of the new Protestant church which was
built on the other side of the road, with its new graveyard, in
approximately 1832. The old graveyard was then abandoned and left
in the care of the Catholic community. The new graveyard in
Rathnure has long since taken over from the old Killanne one, whilst
the Protestant church with its glebe house, is in present day use as
well as being a feature of the local landscape.

In the early part of this century and in my youth, the annual
pattern in Killanne was a momentous event not to be missed. The
week prior to it, the graveyard would be a buzz of activity, general
tidying up being the order, with the next of kin busily cleaning
headstones, cutting grass, renewing gravel and black sand which
was brought from the derelict copper mines in nearby Caim. Some
laid fresh flowers on the graves of their departed loved ones.

As patterns went, for whatever reason I cannot say, the patterns
of Killanne always had top billing over the neighbouring ones. For
the biggest attendance and atmosphere, it vied with St. Mullins
across the mountain in County Carlow. The churchyard is circular,
which I'm told proves its age. Many of the tombstones are
eighteenth-century. There is one large square slab in the middle with
no engraving whatsoever. Whether this covered the site of an old
unmarked mass grave, one can only speculate. The picturesque
grounds are dominated by a massive Celtic cross, surrounded by iron
railings, which was erected over the remains of John Kelly, a
hundred years after his death. The boy from Killanne was
remembered and honoured in his old parish. Apart from the prayers
offered and respect paid to the departed, it was unquestionably a
social occasion; not to mention a boy-meets-girl opportunity. I will
never forget when at the age of six, my mother gave me money for
sweets for the first time (pocket money wasn't invented then), and
allowed me to go alone. It was only a short distance, but it gave me a
booster feeling of being a grown-up. I watched fascinated as the

hawkers set up their stalls. First off all, the ponies were unyoked and put away in a field nearby. Then the shafts of the flat carts were left on the ground with the rear end pointing at an angle skywards. Wide boards were then laid across the shafts from the ground right up along them, then the angled platform was covered with a white sheet. In a short time, these friendly middle-aged ladies, who usually came from the Duffry, Enniscorthy, would lay out a dazzling display of mouthwatering chocolates, sweets and fruit. How I looked forward to it! I would stand there goggled-eyed, in the midst of my own age group with youngsters who had broken away from protective parents and who were armed with similar money for sweets, each holding coins tightly gripped in hot little fists. We would move in closer, eyes widening, to have a more indepth survey of the vast array of goodies stretching from the ground right up to the end of the tilted flat cart.

"Well, sonny," would come the encouraging warm voice of Mrs O'Sullivan (whose face is etched in my memory), "What can I get you then?"

"Give me four of them, two of these and one of those".

As the crowd gathered, shouts came across the evening air, the traders getting fully into the swing of things.

"Oranges. . . apples . . . ripe pears . . . peggy's leg . . . bull's eyes, twelve for a penny . . . liquorice, four for a penny. Nice chocolates here now . . . and so on. I was a liquorice freak, and by late evening, I would have devoured endless strands of the stuff, each measuring about ten inches in length. As I got older I noticed that my annual vast intake of this leathery substance had spectacular impact on a certain bodily function which by chance I detected was taking on a totally different hue!

The pattern was responsible for bringing the generations together, everyone in their Sunday best. You would see a group here and there huddled around a headstone. Sadly, most of the graves were in a state of neglect, due to the passing of the years, or possibly emigration, or perhaps, families becoming extinct, and no one left to care. Grandmothers and grandfathers were easily identifiable, not just by their elderly appearance, but by their irresistible desire to scoop up the toddlers of the family and sway them from side to side, making funny faces in their attempt to extract a word or two from the very youngest of that close-knit family group. Teenagers were eyeing each other across rickety old headstones, indulging in faked interest about the dates.

"Look, here's one that says 1774."

"Here's one that's 1743".

The sudden interest in antiquity was just the beginning of a courting ritual.

A few hundred yards from the graveyard was the precious spring well, dedicated, not to an Irish saint, but to St. Anne, the mother of the Virgin Mary. It was venerated down the centuries. The narrow path to it was over mostly marshy ground, dotted with stones to ensure sound footing, but demanding accuracy of step, a further opportunity for teenagers to scamper and giggle as they brushed against each other, especially when going in the opposite direction.

The shrine is a very touching sight. A little gate opens into a tiny courtyard, surrounded by a low white-washed wall. Concealed behind a neatly pruned holly bush is a miniature grotto, filled with statues of the Virgin and various saints, photographs of popes and other objects of worship. Underneath, the crystal clear water where the spring runs a small pool has formed. Devotees have hung rosary beads at the entrance. Little jars of flowers have also been left there, and a couple of old mugs hang neatly on hooks for those who wish to drink the clear cool water. In extreme drought, whenever the village pump dried up, people were seen carrying white enamel buckets, making the long trek to the well which never failed them.

About eight o'clock, the parish priest arrived in his car. The Rosary then began, everyone going on bended knee. The single voice of the priest created a sharp contrast to the hum of the crowd as their voices droned across the evening air, answering the five mysteries of the Rosary. Once the Rosary finished, it was customary for the men to make a quick departure in the direction of my father's pub, which was just a few hundred yards away. In the warm July evening, the wives and youngsters remained on, forming animated groups, catching up on all the news with relatives and neighbours. The children scampered about, deepening the bond with their cousins.

"Sorry sonny, we're out of bulls' eyes" replied the contented looking woman to a disappointed ruddy-faced seven year-old. She kneaded her fingers through the coin-filled pockets of her pinafore as she spoke. It had been a good evening for traders. The blank spaces on the stalls and an abundance of empty cardboard boxes, piled to one side, were eloquent testimony to the purchasing onslaught.

Invitation

It was about this time of the evening in the year 1916 that Mike O'Brien walked through the door of Rackard's Pub. Bob and his two helpers were going hammer and tongs laying up drinks for eager customers who were bellied up two deep at the bar. "Bottle of Stout" shouted Mike over the din as he caught Bob's glance. He edged in sideways to the counter. His friend laid the drink in front of him and as Mike took an exploratory sip, Bob could not help noticing that sly grin spreading across his face. "You look like a man who wants to have another bet" he said caustically, throwing his pal an irreverent look as he moved away to serve another customer. About five minutes elapsed before Mike vigorously beckoned him. The two pals put their heads close together in order to hear properly.

"Look Bob," says Mike, adopting an advisory stance, "I know that Killanne graveyard holds no interest to you, but all the Dorans are buried here in Killanne. Do I have to spell it out for you? Guess who's over in the graveyard right now?"

"There! Have that one on me" said Bob as he slapped a whiskey on the counter. He untied his apron, had a quick word with one of the barmen and then disappeared into the kitchen. "Sarah," he shouted, "I want you for a second."

His sister who was in a room off the kitchen, detecting a note of urgency in his voice, quickly appeared.

"I want you to set the table with the best table cloth and cutlery – we could be having someone for tea" he announced. "I'll be back shortly and let you know exactly how many. Meanwhile do the best you can."

Pulling on his best jacket, he opened the door and was gone. He knew where the Doran burial plot was located, and as he approached the graveyard, he cautiously avoided anyone who might engage him in conversation. He sidled through the remnants of the crowd, circuitously approaching the area where the Doran family might be. Suddenly he got a clear view. His heart sank, he could only see Statia's sister and her younger brother John. No one else. Having checked thoroughly, he turned quickly, deciding to retrace his steps back home, when his attention was taken by someone calling his name. It was Mrs Doran who had been chatting to a friend, behind a tall headstone. She approached him and in a kindly voice called out, "Bob! How are you? Lovely to see you."

He tried to prevent his face reddening. He was feeling decidedly self-conscious as they exchanged niceties. Then out of the blue, Mrs Doran asked, "Bob, have you by any chance seen Statia? It is getting on in the evening and we are anxious to start the journey home. I think she is gone down to St. Anne's well," she continued, "perhaps if you're going down there you would tell her."

He doffed his hat to the elderly lady, and went in the direction of the Blessed Well. There were about six people standing in a little queue, all women waiting their turn to drink from the well and offer the customary small prayer. She did not see him as his gaze descended on her. She was the tallest. Her black hair was swept up into a coil at the nape of her neck under a fetching straw hat.

His heart thumped. She was, he thought, an exceptional example of young womanhood. As she moved up the queue, he could see her profile. It was as pretty as he had remembered. She radiated all the qualities a man could look for in the opposite sex. He was convinced more than ever that she was the woman for him.

"I would love to, and I'm sure they all would," she reassured him when he invited her and her family over for tea.

As they picked their way back across the marshy ground towards the graveyard, hopping on the odd stone here and there to ensure good footing, there was no evident strain in the conversation. Statia, not given to being a chatterbox, surprised herself with her flow of talk. He was feeling elated because normally she was with other people, cutting out chances for private conversation.

Mrs Doran accepted his invitation with enthusiasm, which sent a warm glow through Bob. His instinct told him that this lady was on his side and was encouraging a closer relationship between her daughter and himself.

"Sure" said Statia's brother John, "but if you don't mind Bob, I have a yen for something stronger than tea."

John, a fine young man was to play centrefield in 1918 on the Wexford football team which beat Kerry, to win four All-Irelands in a row – a feat only once before achieved.

First World War

Whilst Bob Rackard was in tentative pursuit of the delightful Anastasia, grimmer happenings were taking place on a global and national level.

The First World War did not impinge greatly on the quiet village of Killanne. A few of the young local men fell under the sway of the recruiting drive, which had been backed by John Redmond, and joined the British army. Expectations of life, once you landed in France, was mighty short, and some would not return. There was nothing like the shortage of necessities that the Second World War would bring to the civilian community. In fact, it was a prosperous time for the Wexford farmers who had a ready market in war-torn England. Also about four thousand people, both men and women were employed in Kynoch's munitions factory in Arklow. Some others would have joined the fifty thousand men and women employed in munition work in England.

Closer to home and of more direct concern, was the 1916 Uprising. Volunteers were put on alert just three days before Easter Sunday. Immediately two hundred men, along with the Cumann na mBan and Fianna Eireann came together in Enniscorthy. They took over the Athenaeum, (where the ladies of the Cumann na mBan set up a make-shift hospital), and other buildings. Police volunteers in turn, re-inforced the regular RIC, who retreated into their barracks and the Bank of Ireland, which they successfully defended.

All communications with Wexford were broken off and there followed severe disruption of everyday life. Sinn Féin issued a proclamation that the town was now in the hands of the Republicans, and that all businesses and public houses were to close, only gas workers and bakers were to be allowed to continue working. Twenty cars, all available petrol, and an unspecified number of motor bikes and ordinary bicycles were commandeered, as were food and clothing. There were house-to-house searches, and all arms were confiscated. Very soon food became scarce, and by Saturday, the shops were bare. Sinn Féin then ordered rationing. Since widows and pensioners could not collect their pensions, grocery shops were instructed to supply them with necessities against future payment.

In order to stop British troops from coming to the rescue from Rosslare, the Irish Volunteers sent out patrols to sabotage the railway line. Shooting broke out between the two sides, and one RIC man and a little girl were wounded. Paul Galligan led other volunteers into Gorey and Ferns, and the RIC withdrew from these areas to concentrate their forces in Arklow.

On the Saturday, Pearse surrendered in Dublin. Two volunteer leaders, Seamus O'Dubhghaill and Sean Etchington, were dispatched under escort to visit him in prison on Arbour Hill. No one in Enniscorthy could believe that this was happening. They returned the following day with Pearse's orders to surrender. Some, including Pat Keegan, Jim Cleary, Mat Holbrook and Jack Leacy wanted to continue the fight, but they were outvoted and on the Monday the rising in Wexford, was over.

Many were arrested, and though no one was to die a large number were jailed and interned. Worse might have befallen them had it not been for the efforts of the Enniscorthy Peace Committee, who negotiated the truce and surrender, wanting to save further bloodshed. *The Free Press,* the following month, wrote that the families of the arrested men were now dependent on the charity of St Vincent de Paul.

Thereafter, an armoured train, rejoicing in the name of *Enniscorthy Emily* was used on the railway line.

The British military were to be seen in a show of sabre-rattling, doing much drilling and arms practice in Abbey Square. Their manoeuvres were imitated by the local children, using hurley sticks!

CHAPTER THREE

Bob Rackard did not set eyes on his future wife again until the Spring of 1917. What is known as flapper (or flat) racing was popular during that era. Most parishes staged a meeting, and it was run on Bob's land almost adjacent to the house. He was nicely surprised and pleased to see the Dorans (who were keen horse lovers) en famille amongst the throng. Being a member of the organising committee he naturally had a strong input into the running of things. Dressed in his sporting best, he felt he cut a good image. Once again he invited them back to the house and once again there was general acceptance. For a man who had offered such hospitality, it seems strange that there was no reciprocation. He was later to discover the reason. He and his future wife, by virtue of the age gap, were moving in different circles. Mrs Doran would gladly have offered him an invitation, but it appears that her daughter was opposed to the idea. She cared for Bob, but like most single girls of her age, she was enjoying life and was determined to have her fling. This she was doing with great gusto, being a warm favourite at house dances in the district and a regular visitor to the Enniscorthy Athenaeum whenever a dance was held there. However, without realising it, her attitude to life was undergoing a change. Quite a few of her contempories had married, and her younger sister had become engaged.

It was the end of summer of 1917. Bob Rackard was driving his motor car along the main New Ross – Enniscorthy road. He turned left at a cross known as The Leap, and left again to shorten the journey back to his home in Killanne. Taking this turn he realised that it would bring him past the avenue entrance to Moneyhore House, which ran almost parallel to the road. He had no particular thought in mind, but as the avenue entrance loomed closer, he was suddenly overcome with a surging conviction. Braking slightly, he drove in the entrance, up the long avenue. As he progressed his convictions evaporated into self-doubt. By the time he had brought the car to a gentle halt on the gravel in front of the hall door, he had worked himself into an emotional frenzy.

He got out of the car, and for a few seconds, he was contemplating jumping back in and making a fast exit, when the hall door opened. It was Statia's younger brother Pat.

"Bob," he said, offering a calm friendly smile, "Come on in".

It may have been an impulsive decision to turn up that avenue, but as events were to unfold, it was the most fortuitous one he would ever make. Going through the door, he was impressed by the size of the hallway, which had a fine stairway leading to a broad upper landing. He quickly observed that pride of place was given to a gilt-framed painting in oils of Mrs Doran's uncle, the late Dr James Keating, Bishop of Ferns as you entered it was impossible to avoid the stern gaze of his lordship.

"This way," said Pat tapping Bob on the shoulder and directing him left, through a door into a lovely spacious sitting room. He noticed the high ceiling edged with a beautifully moulded cornice. Beyond the nicely draped bay windows was a formal well-kept garden.

Mr Doran Senior was reading a local newspaper, with his feet stretched out in front of him. As they entered the room he looked up over his spectacles "Bob!" he said. "The very man, come over a minute." Slapping the newspaper with the back of his hand, he pointed his finger at an article in the paper. "Look at that!" he said. Bob leaned down to decipher the article.

"I know," he said "Cattle prices are always better on the Dublin market. The farmers should organise themselves to do something about it."

"Never mind that," said Pat, interrupting the conversation, "Come and sit in here, we know you're fond of a game of cards.

Seated at the table with Pat were John, his younger sister Molly, and her husband-to-be, Jim Bowe.

"A game is always more interesting with five playing," announced Pat as he dealt Bob his hand of cards.

This was to be the forerunner of many card games for him at this very table. Three-quarters of an hour had elapsed and there still was no sign of the elusive Statia or her mother. He was beginning to think, having taken his courage in his hands, that this visit was all in vain when there were audible sounds of a horse and trap going past the house.

"That'll be mother and Statia" said John, "They've been visiting relations."

He felt his pulse rate quicken at the mere mention of Statia. He was annoyed at himself having to strive at remaining calm. After what seemed like a year, he heard footsteps, the door opened and there stood Statia. She was wearing a trim-fitting tweed suit, and looked a picture of rural elegance. She pulled a beret from her head, shaking her dark hair as she did so. Her cheeks showing a healthy flush from the evening air as it enveloped her face on the drive back home.

"Bob! What a nice surprise!"

She had barely said so when Mrs Doran came through the door behind her. He stood up from the table, but both women immediately gestured at him to sit down.

"You are staying for tea" says Mrs Doran "and we are not taking no for an answer."

He felt enormous relief and had a strong feeling that everything was going his way. As darkness closed in and the evening lengthened, every member of the family tactfully took their leave, abandoning the room to Bob and the girl he had set his heart on.

Late in the evening a fire had been lit. Its dying embers in the small hours of the next morning, bore witness to the beginning of a love affair that was to end in Statia Doran becoming Mrs Robert Rackard.

Wedding Bells

It was late spring in 1918 that Bob Rackard, surely one of the proudest men to make the short walk down the aisle of the parish church of Davidstown, emerged into the sun light. Clutching his arm was Anastasia Doran, the girl he had fallen for four years previously. It was an ecstatic moment for the happy couple as they were showered with confetti by members of both families and a host of friends and well-wishers. The honeymoon, as with all couples in those days, was spent in Dublin city.

When Anastasia returned to Killanne with her husband after their honeymoon, she was not going back to what could be considered a normal scene for a newly-married girl. First of all, the house she was going to live in displayed all the symptoms of a well-established bachelor pad. It was badly in need of a woman's touch and as a lot of wives will testify, bachelor habits become ingrained, but in this case it was even more so. She would also be saddled with the arduous task of seeing that six maybe eight people were fed three times a day. However, luckily for her new husband, she was a well-trained competent young woman, who was not afraid of hard work. She was an excellent cook and capable of shouldering more than her share of responsibility. Her upbringing had given her good qualifications in all these matters, and especially where running a farm was concerned. However, the business that was going on around the house was a different matter. Apart from a pub, a country store of that period stocked groceries, hardware, coal, manures, petrol; then there was the buying of wool, and feedstuffs. Most people were totally dependent on their local shop. The other alternative was a bumpy journey of seven miles over a dusty pot-holed road to Enniscorthy. While some people made that journey once a week, the majority only made it once a month. She was not accustomed to this. I once heard my mother say that the house was a bit like living in a railway station. You never knew which door would open, or who would come through next.

Shortly after returning to Killanne from the honeymoon, my mother was to experience a strange happening. (She was not someone who concocted stories. Nor was she a nervous individual who easily imagined things or jumped to conclusions quickly). One Sunday evening, she was reading a book in the good parlour, sitting by the window, in order to catch the remaining daylight, when she heard a thump coming from the upper room known as the parlour. The good parlour has a small passageway to the parlour which was connected to the kitchen by another small passageway. She left the book down and went up to investigate. There was nothing detectable to indicate the cause of the noise. She returned unalarmed to her book, when after a few minutes she heard it again, only this time much louder. There was a piano in the room and her first thought, was that it was a cat trapped somehow inside the piano. So she opened the top of the piano but there was nothing. She remained calm. She returned to her book. She had barely started reading when the entire room erupted with a cacophony of noises, which included the movement of chairs. She immediately jumped up, put on her coat, and set off on foot to meet her husband, whom she met coming back up the road having visited his family on horseback in nearby Ballinlug. He jumped down from the saddle when he saw her. "Statia! What's the matter?" he asked, detecting signs of unease about her.

When she told him, he said it was her imagination. They didn't row over it, but next day she got in touch with the parish priest, who was more than helpful. Not alone did he bless the entire house, but he was most sympathetic. In fact, he chided my father for his lack of understanding and concern.

Cat in an Iron Mask

My mother took great pleasure in relating another story about things going bump in the night. Contrary to the previous incident the reasons for the noises in this case turned out to be of a hilarious nature.

It was a sad night in Moneyhore. That day James Doran, my grandfather, had been laid to rest in Davidstown churchyard. It was approaching the stroke of midnight and the entire family, including my grandmother, had just climbed the stairs and were at that very moment gathered on the landing heading for their beds when the most horrendous noise came from the dining-room below. It seemed like all hell had been let loose. Everyone stood looking at each other petrified. The noise stopped, but started again. My uncle John turned to his brother Pat, who was ashen-faced. "If you come with me, I'll go down" he said.

A bizarre sight met their eyes. There were various jugs on the table, one of which was a large narrow-necked enamelled jug. A sizeable tom cat had found his way onto the table, decided to have some milk, put his head into the jug, but then got stuck. Naturally, he panicked with the jug jammed on his head and milk splashing in his face. He careered about the room, scattering cups and saucers in all directions. On the landing above, the other members of the family stood transfixed with fear. They could not believe their ears when they heard laughter emanating from below. The dining-room door opened. John's face appeared wearing a large smile.

"Come on down" he shouted amidst the din, as the cat continued on its merry-go-round. "We need help." There was a certain amount of relief mixed with perplexity as the rest descended the stairs: "What is it?"

"We need a cat posse," called John, forgetting about his grief. Eventually the cat in the iron mask was finally set free.

At Home in Killanne

It was in the parlour that the family spent most winter evenings, although the kitchen, with its open fire and wheel bellows was a great favourite. You could look up the chimney on a bright winter's night and view the stars. The hob corner became one of my favourite spots, listening to the locals spin yarns, as they talked hurling or told hair-raising ghost stories. The open fire was located in a corner of the kitchen with a long wooden bench seat against the wall. On the other side was a draught-protective partition that went up to the ceiling, shielding a similar bench. Whenever the neighbours called for a chat, it was usually around the kitchen fire we would congregate on a cold winter's night.

Looking from there through the kitchen window, you could see the top of the Blackstair mountain protruding above the farmyard buildings. Outside the presence of snow on the mountain top or frost on the hills nearby always seemed to make the fire burn cosier and brighter. On such a night, the hob corner was a heavenly spot. The kitchen then had a plain cement floor, which was scrubbed once a week. Most of the houses of that era did not know the luxury of tap water or flush loos. Water was brought by bucket from a large hand pump located in the farmyard. As the years progressed, water from this particular pump was to become a serious health hazard resulting in practically the whole family and a few workmen contracting typhoid fever. Toilet facilities were a commode in each room and a 'jerry' under every bed. Likewise washing facilities in a bedroom consisted of the wash stand, which contained a pitcher of cold water and an enamel or delph basin. Every house of that period had an outside toilet, usually located near a small stream (if possible). The outside toilet I remember, was a nice wooden building actually boasting of 'ladies' and 'gents,' built across a little stream which flowed past the end of the garden. One of my earliest memories was listening to my mother chatting excitedly to her housekeeper.

"I know he will" she said, her eyes lighting up, "He's like that. Once he's made up his mind, he moves quickly and gets it done."

She was referring to my father who had just given the go-ahead to install a bathroom and proper toilets. There was no present day equipment for pumping water in those days, a method was devised to collect rainfall off the larger yard roofs, and direct it into a big cement tank, which was built as high as possible to allow for a gravity flow. The bathroom, a new building which was added onto the end bedroom, offered a pleasant view of the nearby mountains. The S-bend, which was probably the single most important invention after the wheel, was about to hit Killanne.

I will never forget the first night it was operational. There was a queue of young Rackards, all demanding to be first, as my mother consumed with delight, turned on the hot water tap.

"Look!" she exclaimed, as we all gathered around her, "it's boiling hot".

That was certainly one night the entire family went to bed squeaky clean. Prior to that I can remember being bathed in a wooden tub in front of a glowing kitchen fire, the water supplied from kettles that boiled hanging over the open hearth from what was called a crane. The crane was a straight piece of iron attached to an upright on one side and could swivel out from over the fire. It was always a source of fascination to me, and usually had a big black kettle hanging from its downward arm, an arm which had adjustable holes in order to raise or lower whatever was attached. Likewise, the arm could be pushed to either side of the fire. Many's the time I watched as the fire appeared to aggravate the kettle with extra heat, causing it to complain and spit until eventually it would boil over onto the offending flames. This was usually accompanied by a shout "Will someone lift up that kettle?"

Civil War

"How many bedrooms have you overhead, Bob?' enquired Mike O'Brien of his newly married friend as he sat up to the pub counter. one evening.

"Six," says Bob as he poured out Mike's Guinness.

"Six!" laughed O'Brien. "Too many Bob, you'll never fill 'em all up." Years later, with a few drinks on board, I once heard my father recall that, he eventually put a complete stop to such remarks from O'Brien as nine children were born. Sally and Essie arrived first, followed by five boys, Nickey, Jim, Bobby, John and myself; then two more girls, Molly and Rita. There was just a year to a year and a half between each. My mother, in more ways than one, was proving her worth and versatility.

It was Monday evening, 3rd July, 1922. My mother was seated at the parlour window with three month-old Nickey in her arms. and the two little girls were playing at her feet. Glancing through the window, she could scarcely believe her eyes. There were two men coming into the yard; one extremely tall, approximately six feet three inches, his height accentuating the other, who appeared to be limping. Taking a closer look, she was astonished to see the bedraggled lame figure of her brother-in-law John A. Rackard, who like my father, ran a similar business of pub and general stores in Enniscorthy, now know as the Club. John A. Rackard was a dapper little man, always formally dressed, complete with trilby hat and Hitler moustache, and usually arrived in his motor car. She was startled by his dishevelled appearance. The other man was a close friend of John's, big, happy Joe O'Malley, manager of a wholesale business in Enniscorthy. She ran frantically to open the door.

"Good God, what's happened?' she asked.

"We're lucky to be alive, and that's a fact," said big Joe.

It was obvious to the two men that my mother had no idea of what was going on in Enniscorthy.

"Look," said John, a grim shadow crossing his face, "Enniscorthy is no place to be right now. It's the luck of God we weren't killed with those bloody fools shooting at each other".

"But what happened?" my mother interjected, "Come on into the parlour and have a stiff drink".

"Why did you have to walk here? Where's your car?" she asked.

"Look Statia," said John, shifting uneasily in his chair. "Myself and Joe were just out for a walk, when suddenly it all started. Bullets were whizzing in every direction, windows were blown out. It was terrifying. I wasn't going to risk crossing over the bridge to Templeshannon (where he had his business) and neither was Joe.

Half the town has left to stay in the country until it's over. No one would risk driving a car out of town through all that. The IRA or irregulars as some call 'em wouldn't think twice about taking it or if it goes to that, they would also clean out your premises to keep them in supplies."

As it transpired, the irregulars raided many premises for supplies of clothing, food and drink, sometimes with a promise to pay later.

"You know what all this bloody business is about?" Joe asked, looking towards my mother, "well, if you don't, I'll tell you right now."

His face changed to a painful expression. "The whole damn lot of them are Irishmen, and not so long ago they were all fighting together in the name of Irish freedom, under the Irish Republican army banner. Now you have half of 'em with the Free-Staters, whilst the other half won't agree to anything, only the gun. I suppose it's power that they are both after. Yes, that's it," said big Joe gravely.

Civil war had just reared its ugly head in Enniscorthy, beginning on Friday 30th June, with Free State troops occupying the old castle and barracks, whilst the splinter IRA took over the Protestant church. In the countryside, guerrilla IRA warfare was causing havoc, striking at Free State military outposts and ambushing patrols. This had been the pattern throughout the country, but now it was County Wexford's turn. Strangely enough, Enniscorthy was the only town in the county where rival forces had taken up positions. Late Saturday evening, 1st July, the people of Enniscorthy were to share in the horrors which civil war inevitably brings, with gunfire criss-crossing the town as both sides took up vantage positions.

The battle in Enniscorthy was to last four days. Anyone that could, fled the town. Several were injured. Shops, businesses, banks closed. Bombs exploded shattering doors and windows, some houses later collapsing. My mother was very frightened by the news. She had a lot of friends in Enniscorthy and was naturally concerned.

"You can stay here as long as you wish" she told the two men.

"I want to put these two to bed, it's past their time. Bob should be back shortly; he just went up the land to inspect some cattle. When he comes in, I will fix something for you to eat."

The four days battle in Enniscorthy resulted in one IRA man shot dead, several people injured, many houses badly damaged, including the court-house. Meanwhile, in the countryside, particularly in the Kyle area, midway between Wexford and Enniscorthy, members of the Irregulars or IRA, now supported by the famous Tipperary flying column of IRA men, continued to carry out guerrilla tactics against Free State targets.

One Sunday morning two weeks later, my father and mother came out of Rathnure church after seven o'clock mass. There was a serious look about the two of them as they wended their way amongst the dispersing after mass crowd, towards a nearby farmyard where they had secured a pony and trap. My father untied the pony, hopped in the trap and proceeded towards the roadway. As he reached the gate who was coming through for the same reason only Mike O'Brien.

"Bob!" said O'Brien, looking surprised. "What's a man like you doing driving an outfit like this, and you the owner of a fine motor car."

My father turned a cold eye on his friend.

"So you haven't heard then?" he asked, a grim outline to his mouth.

"Heard what?" asked O'Brien. "Have you crashed the bloody car!"

"Not exactly" said my father, frowning as he hopped out of the trap and pulled the pony to one side. He beckoned his friend towards him. "Look Mike," he said, "You've known me a long time. I have no interest in politics. As far as I'm concerned, the Volunteers, Sinn Féin, IRA, Irregulars, Republicans, call 'em what you damn well like, they are all the same crowd and who are the Free Staters? They're the same too, only they're in power."

"Bob," interjected Mike, "What's the matter? You're in an awful state".

It was the first time he had seen my father so worked up about politics.

"What's the matter?" repeated my father, "The matter is that my car has been taken and not a drop of spirits left on the shelves."

"God, Bob, I'm very sorry to hear that," said O'Brien, placing a hand on his shoulder.

"You know" said my father drawing a deep breath, "We're a long time trying to get the English out of this country, and in the last few years we've finally made some progress, even getting rid of those blackguards, the Black and Tans that Lloyd George sent over to frighten the people. Now look at us, fighting amongst ourselves, even families are split." My father was close to tears.

"We must be the laughing stock of the world. Look Mike, personally I don't care who runs this country as long as they are decent, responsible, able men who have the peoples' interest at heart. But any crowd that goes around interfering with private property. How the hell can that solve anything? It's scandalous, and something that just shouldn't happen."

By 1923, the civil war had more or less ended, leaving the country in a desperate condition, railways, bridges, factories, creameries, shops and houses destroyed. It finally culminated in some sort of peace, with the formation of a Free State government under W.T. Cosgrave.

I never even once heard my father or mother discuss politics, but without question, the taking of his car and the raid on his premises had left its mark on my father.

CHAPTER FOUR

In 1932, two years after I was born, the Rathnure GAA club was formed. A mere seven years previously, Wexford had won Leinster Senior Football championship, and going back a few more years, the county chalked up six Leinster and four senior All-Ireland football titles in a row.

It never ceases to baffle me, bearing in mind, the County's tradition for Gaelic Football, that the Rathnure GAA Club, once formed, had absolutely no interest in the promotion of football. It was to be strictly hurling, a phenomenon that applied to a few other parishes, including the neighbouring parish of Cloughbawn. Prior to the formation of the Rathnure club, the game was played extensively in the parish just for sheer pleasure. Anyone who knows the joy of stroking a hurling ball up into the air will understand that; or the fierce tackle to possess or dispossess that is another joyous aspect of the ancient code. It now appears that at that time, the parish of Rathnure was a dormant hurling melting pot, which boiled over into a flow of passion and enthusiasm for the game that has never since abated. It is what today makes the parish of Rathnure one of the most revered and synonymous names with the sport. A Rathnure footballer though is a rare species, but he is easily identifiable. He kicks a football with a hurley stick in one hand – a true testimony to the affection he has for the smaller ball.

Wexford is a county that can boast of just moderate success at the game of hurling, nonetheless the deprivation of notable trophies down the years has never eroded interest in the game. When I was once asked to give a talk to a Wexford hurling team, I remember saying "There are no fifteen men in County Wexford, no matter what the code, or under what banner they exist, who will carry with them the hopes, backing and affectionate support that you fifteen will have. From the lighthouse of Hook in the very south, to Tara Hill in the north, they will come out of the valleys and from the hills to be with you, let it be victory or defeat."

"What is it about the game of hurling that makes it touch the very soul of Irishmen?" I once asked a well-known gaelic footballer, Louis Rafter, who holds seven county titles. "I would trade three football medals for one hurling title," was his reply. That huge tide of interest and fascination for the game was the same in 1936, when I was just beginning to understand the meaning of the word 'hurling'.

To become a top exponent in any sport, I am convinced that you must not be denied the opportunity to come to grips with that sport at an early age. Who said, "give me the child at six and I'll give you the man at twelve?"

Our consumer society today, I believe, with its wide sporting menu, has resulted in a dearth of specialists. When you only concentrate on one game your chances of reaching the top in that game are greatly enhanced. Had I been offered a wide variety of choices it's likely that my record wouldn't have included three All-Ireland medals. My love affair with the game began at the age of five. To me, hurling is the fastest, most exciting and skilful field game that this planet has ever seen.

Mrs Dreelan and the pot sticks

Mrs Dreelan put her head over the half-door. "Mrs Rackard," she shouted, "them chaps have gone off with those pot sticks again." "Them chaps again," was her usual war cry. As we got a little older, the situation for a different reason between Mrs Dreelan and ourselves was to worsen. Our mother was to intervene once with almost catastrophic results, as far as we boys were concerned.

However, it was Mrs Rackard, and not her husband, that noticed that her sons needed something more than pot sticks. I shall never forget that joyful day. Nickey had started college in St. Kierans, Kilkenny, his parents had just returned from leaving him there. She came into the kitchen, depositing some of her purchases on the table;

most of the girls and us four boys were gathered around her. She snapped her fingers, her face beaming.

"Right chaps" she says "Do you want to see what's on the back seat of the car?"

We threw her a puzzled look,

"Don't just stand there! Go and see!" she ordered. We fell over each other as we raced outside to look and there on the back seat were four new Neary hurley sticks and a proper hurling ball.

She had purchased the hurley sticks with all of us in mind. The shortest stick was obviously for me, being the smallest; but a fight erupted over who should have which one. We grabbed them from each other, testing the spring. I often heard old-timers pontificate that a stick made from the young ash tree, if it's really a good one, should almost wrap around your body. My mother finally swatted us into submission.

"If you don't stop fighting this very minute, I shall burn the lot," she threatened, her face displaying unconcealed annoyance as she spoke." "Now there, that's yours and that's yours," and so she continued "and if there is any more scrapping, I shall burn them. Do you understand?"

Burn the lot! A terrifying thought. With the passing of time, my mother discovered that such a threat always brought co-operation.

"Who's going to keep the ball?" asked Bobby, a question that seemed to take my mother by surprise. I could almost hear her mind ticking. Four hurley sticks and only one ball – a tricky one. She turned to Jimmy. "You are the the eldest, you take it and when you're finished playing bring it back to me; and you are not to play in the front yard. You know how your father feels about hurling, and if you were to break a window, you can imagine what he would be like. Go up to the haggard or down to the Barrack field."

The Garda Barracks or RIC as it was originally known, was built on my father's land and behind it was a perfect spot for practicing. However we did not play in the Barrack field continuously until we were older. This field about two hundred yards from the house and with my father's permission became the official local practice ground. I remember seeing on one occasion, up to forty-five players of all age groups pucking about there. As we grew older, the Barrack field was to bear witness to some horrendous hurling dog fights. We called it 'In and Out' or 'Backs against Forwards', with someone outfield repeatedly pucking the ball back in as it was cleared out. However, for most of our early years we got permission to play in the front yard which measured approximately thirty-three yards by sixteen yards. The house and shop windows were to one side and, apart from the entrance off the road, the yard was more or less encompassed by store houses and a garden wall. By the time the Rackard boys graduated to playing with adults in the practice field, skills were already well-honed, a byproduct of the struggles that had taken place in the front yard.

An old store about thirty yards away with a loft overhead, the outer wall of which faced on to the road, was another favourite spot. There were no windows or doors – just plain wall facing the roadway. This was ideal for a puck about solo. Each one of us spent hours and hours bashing a sponge ball to and fro against this wall. We also played handball against it. During the warm summer days and long evenings, this area was to play a big part in my life, not just in developing my hurling skills, but also in making contact with locals. I would stop to allow a pedestrian or bicycle go past or perhaps, someone driving their cows home for milking nearby.

The village pump, known as Riley's pump simply because it was located close to Riley, the school teacher's house, was also a cause of passing traffic that now and then brought a halt to hurling against that wall.

Fred Crabbe, the local postman, was a regular with his two enamel white buckets, and I always hoped that he would not meet a neighbour coming from the pump. Old Fred, a crooked pipe wobbling about in the side of his mouth, usually had a new yarn he wanted to test on someone, and that could go on and on. I often cursed under my breath when this happened, but the worst offenders when it came to stopping play, were without question Coakley's cows. When they came ambling past, especially on their inward journey from grass for milking, they never missed without one going plop plop plop; not just heaps, but a steaming gooey, thick green liquid trailed along the dusty road. Whenever Jimmy, Bobby, John and myself were playing, we had an arrangement to try and counteract the unwanted mess. The Coakleys were very good friendly neighbours, but old Mr Coakley with his bowler hat and handlebar moustache looked too formidable for us to try our first gambit at prevention. If he wasn't driving the cows, the four of us would shout, banging as many cows as possible on the rump with hurley sticks. "Shoo! Shoo!" we would shout, working them into that silly trot, their udders swinging from side to side. The trouble with this system was you could have a clear run or a disaster. They could all let go simultaneously, creating an impossible mess. The second answer to the problem was taking turns with a yard brush, sweeping it to one side near the entrance to the yard.

"It's your turn Jim" shouted John as, sure enough, one of Coakley's cows found that patch of road irresistible. Jim dropped his hurley and ran to the back of the house. He quickly re-appeared with the yard brush and started brushing towards the low wall with his head down, it was obvious that he was in a foul mood. At that very moment my father, who was becoming interested in seeing his sons banging the ball to and fro, strode out from the shop, a happy look on his face and placed his elbows on the wall. Jim was brushing furiously, totally unaware of his presence. "Them fucking Coakleys and their shittin' cows!" My father was horrified at any youngster using a four-letter word, not to mention one of his own sons doing so. Looking down at Jim as he brushed towards him, his benign countenance altered to an explosion of repellance. He looked as if he was struck by lightning.

I have many memories of that patch of roadway just in front of that old store, where John Kelly used to hold meetings during the organisation of the United Irishmen prior to the rising of 1798.

The new hurley sticks which our mother had given us were the pride and joy of our young lives. They changed colour from the clean, smooth-shaven bright ash to a grimy dirty colour; the backs of them were frayed from continuous contact with the hard surface of the yard. One was kept intact with metal bands around what's called 'the boss'. It didn't matter; like a good fiddle they seemed to improve with age, and the pride in personal ownership was just as strong as the day we were first given them. However, for me the pleasure and excitement I was deriving from all this was to end abruptly.

CHAPTER FIVE

As I looked up from my bed, I could see my mother's face swimming about the room. She was talking in hushed tones to a person I could not identify. Then I heard the cultured voice and gentle comment, and I knew immediately that it was the family doctor, Dr Bowen from Enniscorthy. Putting on his warmest bedside manner, he leaned over me. Placing his hand on my forehead, cajoling as he inserted a thermometer under my tongue, "That's a good lad" as he encouraged me to keep my mouth tightly shut. Neither spoke until he had retrieved the thermometer. Digesting the results, he moved towards the windows. He turned to face my mother, a grave look on his countenance, and in a quiet whisper, although he may not have realised it, I could hear him say, Mrs Rackard, I'm afraid this little lad is very sick. Right now he has a temperature of 104°. It looks like he has contracted double pneumonia. It's a dangerous situation - that temperature must come down right away. The only cure at the moment is to make a huge bran poltice, smear it over a clean sheet and wrap it around him as hot as he can bear it. You repeat this as soon as the poltice gets cold. Get some cold water immediately and begin swabbing his forehead and chest. A further rise in temperature could be fatal."

I must have been near death's door, because I can quite clearly remember the local Parish Priest going over me with the last rites. My mother was deeply religious and had unmitigated belief in the power of the priest. Like a lot of her contempories she felt that some priests were saints and had special access to the Good Lord when it came to asking for a little miracle.

Her favourite clergyman was from her former parish Davidstown, rumbustuous old Canon Power who spent a lot of time in the Doran household. I heard my granny once say that he was a great man to pray over people, and sure enough, my mother sent word that one of her brood was in need of assistance. Although very doddery, he made the eight-mile journey in his horse and trap and I can still see him in his long-skirted soutane. A tall man resembling a large wounded bat as he waddled through the bedroom door, he was from a horsey family and liked hunting with hounds. Accordingly his first words, which struck forever in my memory were: "Foxing, are you?". He then exploded into loud prayer. It was almost frightening, but my mother's satisfied face as she looked and listened to Canon Power's prayers just for me, her son, abated any apprehension that may have been lurking inside my fragile little frame at that moment.

I was to convalesce not for weeks, but months, and when it was all over, if I started running my breathing would resemble that of a broken-winded horse. I was compelled to wear a red flannel vest, something which I found humiliating and which brought derisory comments from my brothers. My father was a firm believer in the worth of red flannel and always had a piece tacked on his waistcoats, to cover the small of his back. Whilst I derived some solace from that fact, it was a moment of uncontainable joy when my mother changed me back to the usual pure wool white vest worn by most people in those days. Unlike the present day, houses were cold; there was no such thing as central heating! And when travelling by pony and trap in the winter time, it was essential to be well-wrapped up. Country people had a strong belief in the benefit of pure wool next to the skin. As each year passed, my breathing improved, but winter and summer my mother insisted that I always wore a pure wool vest.

Little did I anticipate that a few years later, my family and I were to go down with typhoid fever and before I reached my middle teens, a more serious illness was to hit me. It looked like I was destined to be the seven stone weakling on the beach.

Recovering from the pneumonia meant spending a long time in bed, and as the days passed I found myself paying more attention to the noises coming from outside. Farming then was practically all mixed and unlike most farms of today, a lot of the work was carried on much closer to the dwelling house. Lying on my back, I could guess by the sounds coming through the window exactly what was taking place. The dull thud of the cow's hooves as they slowly shuffled from the back yard to the front on their journey out to grass. Without looking I knew that the big strawberry roan was leading the bunch, she was usually tied up first when coming in and first unchained for the outward journey. I often watched them, generally about fourteen in number, as they entered the old fashioned cow house. Each one knew her berth, and would shuffle into the correct spot to be tied up for milking. Should there be a newcomer, it took Mrs Dreelan just a few days applying corrective measures with voice and pot stick to let her know which stall was hers.

Shep was a long-serving big, black and white sheep dog, who spent about thirteen years with us. Every morning, I could detect his admonishing barks at that old black cow, telling her to keep up, but due to her advancing years, she was now having difficulty in doing so.

Away in the distance I could hear faint squeals. I knew it was Tim Breen just pulling the lever on the shuttering that prevented the pigs putting their heads in the troughs as he bucketed in their feed. Silence. I knew then that he had pulled back the shutter allowing the pigs to get their breakfast.

Empty buckets clanking as they pushed against each other on the cement floor of the dairy were easily identifiable. Such noises were soon followed with the high-pitched sound of the milk separator as it got up speed, reminding me of my mother's voice. "Come back here, you! Give Mrs Dreelan a hand with those milk buckets first and take your turn with the separator. You can hurl then."

How often did those words uttered by my mother bring me to a halt as I rounded the house at full gallop with the ball on my stick.

I liked working with sheep. Lying in my bed, I could hear clearly the din from the haggard as lambs baa-ed and ewes bawled, endeavouring to keep in contact with each other during the assembly for movement of the flock to a change of pasture.

We kept a sizeable number of hens, and each evening, for their safety, they were called together and locked up – a little whole oats followed by a few loud 'Chuck chucks' usually did the trick. That golden grain was irresistible to them, and knowing what to expect, it resembled a relay race as they appeared from all directions, each in a silly sprint to get there first. Lying on my back now, I could hear "cawk, cawk, cawk," a reverberating melody, but coming from the wrong area. They usually spent their time picking and scratching their lives away between the back yard and the haggard, but this hen had wandered casually into the front yard, a forbidden territory for a hen as far as a certain individual was concerned. I didn't have long to wait. A loud couple of distressing 'cawk cawks' followed by a panicked flutter of wings told me that Shep had spotted her, and one thing he would not tolerate was hens in the front yard. It was a nice job of policing – he didn't do her any damage but she more than quickly re-joined her friends.

The noise of chains meshing, followed by a deep-sounding 'clunk clunk' meant that Joe Hogan had just asked that big dray horse to get his shoulders into the collar and move off with a load of dung topped high on a common cart. The echo of mens' voices, especially my father's, asking questions or giving instructions to someone, was a familiar occurrence.

"Have you seen that Tom Dreelan around? I sent him off to clean a bit of a ditch. He should have been here long ago," barked my father at Mick Sinnott, the lorry driver, who was busily cleaning its plugs.

"He's probably collecting the cows on the way home," answered Mick, half of him still submerged under the lorry's bonnet.

"Indeed! He has more brains than I thought," responded my father angrily marching back into the shop.

One sound was unmistakable and that was the peculiar method of whistling – a distinctly audible trade mark that belonged solely to Peter Byrne, a reliable old man who ran the shop for my father. On a fine day as he crossed the yard to an outside bacon house, such a trip triggered off a virtuoso performance in old Peter; but in all his years with us we never sussed out what that tune was.

'Who goes to heaven?'

By the end of the summer, under the ever watchful eye of my mother, I made good progress. I took full advantage of all the perks and privileges that are granted to a youngster who has been seriously ill. Come the start of school in autumn, I was ready to take up my position with the rest of the hopeful young scholars in the old Rathnure schoolhouse. By virtue of getting first preference everywhere, and at everything, it's true to say those nine months turned me into a spoiled brat. "Specially made chicken soup – don't touch that – it's for Billy". "If there's any left you can have it", or if bananas or oranges came into the house; "Don't touch those until Billy is finished with them". I made full use of my frail condition and recovery, and by the end of it the abundance of sympathy and concern had now completely evaporated. Being given priority in so many ways had seen to that, and whilst my sisters were still concerned for me, it wasn't long before I was back to fighting my corner again amongst the lads.

The two-mile journey from Killanne to the Rathnure school house in those days was over a dusty road. County council workmen engaged in an endless battle, endeavouring to keep rotational pot holes at bay. In my earliest school days, a retired old ploughman, who had worked for my father and the previous owners of Killanne, drove us youngest in his prize-winning donkey and flat cart. Auld Johnny O'Neill had the reputation of being a true artist when it came to opening a field and his drill-making was revered for being as straight as the barrel of a gun. Many's the comment I heard in my father's pub. "I'll grant you he's good, but he'll never be a patch on auld Johnny."

His donkey and cart turn-out had seen off all comers to take first prize in the category at Enniscorthy show. It was an honour to be driven by such a prestigious ex-ploughman, and three or four of us sat in the well of the cart, knees together, warmly covered up with a wool rug. My father occasionally drove us in his motor car, but we never liked to see him behind the wheel, because it meant we would have to walk the last quarter mile. He would pull up and open the doors, telling us: "The walk will do you good – make you hardy."

Whenever we saw Mick Sinnott behind the wheel, we knew it would be all the way to the school door. As we got older we resorted to bicycles. In those days, on a fine day a number of young lads walked to school in their bare feet. I became envious of one of my chums who was constantly doing it, so with my mother's permission, I achieved the distinction on one occasion and the warm dusty road made it quite pleasurable.

In Killanne was the Protestant school it didn't have as many pupils as in the Catholic school, but travelling in opposite directions we would meet in the morning and on the way home in the evening. Nothing untoward ever happened as we went in opposite directions, but there was never any recognition of each other or social niceties. One lad in my age group, Hugh Rafferty, for no apparent reason, took a deep dislike to one of the Protestant lads we saw each day – a lad by the name of Pollard. Rafferty who was a slow learner, was almost a lost cause when it came to drumming the smallest particle of knowledge into him. Everyone, including our teacher was more than aware of it. Sitting two youngsters to one school desk and approximately nine desks neatly arranged we gazed up at Mrs Skelton. It was catechism class and she had just conjured an image of what would happen if we didn't grow up into good catholics; when we died, it would be Hell fire. The very words struck basic terror into our young hearts. On the other hand, if we behaved ourselves, didn't commit a mortal sin and said our prayers, then when we died it would be heaven, which she hinted was mainly for Catholics and the place to be. It sounded fun and games to our tender ears. It was rivetting stuff and we were hearing it for the first time. Joe Dempsey put his hand up. "Will St Peter be there?" This question drew a compatible "yes." Another little hand went up. It belonged to young Martin Nolan the local builder's son. "Will St Joseph still be doing carpentry?" asked little Martin. Mrs Skelton's eyes visibly narrowed, but she just nodded. There were several more questions, but it was obvious that Mrs Skelton was growing weary when young Lar Fenlon requested to know how long it would all last for. She was about to call a halt when to her surprise and everyone else's up shot Rafferty's hand. Sensing a breakthrough her enthusiasm returned. No matter what she was not going to douse Rafferty's sudden interest. "Yes, young Rafferty what is it you want to know?" I can still see the charmed look on her face change to dismay as Rafferty asked, "Will that Pollard be let into Heaven?"

Going home from school when youngsters, the situation was reversed. We were sometimes collected by old Johnny or someone drove the car to meet us. Like today, the youngsters were let out earlier than the older pupils, but unlike today the girls and boys had separate sections in the old school house. The same applied when going home. The girls walked separately from the boys. It occasionally happened that everyone was freed at the same time, and this meant older boys strolling along with the youngsters. There was sometimes a sneaky individual amongst the older lot – a crafty matchmaker who incited fights between the younger boys, just for personal amusement, but a total coward himself. He was a slick operator. One day walking home he came up to me and whispered, "Pat Morrissey says you're afraid of him."

Pat did not react. He was a pleasant inoffensive young lad who along with myself would later help backbone the Rathnure senior hurling team. But the matchmaker sneakily activated rivalry. "Pat Morrissey says he would box the ears off you," was his next message, and of course he had imparted the same to Pat on my behalf. He finally succeeded in laying a foundation of intense personal dislike between the two of us. He waited his chance and one day as we wended our way home, he brought us face to face. "Well, are you afraid of him?"

"I'm not," said Pat.

"Well, prove it to me," the promoter challenged.

Then he turned to me with the same poison. Finally we were standing there like two bantam cocks staring at each other, when suddenly there was an explosion in my right ear and I found myself lying on the ground looking up at Pat. A satisfied leer spread across the face of the promoter. I have never seen myself as a gutsy individual, and as I lay there on the ground listening to the goading of the older boy, there was a little voice inside saying 'Run'. However, instead, I surprised myself by jumping up, attacking into Pat with both fists flailing, much to the delight of the promoter. We eventually ended up rolling on the ground, each with a bloodied nose. When it was over, the sneaky promoter disappeared leaving Pat and myself to dust ourselves off, the best of friends, but still totally unaware of how we had been set up. Although we were just little lads, it resulted in both our reputations being considerably enhanced.

Typhoid hits Killanne

In the thirties, our little village of Killanne and the Rackard home was to become the topic of the county. There was an explosive epidemic of typhoid fever, and amongst the twenty-one notified cases in the village, nine were from the Rackard household. My father and eldest sister, Sally, escaped but a maid and a farm hand who lived on the premises were also infected. The shop was immediately closed, the entire premises isolated, and the old house turned into a mini-hospital, under the care of a local consultant with two trained nurses in charge. The county medical officer was called in, and the cause was investigated. It's hard to believe that at the time there wasn't even a village pump, so apart from going to St Anne's well, there was no other drinking water supply other than a farmyard pump. The nearest one to the fifty or so people who lived in the little village was the pump in our farmyard, which with my father's approval was frequently used. The cause of the fever outbreak was traced to this water supply.

It had been an exceptionally dry June, when there was an unexpected deluge of heavy rain. It appears that the heavy rain caused an overflow from the cesspit to seep through the earth enough to contaminate the water supply from the old pump. Apart from spending almost six weeks in bed and having heads shaved, it was fortunate in the end that there was no fatality. The result of all this finally put the skids under the Board of Health, and a village pump was installed at a high level drawing from a guaranteed pure source. It has served the villagers well and still stands to the good, it is known as 'Riley's pump.' As well as this pump my father sank his own new farmyard pump on higher and safer ground. Thereby came to an end a remarkable chapter in our village and family history.

CHAPTER SIX

At that time in our young lives, the game of hurling was just a method of achieving some enjoyment from our daily existence. In a parish and a county that were totally devoid of the games tradition apart from a solitary All-Ireland title in 1910 and a Leinster junior win in 1926, there were no ex-stars to look up to or present ones to emulate. We were not starry-eyed youngsters imbued with tradition and skills handed down to us by indulgent forefathers. In that context, we were rudderless. We were merely banging that old rag ball around the place for nothing more than the sheer enjoyment of it, but something was to change all that.

Jim, Bobby, John and myself were in the front yard, tearing into one another, pulling hard, flicking the ball up into the hand with a deft touch and the most favoured of all (which was to be a good servant in later years), hooking. Jim was particularly gifted with the stick and a born stylist. Being the eldest of the four at that time he had an advantage.

"Hook 'im, hook 'im, keep after 'im," Bobby would shout if Jim got it into his hand and started a little solo. Much to his annoyance as the eldest of the group, we often tailed him down and didn't let him hit it, eventually taking it from him. Such sibling rivalry was a common sight. It was just another normal morning and all the activity was going on in the front yard, when we heard our mother banging on the front window, beckoning us to come inside. We ran round to the back into the kitchen.

"What is it, Mum?" queried Jim.

"Come here" she said "I want to show you lads something."

"Show us what?" said John.

"Don't be so impatient," answered my mother. "Just the four of you come over to the kitchen table."

There were two large forms running the length of the empty table, one at each side. We hadn't noticed, but my mother had a newspaper tucked under her arm. She opened up the *Irish Independent*, and spread it out on the table.

"But what is it?" asked Bobby, "what do you want to show us?"

"Never mind, you'll soon see" she answered as she flicked back the pages. We were all four kneeling on one of the forms, still puzzled as to what she was up to.

"There!" she stopped. "Now have a close look at that page!"

It was the sports section. We craned over the page. There was one photograph on it. "Now look close" she said. We craned our necks in further and then we spotted it. It was a hurling picture, and Nickey was smack in the centre coming away with the ball on his stick. One of us slowly read the caption. 'Nickey Rackard who starred for St Kieran's College in All-Ireland win.'

Silence descended as we absorbed it, just staring at the picture. In those few minutes, a change took place inside us – a change, I'm sure, that has taken hold of thousands of youngsters – the flame of burning ambition was ignited. We were playing hurling now for more than fun. Nickey had unwittingly thrown a hurling lifeline of belief and hope, not just to his young brothers, or to his home parish Rathnure, but in fact to the whole county.

There was an unprecedented ripple of excitement and anticipation about this young man. The feeling was that some of the Kilkenny magic had rubbed off on him. The crazed loving followers of the purple and gold could barely wait for him to grow up, and they were not to be disappointed. Everyone was delighted with the prospect, except one man– my father.

One fine summer day, the customary dog fight was going on in the front yard. We were behaving particularly noisily and quarrelsomely, when one of us pulled on a ball that ended up hitting a horse in the belly, causing him to break loose from where he was tied in a corner of the yard. The owner, who was in the shop doing business, came charging out with my father behind him. We skulked off to one side of the yard. The horse was caught and retied. A short time later the owner reappeared, untied the horse, hopped up on the side of the cart, and with legs dangling, disappeared up the road. We re-started our game, making even more noise than before. We hadn't long begun when I saw my father come marching determinedly out of the shop door. Waving his arms, he shouted: "Give me those bloody hurls. I can't even hear myself think with the racket the four of you are making out here."

When he was really angry, and he was that way right now, we were afraid of him, so each of us in turn handed up our stick. For a moment we were horror-stricken, thinking he was going to suggest burning them. We stood there motionless as he went over, and to our surprise, dumped them in a corner. Then he came back. "Now look here," he started "I have no objection to you playing a game as long as it's a good decent game. Now let me tell you," he went on, pointing across at the hurleys, "all you'll get from that is broken bones, and as far as that crowd that run it is concerned, they surely won't do much for you. Now stay where you are," he told us, his mood distinctly undergoing a change, "and I will show you a good game." He turned and went towards the hall door. We stood perplexed, looking at each other. A knowing look crossed Jim's face. "I think I can guess what he is up to." He had no sooner said so when my father reappeared, both arms full of his beloved cricket equipment. He had a genuine love of the game and some of my earliest memories are, when little more than a toddler, I watched him take part in a cricket match as I looked out through the back window of a model T Ford. There were quite a number of cricket teams within the county then, including a Killanne eleven. He put the cricket gear down on one side of the yard. There was a little heap of sand in a corner.

"Bobby," he said, "get me a bucket of that sand." He then proceeded to erect the three stumps with sand packed at the base. The wickets were placed in position. Picking up a bat, he called Jim over. A painful expression crossed Jim's face as he responded. The resultant attempt to introduce us, his sons, to his beloved game of cricket turned out to be nothing short of farcical and we weren't helpful, dragging our feet at every opportunity. Endeavouring to ignite enthusiasm amongst us, he tackled the situation from all sides. He explained the rules, then asked each of us in turn to bat whilst he bowled. It was a disaster. Having bowled the hurling ball yet again at Bobby he roared, "God damn it, if you would make half the attempt to swing the cricket bat as you do that bloody hurl, you would have hit that!"

It was equally as disastrous in reverse. The fast-moving play, physical contact and excitement of hurling was now too deeply rooted in us. This sudden attempt at our metamorphosis was inevitably doomed. Our derisory looks, lack of enthusiasm and clumsy attempts at co-operation, finally proved too much for his mounting frustration. He called a halt, picked up all the cricket equipment and dropped it beside the hurley sticks. To our surprise and delight he then scooped up the hurleys, flung them into the centre of the yard, accompanied by the admonishment, "I still say all you will get from that game is broken bones." At this stage in our young lives, we never knew or asked, or in fact cared, why our father made the odd derogatory remark about the game we loved, and on the one occasion I saw him standing by the goal posts in the barrack field watching the action, I thought he was an incongruous figure.

'Pull on it more often'

I never heard him referred to by another name, other than 'Auld Tommy'. When I first became aware of his existence, he was probably only about sixty years of age, but he was then 'Auld Tommy' and so it remained. He had one expression which he constantly used. It was "Feck ya man." Instead of saying "Excuse me, I don't understand", Auld Tommy uttered an emphatic "Feck ya man, you don't know what you're talking about." It was in regular use. "Excuse me, I need to go through here," instead, it would be "Feck ya man, get out of my way." Tommy White farmed a small holding about three quarters of a mile from our house in Killanne. He had no children. His wife, a very retiring woman, was rarely seen except on her once a week shopping trip for essential household necessities. Her husband was not a serious farmer. As long as he had enough money for a few pints and a bit of tobacco, he was a happy man, and the urge for those few pints might come at an inappropriate time. Making hay while the sun shines was not one of Auld Tommy's mottos. That same hay could be looking up at him from the ground, begging to be cocked, but the strong urge to lap his fingers around a pint of cool Guinness, even at mid-afternoon, put such decision-making for Auld Tommy into an easy category. He may not have been a man of material wealth and a very casual farmer to boot, but he had other riches and qualities that were envied by many. Life, for him, was not to be taken seriously. He was a born funster, with a wry waggish sense of humour, devoid always of even a grain of cruelty. He was loved by all. Auld Tommy, to use an Irishism of the day, was a right pantomime.

My father now and then demanded that one of us give him a hand behind the bar counter. I never liked working behind the counter and could not understand why people drank that awful tasting Guinness, and as for whiskey – it mystified me, especially when they had the choice of lovely fizzy red lemonade and lemon soda. It took a number of years, to change my mind about all that. One afternoon, I was left alone to mind the bar when who came through the door only Auld Tommy. A couple of local men inside were seated at the counter. Being a prisoner behind the bar with Auld Tommy there was different. His presence had a way of lighting up the room, injecting a little levity into even the most moribund.

"Hey young fella! Give me a bottle of stout there and take your time pouring it. You destroyed it on me the last time," he grumbled. "I know you're a bit young yet, but when your time comes you should go off and learn the trade properly like your father did," he further advised, drawing the back of his hand over the ring of froth around his mouth.

"Thanks, Mr White," I said and put his change on the counter. His response was characteristically adamant.

"Feck ya man, I'm not a Mister. Just call me Tommy." This harmless positiveness, combined with a pair of twinkling eyes set into a roguish button-shaped face with a cap perched on top, gave him the appearance of a stand-up comedian. As I sat there looking at him, I found it difficult to keep a straight face.

"Another thing, young fella" he went on "I see you out there on the road hurling that ball against the wall. Let me tell you, you're lifting it too much. You should pull on it more often."

Many times I heard this advice. Auld Tommy was a member of the old school of hurlers. In those days sticks weren't designed for lifting. In his day it was pull, pull, pull, which means whacking the ball at ground level.

Auld Tommy does sideline

The spectators were milling about in the centre of the pitch like pigeons looking for breadcrumbs. The rickety goal posts stood alone, defiant at each side of the field with equally rickety crossbars in position. The playing area was marked out with rows of gorse bushes, the ends trimmed and stuck in the ground. I had just travelled by bike the seven miles or so with my brother John to see Rathnure (parishioners say Ranoor) take on Ballyhogue in Junior hurling. I think it was 1939. Having left our bikes lying against a hedge in a corner of the field, we were strolling towards the centre to join the rest of the crowd, when the ref's whistle sounded. The shrill 'Toot! toot!' was interspersed with shouts of "Clear the pitch – everybody to the sidelines." Then there seemed to be a problem, the ref and an official raised their hands to shield the bright sunshine from their eyes as they scanned the crowd. John and myself came within earshot as they walked towards the spectators, who were now taking up position outside the row of gorse bushes.

"We need someone to keep sideline. A Rathnure man," one of them shouted. "The other side has a Ballyhogue man. Anybody here from Rathnure?" There was a pause and then I heard the familiar voice.

"Certainly son, I'm from Ranoor, and I'll do sideline," came the firm announcement. It was the unmistakable voice of Auld Tommy. The rival players came trotting through a gap from the next field, resplendent in coloured jerseys. Black and gold for Rathnure and all blue for Ballyhogue. Meanwhile, with the ref's approval, Auld Tommy plucked up a piece of gorse and started patrolling one side of the playing area. The players lined out, the whistle again sounded, the ball was thrown in and the game was on. Everything was okay for a while, but approaching half-time there was growing bewilderment amongst the Ballyhogue spectators about some of Auld Tommy's decisions. Their tolerance level was being stretched to its limits.

One rather stout-looking man with a red face was particularly annoyed, claiming the sideline official had yet to give one ball in favour of his team. As the game re-started, this man was to pay particular attention to Auld Tommy. When a ball went over the line and it appeared almost certain that the resulting free stroke should go in favour of his team, Auld Tommy again gave a firm wave of the gorse bush in the other direction. This proved too much for the Ballyhogue supporter. Cupping his hands around his mouth, he bellowed "God damn it, you must be blind." It had no effect, except to extract a further wave of the gorse bush from Auld Tommy confirming his decision.

As the game progressed, what looked like a few more fifty-fifty decisions all went instantly in favour of Rathnure. The Ballyhogue contingent of supporters on the sideline were now very irritated and started cat-calling at Auld Tommy, who appeared totally oblivious to their angry mood, as he cheerfully marched up and down with the piece of gorse in one hand. It was the last straw for them when a ball that was blatantly in favour of Ballyhogue was yet again given to the benefit of Rathnure. I threw a glance at the stout red-faced man. The veins were out on his neck. He looked ready to explode as he cupped his hands around his mouth again and shouted: "I thought you were blind, now I know you are f - ing blind," he roared. Auld Tommy's response was three waves of the piece of gorse, each one more vigorous than the previous one, only this time accompanied by a loud "Feck ya man," followed by "Ranoor ball."

I was beginning to fear for Auld Tommy's safety as the Ballyhogue supporters were now in implacable mood, but fortunately the final whistle sounded; Rathnure the victors. Pockets of Ballyhogue supporters hung about the pitch throwing scornful looks at Auld Tommy, who was in a world of his own, and failed to notice their irate feelings. He was too busy anyway chatting excitedly to Rathnure fans.

I watched him as he merrily strode off to the end of the field where he had his pony and flat cart tied. The field was above the level of the road, which ran parallel to it. He was sitting on the sidelace with a carefree air, his legs dangling down, as he steadied the pony in the mad descent to the exit. At this stage, I saw the big red-faced man half-trot, half-walk towards the fence which gave him a view onto the road below. Unknown to him, John and I ran behind to watch, fearing he was going to chuck something down as the pony and cart passed underneath. He glowered as Auld Tommy came into view. We watched as the pony and cart went smartly up the road, the pony's shoes knocking sparks from the surface. Then we heard a loud war whoop, "Go on, Ranoor." It was Auld Tommy unwittingly putting the final nail in the red-faced man's sporting coffin, and again he was totally oblivious to the fact.

I was later to discover that Auld Tommy's interpretation of the rules were rather unique. He firmly believed that the Ballyhogue man on the farside was making all decisions in favour of his team, whilst it was his duty to do likewise at his side for Rathnure.

CHAPTER SEVEN

Nickey Rackard won two All-Ireland college titles outside his own county, with St Kieran's of Kilkenny and his first medal within his native county also came from outside his own parish in 1939. The Rathnure club had yet to enter a team in the minor grade, so Nickey, along with two other Rathnure lads, Spud Murphy and Nicky Carr were scooped up under the isolated players ruling which qualified them to play with the parish of Glynn, about ten miles from Rathnure, by a future president of the GAA, the late Micháel Kehoe. In that same year young Rackard was selected on the Rathnure Junior Hurling team. The Club, founded in 1932, concentrated on winning a junior title and made steady progress through those years in a grade that was far more competitive and exacting than its contemporary senior competition. The seventeen year-old Nickey was not available for the earlier games in that junior championship, but took part in the semi-final and final in which Rathnure were beaten. This was the first glimpse of the rising young star in his club colours. He had also been closely monitored in the Glynn minor victory of the same year, and apart from getting a tough time from the much older and more experienced St Fintan's men in the junior final defeat, he still managed to add further lustre to his fast growing reputation. However, significantly the Rathnure junior team made the breakthrough in 1940.

> Come all you lads and lassies, unto me lend an ear
> It's of our dashing hurling team, I mean to let you hear
> The 1940 championship our boys they did make sure
> To win the county honours and bring them to Rathnure

That is the first verse of a song celebrating Rathnure winning that junior hurling title. It was to be the first of many songs written about the Rathnure hurlers.

In this junior championship, in which they won the county title, the now eighteen-year-old Rackard was to rip opposing defences apart. His speed, strength, athleticism, and hurling artistry, combined with brilliant overhead and ground striking was a complete contrast to his style of latter years. In the district final of that championship against Blackwater, had a visitor from Mars been watching, he would have been entitled to think that the Rathnure centre-forward was from a different planet. I once asked Nickey when he felt he was in his hurling prime and he replied, "between eighteen and twenty". Unlike Bobby and myself he was an early developer, he was never a gangly youth. In athletics competitions of that period he was quite successful at long jump and high jump, but the most astounding aspect to his hurling then was the power he packed into a shot from a twenty-one yard free or from anywhere within thirty-five yards, as in this incident.

One day in the Barrack field around this time, he was practising the taking of the twenty-one yards pile driver. The goal posts in the field were about twenty yards out from a clay bank where people sometimes sat and watched. In the goal, was a player, who had an excellent eye for stopping a rasper. Nickey fired this twenty-one yard rocket at him. The lad in goal braced the boss of the hurley flat to take the impact dead centre. He knew what was coming so he gripped the hurley stick extra tightly, but the boss of the hurley disintegrated as if it was hit by gunshot and the ball was subsequently retrieved embedded in the clay bank twenty yards away!

Now let's go back to that junior hurling championship, and to one match in particular, the district final against Blackwater. In the goal for them that day was five foot five Joe Murphy, a member of a highly- respected Blackwater hurling family and known to everyone as Wee Joe. He never wore togs, always appearing in goal, the jersey pulled down over his pants which weren't as tight fitting as they are today. Back and front Wee Joe resembled the rear end of a pantomime horse, and he also wore long johns. His brother Johnny, a close friend of mine in after years, told me that Wee Joe's baggy pants and underwear were instrumental in saving his life that day. Nickey Rackard at centre-forward cut loose in that match to fire the type of rockets at a goalman that had never previously been seen in Wexford hurling. I still have a mental picture of Wee Joe in mid-air, legs askew, as those pile drivers whistled between the legs of his baggy pants.

Bill, the chestnut cob

I remembered back to that spring day of 1940, when Bill, the chestnut cob entered our lives. I was out on the road banging the ball against the old store wall. My skill was showing tremendous improvement. I could keep that ball going to and fro for minutes without losing control. I could pick my spot on the wall, knowing where it would bounce. Moving in, I would hit high before it touched the ground. Next time, I would move back, hitting a drop shot, the feeling of developing more control over that ball was very satisfying. Whilst all this was going on, I was constantly gazing down the road which was straight for about a quarter of a mile until it disappeared from sight downhill. From where I stood I could just make out approaching traffic as it surfaced the brow of the hill, but it was impossible to identify until it came closer. My father was back from the fair at New Ross now about two hours, having informed us that he bought a 15.1, three-year-old chestnut cob that was just broken. Any addition to our equine family was always greeted with excitement by us lads. Most of the horses we had were Irish draught types, some of them excellent bank jumpers and also able to gallop around the four fields above the house, where the flapper races were held in the past. We were all reasonably adept at riding, either bareback or in the saddle, so the prospect of a new addition to the stables was a time of eager anticipation. There was a distinct twinkle in my father's eye when he talked about this new cob.

Tim Breen had ridden him bareback to New Ross, I reckoned he should be getting near Killanne by now. As I was banging the ball, I kept throwing glances down the road. A couple of times I had convinced myself that they were approaching, only to find it was some large local man on his bicycle, but now there was something appearing on the brow of the hill, and yes, this time it was without question a man on horseback. Closer and closer they came. I stopped hurling, stared and waited. Even from that distance I liked the look of him and that step, there was something about it. His head was held high, with ears cocked.

"Whoa, boy," called Tim, as he took a pull on the bridle and hopped down. I moved closer to have a good look. The more I surveyed the more my heart danced inside my rib cage. My father was seen by many as a shrewd judge of a horse. Bill, a nice chestnut with a white blaze and two white socks behind, lifted his head, twitched his ears, and looked in at the old house, flared his nostrils and gave a loud neigh. He was looking a bit disorientated as he vented his feelings. "Was he going to stop here or continue on?" he appeared to be asking. Fate had already decreed his future. He was looking at his new home and for an animal he was to have an inordinately long lifespan, spending thirty-two years with his new owner, becoming part of a large family. Having proved his worth and versatility so magnificently in a short space of time, owner and family decreed that Bill must never be sold. Over the years many offers were turned down; he was allowed to live out his old age in dignity and comfort, leaving behind a cavalcade of fond memories, a lifetime of dedicated labour and loyalty, and a contender to any canine for the title of 'man's best friend.' He was a kindred spirit, one who had been a permanent fixture in all our hearts, someone in whose company we had spent many happy hours, especially when we were both youngsters together.

My father had by now spotted his arrival and with much alacrity came out to where we were standing. Anyone who has ever been through the mental trauma of buying a horse, will tell you that once you've paid for him, given a time lapse, and now that he is yours, the next time you view him, you do so through a completely different set of eyes. Your earlier doubts will have vanished or will have doubled. You have done the right thing or the wrong thing. This is a well-known feeling in horsey circles. As my father approached he stopped in about ten feet of the cob, his eyes swivelling as they criss-crossed, taking in every bit of him; then a broad smile lit up his face as he walked quickly over, patting Bill on the neck.

"Thata boy, thata boy." He had no doubts about this purchase. He was delighted with himself and his judgement of horseflesh. A neighbouring farmer on his bike came sailing down the hill towards us, the wind catching his unbuttoned jacket, the tail ballooning up behind him. Applying the brakes, he became another connoisseur.

"After buying, Bob?" he queried. It was Pat Lynch, known to start every conversation with "Be me sowl (soul)." My father turned. "What do you think Pat. Have I done the right thing?"

Pat gave the cob a long searching look, going from head to tail and eventually his opinion. "Be me sowl, Bob. He looks a right one." Then he pushed his foot against the ground and off down the hill he went, the tail of his jacket again rising with the force of the breeze as his bicycle gathered speed. Standing looking, admiring his new purchase, my father, without realising it, gradually clicked into an expansive mood.

"Now. See here," as he looked towards me. "Young fellas like you should pay attention and learn to understand the points of a horse. Stand back and have a look at the way this fella is balanced on his legs. That's good. Now let's take him piece by piece."

Getting deeper into his favourite subject, he started on the hind legs.

"See those straight hocks and strong fetlocks? That fella will never get a curb. Now look at his front legs. Good flat knees, short cannon bone, again well up on his pasterns and good span of bone under his knees – that fella'll never go lame."

There was no stopping him now as we went to his head.

"See that kind eye with plenty of space between both eyes; and for a cob he has fine sloping shoulders. That is why he is such a good mover." He went on and on, finally slowing to tell me something that many others were to hear on countless occasions in the future.

"You see the thing about this fella, really, is the way he's bred. He's by a thoroughbred horse out of a mountaineer pony. (That description of a pony was solely my father's and I regret never asking him the full meaning). This fella will combine the speed of a thoroughbred and the strength of a halfbreed, and being a cob, there'll be no end to him. "Wait till you see" he enthused, "he should be able to do anything as well as making a smashing hunter."

How right he was; between the shafts of a trap, with a saddle on him, or even a common cart – it was all the same to Bill. Lastly, seeing my eye drawn to the excessive hair growing from the cob's fetlock, "don't mind that," he reassured, "that comes from the dam and when it's trimmed off he'll look like a little thoroughbred", which Bill did once that growth of shaggy hair was dispensed with. Tim Breen was still holding him by the head.

"Come on" said my father, grabbing at one of my legs, "get up and give him a walk about."

I hopped aboard, catching up the bridle rein. He responded left or right to the smallest pull, and the walk! Oh, what a joy after big farm horses. He was so light, you felt he couldn't break eggs should he walk on them. I was overjoyed with the prospect of slapping a saddle on him.

"Okay, that's enough," called my father. "Put him away, Tim, in the second stall on the left. Make sure he has hay and water and give him a chive of oats." And so I watched, delight sweeping over me as Bill the cob, stepping adroitly, was led for the first time around the house towards his berth in the stable which was to be a permanent home to him for the rest of his days.

No hurling at the dairy door!

Mrs Dreelan's voice reverberated around the old farmyard.

"Them chaps are gutlin' in the dairy again, Mrs Rackard" she shouted. After a few hours hurling on a warm day, especially coming back from the barrack field, it was impossible for us to pass the cool dairy as we made our way around the house towards the kitchen. This was about the fifth time now that Mrs Dreelan had caught us red-handed, heads down, gulping copiously from enamel buckets of fresh milk or better still fresh buttermilk. As we drank, we had to keep a weather eye out for fear of her sudden appearance; knowing that such a compromising position made our rear ends vulnerable targets to a pot stick attack, something that had happened a couple of times as she walked in unexpectedly carrying one in her hand. However on this occasion as she appeared, it was just admonishment followed by a threat.

"There's no rearin' in youse, that's all, and I'm going straight in to tell Mrs Rackard." She was back in seconds with my mother, the four of us standing just outside the dairy door, guilt written all over us and looking like condemned men. John in particular with an impressive moustache of cream beneath his nose. My mother marched towards us with Mrs Dreelan in the rear. She had a strange expression on her face, throwing each of us in turn a dissociative look.

"I'm ashamed of the four of you. That's all. You're no better than little pigs. There are cups in the dairy for the purpose if you want to drink milk. Mrs Dreelan must think that I've never tried to put manners on you. I'm ashamed. That's all," she reiterated. But there was something about her expression – it was her eyes. Her face was serious but her eyes were not. She was, we sensed, hiding her true feelings behind a pseudo-display of indignation which was principally put on for Mrs Dreelan's benefit. I really think she was not overly concerned by our lack of etiquette inside the dairy. Her sons were growing up active, with an admirable interest in healthy hobbies and an intake of fresh milk by whatever means could only strengthen and do them good. However, as we got older there was another aspect to the dairy that was to put us in very hot water, it was strangely enough to be the dairy door itself.

Mrs Dreelan, whose son Tom also worked for my father, lived in a cottage just a field away from the house, and was for years part of our family set up, so much so that we referred to her as 'Auntie.' She was a very reliable person, with a good sense of fun but now that she was getting on in years, she was finding it difficult at times to cope with four young lads rampaging about the place. My mother trusted her judgement implicitly, so whenever there was a showdown, Mrs Dreelan always had my mother as an ally. She had warned us about hitting the ball against the dairy door, and had brought the matter to our mother's attention. For a few years now as smaller lads, we had developed a habit after the dinner (never called lunch) of picking our hurleys from beside the dresser and going out to the yard with a sponge ball. The most inviting target was the dairy door. We weren't strong enough or accurate enough then to make much impact, especially with the light ball, but now that we were older and using a proper ball and with much improved accuracy, it was a different matter. We had run the gauntlet too often and had been given a firm warning by our mother.

"Poor Mrs Dreelan," she would say, "you know she's getting on in years. Her nerves are not what they used to be and that ball banging off the door frightens the life out of the poor woman. It's disgraceful; it surprises me that she continues to work for us. There are plenty of places to bang that ball against, besides the dairy door. So don't let it happen again."

The dairy door, however, retained its seductive appeal as a target, especially as we stepped out of the kitchen. On this particular day as usual after eating we grabbed the hurley sticks and headed outside. Bobby was holding a brand new hurling ball we had just been given. A few steps into the yard he angled towards the dairy door, mocking a shot at it.

"Go on," said John "I dare you."

"She's probably not in there anyway" was Jim's encouragement. Holding the ball in his hand, Bobby's eyes were rivetted to the dairy door.

"I'm going to have a crack at it, but the second it bounces back from the door, let's run, pick it up on the way and disappear up the haggard. Just in case she's in there."

He threw the ball up, made perfect contact with the stick. Bang! As the dairy door exploded with the noise of the impact it went careering about on its hinges. We moved quickly, one of us picking the returning ball onto the point of the hurley, and all disappeared up to the haggard, stopped, turned and listened silently. After a few seconds, we heard the dairy door open and shut, followed by a scuffling noise that suggested running feet. Mrs Dreelan was obviously running at top speed to our mother. There was dead silence as we turned and exchanged fearful glances with one another. Our father would explode in such a situation, but his bark was worse than his bite. Our mother was not the same kettle of fish. A short reprimand was followed by what was known as a good leathering. With a small ash plant in her hand, we were bent over to receive a few whacks on the backside or bare legs. It was hard medicine, but whenever it was administered we took it in the full knowledge that we deserved it. Now we were filled with trepidation as we lay hidden behind the wall, expecting our mother to call out our names at any second. There was a consensus amongst us that such a clanger against the dairy door was the last straw for old Mrs Dreelan and we had been warned, but strangely all was quiet, but somehow uncomfortably so. We remained about the haggard for about an hour, afraid to go near the kitchen, and to our surprise there was still no action being taken. John was the first to crack, showing a crisis of conscience. "I'm going down to the kitchen and offer to help."

As he walked in our mother was busy re-arranging the dresser. "Mum. Would you like me to get a bucket of nice spring water from St Anne's well?" he asked.

"What's come over you?" she replied, throwing him a cursory glance. "No thank you." He soon reappeared, his facial expression a strong testament to the chill she had put on him.

"She's probably not going to do anything," we nervously vouched.

"She is, I know she is," he warned.

We came in later on as supper was being prepared, sitting around the table in silence.

"Anyone for more tea?" asked my mother as she went round with a large teapot in her hand. She poured out the last cup for one of us, and then, with a palpable thud, she put down the teapot on the table.

"Right then," she said, folding her arms with an air of finality. We knew what was coming as we looked up at her, our faces a mixture of wide-eyed innocence and pained surprise.

"Right then," she repeated, this time articulating slowly; "Which one of you hit the ball off the dairy door?"

The silence continued as all four of us stared down at the table.

"So that's it," she said drawing a deep breath. "I will ask the question one more time", she said, giving each of us a searching look. Again the same reaction. Still silence as we stared through a crack in the old wooden table. She thumped the floor loudly with the heel of her shoe.

"I see. So that's the way it's going to be." She then turned, went over to the side of the dresser, scooped the four hurleys up in her arms and marched straight towards the big open hearth. She made a gesture of throwing then onto the fire. This instantly broke the silence and brought us to our feet.

"Mum! You're surely to God not going to burn the hurls," we begged in plaintive tones, our boyish faces wrinkled with what innocent beseechment we could muster. She stopped, turned and looked at us, the hurleys still in her arms. "Right then. Which one of you frightened the life out of poor Mrs Dreelan again today?" There was a chorus of voices. "It was me, Mum." A long pause followed a long silence, as she stood embracing the hurleys. She then dumped them on the floor.

"I see," she said "Well, remember this. Next time there will be no questions asked. They will be put straight into the fire. Do you understand? No hurling at the dairy door!"

CHAPTER EIGHT

"Please Granny, let me stay and listen to the match. I promise I won't be in the way."

"You're not going into that room with all those men sitting around the wireless. You're too young and anyway they wouldn't want you in there. It's fine outside. Some fresh air and a paddle will be much better for you and let me remind you that's why you're here with me and your sister. You're still wheezing a lot you know, and your mother wants to make sure that you get plenty of sea air."

The thunder and lightning final of 1939 between Kilkenny and Cork was about to commence. I was on holiday with my granny and my sister Essie in Kelly's old hotel at Cullenstown beach in South Wexford. The argument between my grandmother and myself had reached stalemate as Michael O'Hehir's voice, in spite of competing with incessant crackling from the old fashioned radio, still came across shrill and clear. The men, some in hats, others in caps, were huddled tightly together. The odd older one had a hand cupped around his ear. I was about to lose the battle with my granny, when the door into the room swung open a bit more. From the inside, a tall fine-looking man reached to pull it closed, then he turned and called out:

"Ah! Mrs Doran. How are you?"

My grandmother coyily switched her attention from me.

"Oh hello Mr Gallagher. Nice to see you again this year. You're enjoying your stay in Cullenstown?"

"Yes indeed," he answered. "I always do. I love this place. It's my intention to make an annual trip here until the kids are grown up." He then turned towards me. "Who's this? Another grandson?"

"Yes, said Granny, "but I'm afraid at the moment we are having a difference of opinion. He wants to listen to the All-Ireland hurling final, but his mother gave strict instructions for him to get plenty of fresh air and paddle in the sea. You know he has had two serious illnesses and he's not as strong as he should be. Anyway it's no place for youngsters in there", she said nodding her head towards the room.

I obviously looked downcast because suddenly Mr Gallagher came across, placed his hand on my shoulder, and to my sheer delight turned to my grandmother and said, " Mrs Doran, let him listen to the match. He'll be alright, I assure you, and he can sit alongside me." Mr Gallagher was a much respected secondary schoolteacher from the Midlands, well-liked by the locals, and this request coming from him proved too much. A smile broke over my grandmother's face as she said, "You look after him then, and when the game is over, please hunt him down to the beach. He'll know where we sit."

"By the way," said Mr Gallagher addressing my grandmother as she was about to leave, "I hear great talk on the hurling grapevine about your other grandson. Is it Nickey? I take it he is this chap's older brother. Teachers from St Kieran's have told me he is one of the strongest and finest hurlers that they've had in the college for years."

As Mr Gallagher was speaking, I caught sight of myself in a full length mirror across the hallway. The words 'finest' and 'strongest' seemed to hang in the air as I gazed at my skinny legs and arms, complete with dodgy chest. I was probably a mere four stone. Would anyone ever say that about me, I was thinking when Mr Gallagher turned, placed his hand on my head and with a pleasant smile said, "Wait till this fellow grows up and who knows, one day he will play for his county and mark, maybe, the great Jim Langton of Kilkenny."

Little did I or Mr Gallagher think at that moment, that fifteen years later that was precisely what happened when I took up position in Croke Park to mark my idol, the Master hurling craftsman himself, Jim Langton of Kilkenny. The legendary names that came across the crackling airwaves on that occasion were to stay forever embedded in my mind; Corkmen such as Alan Lotty, Jack Lynch, Johnnie Quirke and Batt Thornhill (how could you not remember a name like that!) to name but a few. But it was the Kilkenny names that held more significance for me. Perhaps, that was because Kilkenny was nearer home. In fact, I often thought that not far over the blue mountain behind our house, were the men I admired most in the whole world like Paddy Phelan, Bobby Hinks, Paddy Grace and Terry Leahy. Terry, I think, scored a point that day from his knees. "Terry Leahy has put it over the bar and Kilkenny are in front." It was the dying seconds as Michael O'Hehir brought across a vivid picture of the scene as it was at Croke Park. Wexford men in that room, were absorbing the Kilkenny win as if it were their own.

I was as quiet as a mouse during that broadcast, but there was a strange feeling inside me and it was interconnected with the photo of Nickey starring for St Kieran's in that All-Ireland Colleges win. Stranger still that feeling was a mixture of conviction and unshakable belief and was as buoyant inside me as if I were a grown man. Yes. One day I had a far-off dream and this same dream wasn't just peculiar to me or the Rackard household, it was one shared by the parish of Rathnure.

"Thank you, Mr Gallagher, for getting me in to hear the match," I said, looking up at him as everyone traipsed out of the room. "Not at all. It was a pleasure and you run along now, otherwise your granny will be getting concerned."

He left in front of me and went walking up the road. I was just outside the door and about to go towards the beach, when there was a tug at my arm. I turned, and there sitting on the window sill were two fine looking and friendly middle-aged men.

"That's him alright," said one to the other as he looked at me, and with his next breath he asked my name.

"Billy Rackard," I said.

They looked each other in the eye, then turned to me.

"That's not a Wexford name. Where are you from?"

"Rathnure," I said, as one of them scratched his head in puzzlement.

"I know", said the other man, "It's up north somewhere near the Blackstair Mountains." I instantly cut in, "You've heard of *Kelly, The boy from Killanne*?" "Oh yes" chimed the two, "We know that song well and where Killanne is."

"Well, I live in the house where Kelly used to live."

"Is that so? Is that so?" they parroted. I was beginning to wonder about their interest in me when one said: "I just want to say something to you. We've been watching you down in the ball alley hitting that sponge ball," (the ball alley in Cullenstown was embedded in the cliff. Walking past on top you could peer down into it. There were always heads looking down.) "and we have never in all our time spent looking into that alley, seen anyone that can keep that sponge ball going the way you do. You're going to be a good hurler one day." And then throwing me a standard question for any ambitious youngster, he asked blithely "How would you like to play on Terry Leahy when you grow up?"

How I wish the ephemeral fly had come down from the wall and told us all right there and then that eighteen years later, in 1957, I would have the honour of marking Terry Leahy as Wexford, the All-Ireland champions played the New York All Stars in the Gaelic grounds, New York. Terry Leahy was way past his best then but still made me fell inadequate as he demonstrated his skill hitting the type of overhead and ground shots I could only dream about. I was about to take my leave of the two men, when one started again scratching his head.

"Rackard. Rackard," he repeated. "I've read something somewhere, ah yes," he slowly drawled, "have you an older brother who plays with some college somewhere?"

"Yes," I said. "Nickey, he won an All Ireland medal with St Kieran's, Kilkenny."

"Ah, that's it; and you're a brother of his?"

"Yes. I am."

"I see, I see," he went on. "Now tell me, how many brothers have you altogether?"

"Five, including myself," I quickly answered. "And where do you come in?"

"Oh, I'm the youngest," I said as I took my leave and headed off to find my sister and grandmother, but with the scrawny image of myself in that mirror now beginning to haunt me more than ever.

Unruly hormones

"Come on out from behind that garden shed, whoever you are!" It was a dark winter's night as Fred Crabbe, the village postman, from the corner of his eye detected a slight movement outside his kitchen window. A local youth, whose hormones were proving too unruly, was caught as a peeping Tom behind Fred's garden shed. The object of the youth's passion was Lydia, the second youngest of Fred's seven daughters. As Fred shone his bicycle flash lamp on the trapped youth, he was to suddenly suffer a conflict of interest. The age-old instinct to protect his daughters' virtue collided with the possibility of this particular young man paying proper court to his Lydia. He was bearing in mind the future prospect of settling seven daughters.

Fred Crabbe, an Englishman and a Protestant, married Florrie O'Lord, surely two of the most unusual names ever to confront a preacher. Shortly after they were married at the beginning of the First World War, Fred joined the British Army, and having done his basic training in England, was sent with his regiment to France. There, it is believed, he fought at the battle of the Somme. After being demobbed at the end of the war, he eventually arrived in Killanne to become the area's most unlikely postman. In due course, he was to raise a large family of seven girls and three boys, with he and his wife becoming popular and prominent members of the local community. When the Crabbes arrived in Killanne they brought with them more than their luggage. They also brought a different culture and different customs. Right now as Fred confronted the young man, he realised that perhaps the youth was a victim of the Irish 'Sub Rosa' culture that existed in the country at that time – especially where boy-meets-girl. The clandestine date was the modus operandi and the acceptable face of romance.

"Now, see you here young man," Fred's English vernacular as staunch as ever, "If you want to court my Lydia you go to the front door, come in and have a cup of tea and then take her out."

This was the last thing a tempestuous young suitor of the day wanted to hear. In more ways than one, his idea was to feel his way into the relationship, and that unbeknown to everyone. The idea of going into the girl's home, meeting her parents and drinking tea was to him horrific, and tantamount to what was known then as 'putting your feet under the table', as well as being almost a public declaration of marriage. On the contrary, a secret romp in a nearby hayshed was looked upon as the ideal starter. Today, via the media, be it TV or your average newspaper, a young man's sexuality is encouraged.

Back in the thirties and forties a young man with the same glowing hormones coursing through his veins was not so fortunate. On the contrary, there was a formidable array of weaponary lined up to challenge his sexuality and to keep him in check, fill him with guilt, and if possible snuff out the very idea of catering to his biological needs – that is until he married. 'Can I keep pure?', 'How to remain pure', booklets with such titles were in an abundance inside every Catholic Church door. From the pulpit, impurity or sins of the flesh was the only commandment that really caught the congregation's attention. Others, such as dishonesty, carried no real threat of hellfire. Catholic guilt weighed heavily on every young man's shoulders. In order to save his soul, he carried the battle against Satan's temptations with constant purpose using weekly or monthly confession, accompanied by a fervent promise of amendment, but knowing in his heart it was futile. Stemming the ever increasing tide of sexual desire generally proved impossible, and should a young couple mutually capitulate to each other's passion, the subsequent remorse was inevitably followed by the usual rotation of guilt, fear of hellfire and another obligatory trip to the confessional for forgiveness.

In rural Ireland then, the church's teaching and preaching on the rest of the Commandments appeared light fingered, compared to the heavy hand that was used in an attempt to stamp out sexual desire and lascivious thoughts. Most clergymen were ill-equipped to deal with the subject, freaking out at the mere mention of the word 'sex'. The traditional teaching of the Catholic church naturally frightened them against saying anything that could be construed as encouraging a natural relationship between a couple, that is again until marriage. Whenever they were compelled by peers to give a sermon on the matter, it was commonly and euphemistically referred to in a cop-out Hell-fire threatening sermon as 'company keeping.' Today, from the pulpit, sexual peccability is in the main unchallenged and unmentioned. Sexual relationships with a Church of Ireland girl was, however, in those days a different matter for a Catholic youth. Should the wrath of God descend, his feeling was that the main brunt of it would come to bear on him. There was a strong belief amongst Catholics that the Protestant God was not as ferocious as theirs, and neither was he of the same kill-joy nature, which perhaps accounts for the fact that the average Protestant parent may have seen the average Catholic young man as something as an opportunist.

All the Crabbe girls were given a strict upbringing and were lucky to benefit from parents who had travelled, and experienced different cultures. They were gifted, with natural outgoing personalities which they projected in the gentlest way, and a refreshing openness and interest in other people and were lacking the social insecurity which plagued a lot of young girls at that time.

The young man in this story who had regularly watched Lydia as she tripped her way to and from the village pump for a pail of drinking water, may have got the wrong impression, but was certainly not the victim of a crisis of conscience. Her skirts about two inches above her knee, laid bare a pair of shapely legs which were ample evidence as to what the rest should be like. He was filled with such passion that he would sacrifice anything to be given an opportunity of tumbling her in a nearby meadow. Lydia was totally unaware of the flutter she was causing to this young man's libido as she made her way to and from the village pump. He decided therefore to bite the bullet and take Fred Crabbe at his word. Yes. If he had to call to the front door and socialise over a cup of tea he would, because he could then walk off with Lydia and head down a neighbouring boreen. But there was a snag. The Crabbe household and wicket gate faced the crossroads in the village, and usually sitting there on varying levels of stones set into the fence were some of his local contempories and older men, most of whom were sexually repressed and had never been seen alone with a member of the opposite sex. On the other corner of the crossroads was the garda barracks, so there was also the possibility of four garda sitting out. He would have to run the gauntlet of leers and looks as he walked past. Weighing up the situation, his intense feeling backed by the reward of being alone with Lydia, proved too attractive. He would call to Crabbe's front door, and so he did, until one morning Old Fred awoke to the realisation that the young man's intentions were somewhat less than honourable.

It was the end. Fred Crabbe was not one to indulge in circuitive discussions. What you saw was what you got – he spoke his mind openly. Ferociously and defiantly English, was he staunchly proud of the Empire. He still proclaimed undying loyalty to both King and country. During his time in Killanne as well as his postal delivery, he also was caretaker of the local Protestant church. Many a time during the course of the Second World War, was he heard to reiterate Churchill's immortal words – "We will fight them on land and sea, in the air and in our own back gardens etc." Yet, I can never remember one untoward, sectarian incident involving a putdown of Fred's nationalistic zeal or beliefs. Whilst Fred's forthrightness and unbending moral fibre were admired by all, Mrs Crabbe, on the other hand, was the very epitome of drawing-room reticence and gentility. I always felt that she arrived on this earth with the wrong label. She was, to me, a dowager duchess who had married a postman, and I say that with the greatest of respect for her husband.

The Crabbe family lived in a modest little house that belonged to my father. A look through the door gave full meaning to the old adage of a man's home being his castle. It never ceased to fascinate me, with its pieces of home-made-to-measure furniture. Little cabinets filled with bric-a-brac and photos of all the family tastefully displayed. Although a modest abode, it was truly a treasure trove, crammed full of cosy joy. Her gatherings were by invitation only, though many a gate-crasher wangled his way in. We would crowd into the little room where our hostess presided over a huge teapot of steaming strong brew, and the best plates were laden with barm-brack, sandwiches and home-baked apple pie. Her tea parties were elegant and she went to great pains to draw out her guests in conversation and was altogether a marvellous listener. You left her house feeling somehow special and that you must be a more interesting person than you had thought you were. She and her daughters brought a colonial style and levity to the little village of Killanne that will be always be remembered by those who knew them.

CHAPTER NINE

In the Autumn of 1939, in fact the same day as the All-Ireland Hurling Final, World War Two began, resulting in catastrophic effects on many countries and millions of lives being lost. This present generation can be forgiven for thinking that, because of Ireland's neutrality, the war did not impinge on the lives of its citizens. Not so. Even in sleepy Killanne, in the self-sufficiency of a farming community, we were subject to the shortages and deprivations inevitably caused by our gallant merchant ships running the gauntlet of the naval battles being fought off our coasts, and suffering heavy casualties at sea.

> In nineteen thirty-nine or so
> The Emergency began to grow
> and Dev, he says to me "What ho"
> "You're just the man for me!"
> "Why Dev" says I, "Why so I am.
> We may be running short of ham
> and petrol, coffee, tea and jam
> and ships that go to sea."

Author unknown

By 1941, rationing had been introduced and I well remember the individual bowls of sugar and butter each member of the family was issued with by my mother. Raiding another's bowl was a heinous crime, with only half a pound of butter to last a full week. Sugar was also a problem although it helped that Ireland grew its own sugar beet. By 1942, tea was reduced to half an ounce per head a week which was serious to a nation of tea drinkers. Soap, candles and paraffin oil were also rationed. The biggest shock of all to people was the disappearance of white bread. The white loaf was replaced by something resembling a grey-brown brick, which was not only difficult to slice but worse to digest. Coal was also impossible to obtain but not so serious for country people because wood and turf were locally available. Gas and electricity were also a problem as there was no coal to power the plants and the trains were reduced to running on turf, rotten leaves and twigs. Travelling to Dublin must have been hell. One train was reported to have taken twenty-three hours. The Wexford fishing fleet was also seriously affected by the lack of petrol, which in turn added to the food shortages.

My father's car had to go up on blocks as there was no petrol to run it on. It was covered down with two large worn-out sheets stitched together. He had just bought it. It was new Hillman. We all marvelled at the slim-line exterior and beautifully fitted interior. During the next five years I would climb in behind the wheel and take off on imaginary drives through the countryside. Sadly, I can still hear my father instructing Mick Sinnott to paint red lead under the mudguards to prevent rust.

The Taoiseach broadcast to the nation, warning us all to tighten our belts and announcing that there would be no further petrol coupons except for vets, clergy, doctors and other key people. This caused great annoyance to the few car owners who had just paid their tax for the year weeks before. No private cars meant rural communities became quite isolated. The result of living through those five years of sacrifice and shortages was to imbue most people with a sense of thriftiness and abhorrence of waste that stayed with some for the rest of their lives. Our present day disposable world and rampant consumerism is still a sore bone of contention to those who remember the harsh times of the war years.

The war may have changed peoples' lives and brought about shortages in villages like Killanne and the parish of Rathnure, but there was one commodity that was not affected. On the contrary, it became more infectious and prevalent than ever, and that was the passion for the game of hurling.

> Oh! cut me a hurl from the mountain ash
> That weathered many a gale
> And my stroke will be lithe as the lightning's flash
> That leaps from the thunder's flail:
> And my feet shall be swift as the white spin-drift

On the bay in the wintry weather,
As we run in line through the glad sunshine
On the trail of the whirling leather.

From The Song of The Hurl, Crawford Neil.

Rathnure's first hurling title

Rathnure had annexed its first Junior hurling title and Wexford had made a breakthrough in Leinster in winning the Junior Hurling Championship. In the early rounds of that championship, Rathnure was represented, but by the time the All-Ireland Semi-Final was reached, thirteen of the original team who lined out in the first round win over Wicklow at Aughrim were dropped. It was an extraordinary statistic. There was no Rathnure player now on the team for the All-Ireland Semi-Final against Cork. However, the parish was represented when the selectors gambled in bringing on the exciting young college star Nickey Rackard. Opinions differed as he replaced the established and talented veteran, Larry Harrington. This was to be Nickey's first appearance in the purple and gold, but for those who had witnessed his exploits with St. Kieran's and his couple of outings with Rathnure, they waited with high expectations. They had observed his searing shots to the net in those club games. They now looked forward with bated breath for more of the same. On the other hand, shrewd critics were pointing portentous fingers. "He is too young," they said "and you are expecting too much from him too soon", and sure enough the latter assessment proved to be accurate. It was not Nickey's day. So much so, that amongst followers' opinions as the crowd left the park, one was heard to remark: "It's unlikely that that young fellow will ever again be seen in a Wexford jersey."

Bobby suggests a race

Looking back on one's childhood and adolescent years can be a painful experience for some, but it is my firm belief that anyone who first saw the light of day and grew up on a mixed farm such as I did, can only look back on happy, wholesome memories. The therapy of watching a ploughman with his pair of horses turning the sod in the Spring, haymaking, harvesting and all such activities so close to mother earth are absorbed by youngsters irrespective of the parents' economic situation. Consequently, in latter years whenever I exchange memories with new acquaintances, and find that their growing-up years were spent differently to mine, they immediately evoke my silent sympathy. I would not exchange my growing-up years on a mixed farm for anything. My father was a tough but reasonable taskmaster and delegated small jobs to his sons as soon as he felt they were up to it. He decided that I was capable of counting sheep. At first I was upset at the idea of finding myself committed to the responsibility of a daily chore. However, my mother reassured me that I was well able for it and that it would, in fact, be good for me; and also that I might even get to like it. In spite of her comforting words, for the first time in my life it suddenly came across that I could no longer wander about the place doing exactly what I liked and when I liked. In some cases my father would send my brothers John and Bobby with me, but in the main I set off alone. Once I arrived home from the national school and was fed, I jumped on my bike and was gone. On my return my father asked, "Well, are they all there and are they all right?" As we boys grew older, my father made sure that all of us gave a hand with the various jobs on the farm, from fetching the cows, putting out fodder for the cattle, picking potatoes, thinning turnips, helping with haymaking and harvesting etc.

Counting sheep is a difficult job. I would do my best, but I was never absolutely certain that they were all there. I would, however, assure him that everything was alright. In the summer time, it was essential to have a close look at sheep. In those days dipping to prevent flies laying their eggs and causing maggot infestation was not effective as is now. If an animal is badly infested it is easily spotted as it is usually alone away from the others. If I needed help, I would return home for assistance. I grew to enjoy my responsibility, and throughout the year, from early lambing to separating the lambs from the ewes, shearing and dipping and changing them to fresh grass. Without being fully aware, it had all become a refreshing and pleasing aspect of my youth. My animal husbandry instincts were fully aroused.

For geographical purposes every field on the farm had a name. There was The Hollow Field, The Iron Gate Field, The High Field and The Grove Field, etc. There was a block of land of about fifty acres, which was referred to as 'the land above the house' and 'close to the farmyard.' The rest of my father's land was scattered in parcels literally North, South, East and West. At this time he had about thirty or so strong ram lambs that had been specially selected and fed and were now almost fully grown. Bobby and John were ordered to accompany me to round them up for a close inspection. We had them penned in a corner of the field, one side of which ran parallel to a narrow back road. We were satisfied that they were okay, and about to let them go when Bobby shouted: "Hold it! Let's grab three of the biggest, keep them in check until the rest have crossed the field, then we hop aboard for a race."

We grabbed three big ones and we each threw a leg across and off they went to join the others. After about twenty yards, John had fallen off but Bobby and myself hung on as our two reached the rest of the flock. We hopped off and looking back we could see that the riderless lamb had lost sight of the rest and was stomping off towards the fence that adjoined the road. We tried to intercept, but as soon as it came to the fence, a sort of bank, it hopped up and in a flash was down on the road and to our dismay was going at full gallop away from us. We ran as fast as we could, but were unable to overtake. We must have gone about half a mile, before we found it grazing peacefully at the bottom of what looked like a very high bank. We approached gingerly. We were succeedingly nicely when suddenly a big black face appeared on top of the bank above where the lamb was grazing. It was a fine sized ewe who was looking down from the field that shelved way above the road level. Her maternal instincts exploded on seeing the solitary lamb. She gave a loud Baa-aa. The lamb looked up and in the style of a good hunting horse, jumped up on top of the bank and disappeared. We climbed up and looked. There were about two hundred sheep in the large field. Our hearts sank. What are we going to do? We were already anticipating our father's question. "Well, did you count them and were they all there?" After a lot of deliberation, we decided that discretion was the better part of valour. Our answer would be 'Yes'. We knew the farmer who had unexpectedly gained an extra lamb, and on a few occasions afterwards, when I saw him in the bar with a pint in his hand and huddled in conversation with my father, it gave me a very uneasy feeling.

Unlucky dip

'I now must sing in praise of one who hurled with
might and main to win the honours for Rathnure.
Jim Blackburn is his name'

This line was from the ballad written to commemorate Rathnure's 1940 hurling success. Jim Blackburn, who was a member of this history-making team that brought the hurling-crazed parish of

Rathnure its first title, had now come to work on my father's farm. We young lads were very impressed and regarded him with a fair amount of admiration and awe. Jim, had a mischievous sense of humour and with his shirt sleeves rolled up he displayed massive biceps and granite-like forearms. He looked the epitome of muscled manhood – a fact that drew envious glances from us skinny youngsters. However, one evening in my father's pub I overheard a conversation concerning his hurling ability which made me scrutinise him closer. There were about six men at the counter, all lovers of the game. My father had finished his supper and appeared. The first one to broach the subject of Blackburn was Pat Byrne from Rathduff, a man whose nightly love affair with a pint of Guinness was known by all in the parish. When Pat spoke it was through clenched teeth that were tightly gripped around a pipe. He merely lifted his upper lip and out came the words:

"I say, Boss, I hear you have Blackburn working for you now." His lips curled away again: "He's a tough cut you know. He played a fierce game against Ballymurrin in the district final."

"Feck ya man. You don't know what you're talking about". It was Auld Tommy. "Ya mustn't have been watching Crank Connors or the Mowler Redmond at all that day. There's the men who bet Ballymurrin, and all the talk they had about the great Larry Rath (Auld Tommy was now at full throttle). By God, the Mowler (Mickey) showed him where to get off. There's no stoppin the Mowler, ya know. He'd go through a stone wall when his dander is up."

I often watched my father when there was a hurling conversation going on. He was totally incapable of speaking the jargon. Erudite hurling comment necessary amongst such afficiandos was totally beyond him. He didn't seem to merit hurling lingo. It went on around him and at such times he generally remained silent. A few years later that was to change. Next into the verbal fray was another Rathduff regular, Willie Holohan (a life-long pal of my father's). Willie who always wore a fixed grin and was never seen without that pork pie hat perched atop his head looking like it had grown there, targeted Auld Tommy.

"God damn it, Moloney. You're not being fair. I know the Mowler Redmond is a good one, but so is Blackburn." This remark evoked more vigorous dissent from Auld Tommy, extracting another "Feck ya man, Blackburn pulls on everything that moves but he's not a patch on Connors or The Mowler. He's muscle-bound and a bit fettered as well," was Auld Tommy's final shot. My father intervened.

"As far as I'm concerned, Blackburn is a good workman and that's all I need. His hurling ability doesn't come into it."

He was, however, impressed by Blackburn's strength. In his young days, my father was exceptionally strong, and always seemed to place inordinate emphasis on the glory of physical strength. From now on he was to take an interest in endeavouring to put some sort of muscle on his scrawny-looking younger sons.

About three days later, he turned to me at dinner-time with instructions to help Blackburn dip some sheep that were pastured down in the Larkfield river fields. We had our own set-up for dipping near a stream. It consisted of a concrete tank with a holding pen at one side. First, the sheep were driven in, then chucked into the tank one by one, from which they could scramble out into another pen, where they were left to dry and subsequently released. My job, which was really a bit of fun, was to place a concave wooden mallet attached to a long handle on the animal's shoulders. Before it scrambled out I made sure that it was properly submerged.

"The tank is full; everything is ready. Just round them up. Blackburn will throw them in the tank. You must make sure they go under – that's all," continued my father.

Immediately after dinner, I joined forces with Jim and the ever-willing Shep. All three of us walked the quarter mile or so. On entering the land, we made our base at the dipping area and sent Shep off to round up. It was a difficult task for a lone dog, so we ran here and there shouting and gesticulating helpfully, as we moved the sheep towards the pen. Looking at Blackburn racing about, Auld Tommy's words seemed to make some sense. He wasn't using his arms and likewise appeared to be always back on his heels as he ran. Maybe Auld Tommy had a point after all. Anyway, we finally had the sheep penned.

Before we started, I paused and looked around. This particular part of our farm was one of my favourite areas. It contained four sizable fields, whose sod had never been turned. Irrespective of the season, its fertility needed no assistance as the lushness of its folds rolled downwards in a grassy slope that fell away to a chattering, busy stream. This progressive little brook was given birth about two miles further up under the shadow of the blue Blackstairs. It was now in a compulsive rush to join up with similar juvenile waters, all suddenly becoming anonymous as they were swallowed by the larger river Boro, which in turn lost its identity as it was engulfed by the

Slaney, all on their final journey via Wexford Harbour out into the Irish Sea.

In a corner, adjoining the roadway in this tranquil setting, was sited the dipping tank. It was a warm summer's day. The sun was doing its best to break through the haze of afternoon heat. Blackburn rolled up his sleeves. "Come here you little bastard, and you too." He had a sheep in each hand as he literally cannoned them into the tank. With a sadistic gleam in my eye, I used the wooden instrument, making sure they went under. We were making good progress and both of us were enjoying our work, when I heard a voice. I looked towards the road fence and there was a lad of about twenty. He was from a neighbouring townsland and a slightly gullible young man, but a fanatic on hurling.

"Is that Jim Blackburn with you?" he queried.

"Yes," I shouted back.

He jumped down and went across to Blackburn, who was about to hurtle another sheep towards the tank. After a short exchange of words, Blackburn came across and dumped the animal in. He then turned about and looking back, he shouted, "You're not tough enough. That's why you're not picked on the Rathnure team."

"But how do I make myself tougher?" the young fellow asked. A wicked grin appeared on Blackburn's face. "Hop in there," as he nodded at the dipping tank, "that will toughen you up."

I could scarcely believe my eyes as the young fellow, who hadn't much to shed anyway, quickly undressed and walked down into the dip tank. The water contained a colouring component which was giving the sheeps' wool a yellowish tint. As Blackburn turned about dragging another victim, the look on his face changed to panic. The swift acquiescence of the young lad had made his implausible suggestion backfire.

"Good Christ," he moaned, "if that fellow dries out yellow and his mother discovers who's responsible, I can tell you – I'm in trouble! I would rather take on Tommy Farr any day than square up to that one."

As events transpired, the lad ended up looking a bit jaundiced. (His mother obviously didn't notice). However, more importantly, he never achieved his ambition of being picked for the Rathnure team.

CHAPTER TEN

I spent most of the morning banging a sponge ball against the old store wall that faced onto the roadway. I stopped as neighbours passed. They would just bid me the time of day and continue on, but Johnny Hetterington, an elderly bachelor who lived and farmed with his spinster sister about a quarter of a mile away, always stopped. A smallish man, he and his sister shared a sit-up-and-beg old fashioned ladies' bicycle. I would always know from a distance that it was Johnny as he freewheeled down the hill in an almost motionless fashion. He would stop, hop down beside the bike and stand bird-like, silently watching as I bashed the ball again and again against the wall. Should I miss a shot he would choose that moment to skip past, turn about, and carry on silently staring. The only time he spoke was when he was crossing over, and it was always the same. "Give it the cuts," he would say and repeat it about three times, then stop and carry on with the silent stare. His eyes sparkled with a definite glint of enjoyment as he watched, a fact which inspired me to produce as virtuoso a display as I could strictly for his benefit.

I could recognise from a distance most of our neighbours as they approached, but Auld Tommy was the easiest to identify. He never rode a bicycle; he was always on foot. There was a jauntiness about his gait. He seemed to walk with merry legs, but unlike Johnnie Hetterington, he never stopped. As he came around the corner, on his way to the pub, it was the inevitable admonishment "pull on that ball", more often "young fella, you're liftin' it too much." It must have been about one o'clock because my stomach was rumbling. Just then I heard the rapturous tones of Maggie Somers' voice coming across the roof tops, using every drop of oxygen her lungs could muster. "The dinner is ready," she shouted.

It was sweet music to my ears. Maggie came to work for my parents in 1936. It is now 1996. She lives nearby. Her children are grown-up and she can boast of a commendable quota of grandchildren, but she is still as much a component part of Rackards Killanne as she was throughout her earlier years, when my mother placed serious responsibility on her young shoulders, and my sisters looked upon her as an extension of the family. During the dreadful period of the typhoid fever, even though very young, she was a tower of strength to my Mother in seeing that the house ran smoothly and proper food was supplied to all who were affected. She married in 1946 and became Mrs Bill Clince. Bill also joined the workforce at Killanne and had the ability to cross all job barriers from ploughman to farm manager.

After forty-nine years of work and commitment, he died suddenly in 1994. He was preparing a site for a Marion Shrine at Killanne crossroads when he suffered a fatal heart attack. If you say 'Killanne' to emigrants from that part of Wexford, they will say 'Maggie and Bill Clince.' They were wonderful neighbours and gave much to the community. Bill, a quiet modest man, and a fine hurler in his day was laid to rest by a gargantuan gathering of people from near and far and from all walks of life – a farewell that was a resounding tribute to the memory of someone whose integrity, honest labour and concern for fellow man will be hard to equal.

A ram plays truant

As Maggie's dulcet tones hit my ears, I picked up the ball, ran around to the back yard and straight for the kitchen. The three or so men who worked on the farm appeared one by one from different yard doors, also responding to the 'dinner is ready' call. I hadn't even gone through the kitchen door, when my nostrils had already picked up the delicious smell of bacon and cabbage, quickly activating my saliva glands. Hunger pangs had added a keen edge to my sense of smell. Whatever cooking method was used in those days – for me the smell and flavour of bacon and cabbage today, does not assault the senses to the same extent. Along with the large plate of bacon and cabbage, came a praskeen of potatoes with a large dish of farm butter, and Colman's mustard. Most of us were seated when my father came in and slowly took his place at the table. His plate was set in front of him, but he just stared at it. My mother noticed and eventually remarked, "Are you alright? Either you've lost your appetite or you're a man with a problem."

His head slowly lifted, directing a soulful gaze across the table at her.

"Can you guess what I've just had to contend with yet again?" he asked. My mother looked at him quizzically.

"Well, it sounds awfully like Mrs Tierney and your sheep." "You know," he said, sitting bolt upright in his chair. "That whole situation infuriates and baffles me. Mrs Tierney is perfectly within her rights to come into the shop and castigate me about my trespassing sheep. But what I cannot understand is from time to time every man in the place has been sent down there to fence that boundary, and I know they have done a good job. What's more those blasted sheep have plenty of grass where they are and if they were to break out, I wish the stupid so-and-sos would be more resourceful, because the other fields adjoining that boundary have far more to offer. No! It always has to be into Tierney's land, which has bugger all grass on it. What the hell makes that ground so damn attractive to them?"

My father was now in a furious mood. "I wouldn't mind if I was a careless farmer, but I'll tell you this," as he sought further release to his frustration, "if I have to confront Mrs Tierney or her husband one more time about trespassing sheep, I will be a candidate for Enniscorthy mental home." "Well then don't put them in there." answered my mother. "You don't understand," argued my father. "That's great sheep land, it has to be grazed. You can't put cattle on it all the time. Anyway, I will move those sheep immediately and not until late spring will I put them back there. Then, at least I can be assured of four or five months peace of mind."

About a week later, before bedtime on Friday, my father turned to me.

"You help Tim Breen in the morning to get those ewes down from the Iron Gate field. There's a new ram out there in the box stall. Let him out with them and put the lot over in the Grove."

He bent down to untie his shoe laces, when I overheard him muttering to himself, "They won't trouble the Tierneys from there."

Next morning about nine o'clock, Tim and myself, accompanied by good old Shep, rounded up the ewes and soon had them huddled against a gate in a corner of the back yard. Shep was standing guard over them. Tim was pushing his way amongst the ewes inspecting them closely, when he turned to me and over the collective panting which was interspersed with the odd hoarse bawl and cough, he shouted: "Go and let that ram out of the stall." I ran up, opened the door and out he bolted, but instead of joining the ewes, he went for some reason to the other corner of the yard. I called Shep.

"Shep, bring him back," I instructed. He obeyed and quickly ran towards the ram, but halted and stood uncertainly looking at the newcomer. The ram sensed he was afraid, lowered his head and advanced. To my surprise, Shep backed off.

"Look," I shouted to Tim, "he's afraid of him."

I moved in closer, hushed at the ram who had by now seen the ewes and sprightly crossed the yard to join them.

"Don't mind that," said Tim. "Neither Shep nor the ram is sure who's boss yet, but you'll see, as time passes Shep will establish his authority."

I opened the gate. There was a bit of a scramble as they all tried squeezing out together. It didn't take long until we had them out on the road down to the cross. I went ahead and turned them left towards the Grove, which is almost in the opposite direction of Tierney's. We had nearly half a mile to go. Both of us were in a relaxed mood as we casually strolled behind the sheep who had now slowed to a walk. We noticed that the ram was always in the rear on his own.

The clouds were moving quickly overhead, allowing the odd warm blanket of bright sunshine through. A blackbird flew off at speed, vehement in its noisy distaste at our presence. The ditches were carrying an abundance of blackberries. We stopped now and then, picking and eating a few as we casually strolled on behind the sheep. We were gone more than half-way when Tim asked, "Can you see the ram?" We raked the flock with glances and turned about and looked down the road, but there was no sign of him. "Wait," said Tim, an anxious look crossing his face. There was a gate open back about one hundred yards or so. "Maybe he's gone in." We raced back, turned into the field which was quite long, and there he was in full flight heading towards a gap at the bottom.

"Shep, come here, come here"

"Quick, go get him," we called.

Off went Shep, but as soon as he closed near the ram he stopped and came back.

"Blast," said Tim as we both had no option now but to race after him ourselves. When we got to the gap and looked, there was no sign of him in the next field. We ran around the headland and up to the road.

"I see him," yelled Tim, "He's heading back down to the cross."

He now had a substantial lead on us. We ran as fast as we could but it was of no avail as he kept up a relentless gallop. He was a fit young ram. We caught sight of him as he approached the cross.

"Jasus," said Tim out loud. "The fucker has turned left towards Tierneys," which was about two hundred yards away on the road. "Don't worry," I said, but when I got to the crossroads and looked to see no sign of the ram, I found myself swallowing hard. A look of despair covered Tim's face.

"You know," he said, "If that ram ends up on Tierney's land and your father finds out. Well, I'm sacked!"

We frantically ran down the road. When we got close to Tierney's, Tim jumped up on the fence and looked all round scanning the fields.

"Well, thanks be to God he's not in there."

He had barely uttered the words when he gave a loud gasp, "Get up here quick," he demanded, "and look towards Tierney's back garden." I jumped up and looked. I could make out the three foot six inches privet hedge that surrounded the garden. I had been in that garden and had marvelled at its ordered symmetry of vegetable production, combined with touches of formality that showed a splendid little display of flowers. It was Tierney's pride and joy.

"Look to the far corner," said Tim. I did, and instantly knew why he had gasped. The ram was half submerged in the hedge; his rear end clearly visible. We gazed across at him with mounting disbelief. Furtively we crept around behind the garden hedge. As we came in about thirty yards of the ram, I could scarcely believe my ears. It was Tim 'baa baaing' in desperation, imploringly at the ram. It did not produce the desired effect. We stood aghast watching as his woolly backside slowly disappeared from sight. Like two American Indians, we crept around, and gently lifting our heads we peered over the hedge. He had walked straight across the garden and we caught a glimpse of his backside again as he marched through the wicket gate that led into a little yard in front of the kitchen door which was open. We went a bit further, lifted our heads again, and horror of horrors, we stood dumb-founded as yet again we caught a glimpse of his woolly rear-end, only this time as it disappeared through the kitchen door.

I turned and looked at Tim. Never have I seen such despair on a man's face. We ducked down again and waited for an explosion. We just didn't know what to expect, but strangely all was quiet. We exchanged depressed glances, then Tim in a low whisper said, "The Tierneys must be out somewhere." We tiptoed towards the kitchen door. We both coughed and then Tim called out "Anybody home?" There was no answer. You've heard the expression 'Cheer up, things could be worse!' So we cheered up and sure enough things got worse! It was a bit like that as we gingerly went through the kitchen door and, to our astonishment we saw no ram. Inside the door to the right was a scullery, we looked in – still no ram. At the far side of the kitchen there was another door which was open and led into the Tierneys' parlour. We went and peered in. He was standing on Mrs Tierney's best carpet, with his backside close to her precious china cabinet. His sides were heaving in and out but there was something else going on and I didn't care for the sound of it. From underneath, he was pumping copious jets of piddle onto the carpet.

"Jesus Christ!" said Tim, "let's get him out of here quick, but for God's sake be careful. If he backs up, he'll break that china cabinet."

We sidled up to him gently, stooping down, we grabbed a foreleg each and pulled him out into the yard and into one of Tierney's fields that bordered the road. We were close to the fence hoping to get back onto the road somehow, when we heard a pony trotting towards us. We had a quick look, it was Mrs Tierney sitting bolt upright on a bench seat that was fitted across a spring cart. We were behind the fence as she approached. We upended the ram and lay on him with our heads down as the pony trotted past. Finally, we got him onto the road and with all the energy we could muster, we hurried him back along to the ewes who were now climbing up the road hither and thither, contentedly grazing away.

CHAPTER ELEVEN

During the war years, the hurling craze intensified and not just amongst us brothers, but also within the parish. In retrospect, it is easy now to see that it was the principal combatative sporting outlet for the youth and men of the area. During the summer time, especially on Sunday, nobody dared miss out on first mass which was at the ghastly time of 7 a.m. This early rising had nothing to do with pleasing the good Lord. Its motivation was totally selfish, because on Sunday morning there were usually sufficient numbers in the Barrack field to play a game of In and Out, and that was something you did not want to miss. I often heard it repeated during the week 'Be God, that was a great bit of hurling last Sunday morning in the Barrack field.' Once we were back from Mass, the usual pattern would evolve which was to quickly down our breakfast, and then – complete with hurleys and ball – make a mad dash for the Barrack field.

This game In and Out consisted of six backs opposing six forwards, whose task was to score five goals within a certain time limit. It took place at one side of the pitch in front of the goal posts, with an independent player outfield pucking the ball back into the battle area each time it was cleared. This was thoroughly satisfying entertainment, but it also tested your nerve and competitive edge. I can recall some ferocious pulling and every trick in the game being used to prevent the goals being scored within whatever time was specified. Unwittingly, all sorts of skills were well honed in those dog fights, and were to serve some of us well in the more important clashes that we hoped lay ahead.

On a normal Sunday we reluctantly appeared in the kitchen after several calls of 'dinner is ready.' After dinner a similar pattern repeated itself until we were called in for our supper, again that was quickly downed and off we went once more, to end up literally pushing the gathering darkness away as the craving for hurling continued. The trips back to the house for food were more often than not punctuated by a quick trip in and out of the dairy.

However, this particular Sunday was different. It was the Sunday of the All-Ireland Hurling Final 1940, between Kilkenny and Limerick. The wireless, a Murphy, was located in the kitchen, attached to what was known as wet batteries, and connected to an aerial that went up to a pole above the kitchen window and then a distance of about one hundred yards all the way to a similar pole attached to the gable end of a high out-office. These aerials were connected to a convenient tree within the vicinity of some homesteads which once prompted a comment from a local onlooker - dazzled by the advance of technology. "Never have I heard such music coming from a skeogh."

In 1940, very few households could boast of a radio and on auspicious occasions such a hurling final, interested neighbours were welcome visitors to the houses that had such a modern facility. We were one of those houses, but there was naturally an added attraction where we were concerned, because Rackards was also a pub. After the dinner my mother gave instructions. Turning to John and myself she asked us to bring some chairs up from the room below the kitchen. "There is bound to be a few in this afternoon to listen to the match, and I expect" she said, "we will need those extra chairs here."

About half an hour before the game was due to start, the latch on the kitchen door lifted. The first one to arrive was Tommy Coakley, a founder member of the Rathnure club, a good hurler in his own right, now retired but a perennial selector on the Rathnure team. His opinion about the game was always highly valued.

"Ho, ho, ho," said Tommy, opening the door, "Is it alright to come in Missus?" addressing my mother. A characteristic mannerism of Tommy was always a triple 'Ho, ho, ho,' before starting a conversation. "Certainly Tommy," as she turned to give him a big welcome. "Take a chair and sit down." Then came Willie Holohon (Sen), a famed Rathnure hurling name, my father's old pal. Then Pat Byrne, teeth still clenched on the pipe stem. He was accompanied by his life-long friend Pat Leary. Shortly afterwards, the door burst open followed by a loud greeting "'Morrow Men". It was none other than Auld Tommy. Then a few more locals arrived, squeezing in onto the form behind the kitchen table. The door opened again and it was another neighbour Pat Lynch. He immediately dished out a "'morrow missus" towards my mother, who affectionately acknowledged the salutation, but Pat somehow looked a bit exasperated. He was about to sit down, when he changed his mind, going bolt upright with his cap in his hand.

"Be me sowl, men," he started, with forceful emphasis. "You'll never guess what I just saw down there on the crossroads. It's them Crabbes and you should have seen the caper that was going on. God's truth; but do you know what they were doin' gathered about that donkey. I declare to Christ but they were feedin' 'im sponge cakes."

I had witnessed this on different occasions. A lovely black donkey with extra large ears as he stood swamped in a garland of Crabbe girls stretching from his tail to his head. You would hardly know he was there except for the two large black ears sticking up – a sure sign that Mrs Crabbe was offering him some of his favourite titbits. All the Crabbes had inherited that fatal concern for and tendency to treat animals as humans, something which could not be considered an Irish trait. Pat was reeling from the culture shock, finally bringing the matter to a close with another 'Be me sowl, men, if I had that fella up in my place for a morn, I know the sponge cakes I'd give 'im.'

Nickey was not home on this occasion, but Jim, Bobby, John and myself were seated in a strategic position close to the wireless, making sure we were not going to miss one word of Michael O'Hehir's commentary. Again the latch on the door moved and in came another neighbouring farmer, Charlie Foley. Middle-aged and a reluctant bachelor, his inability or failure to land a suitable mate may have been due to his drinking habits. A sustained spell of hard work was usually followed by a 'pro rata' spell of hard drinking. Many's the morning did Charlie wake up in our hayshed instead of making it home to his own bed. Then it would stop with Charlie rotating back to the work. During these drinking bouts he was known to air his views on many topics including the necessity and advantages of female company. He did marry eventually but rather late in life. As Charlie took his seat he blinked both eyes simultaneously followed by a grimace. Now and then he would repeat this, public testimony that he was on the batter. Like the others my mother gave him a warm welcome. As the conversation on hurling and the match bounced his way, Charlie, not having a clue, but in a desperate attempt at sounding interested, kept repeating "Yis, yis, yis" or "T'would, t'would." He knew nothing about the game and cared less. He was on one of his binges, and the popular and rakish bachelor's sole reason for coming in was to collar my father, when the opportunity arose, to procure a half-dozen or more of soul-sustaining bottles of Guinness.

At this stage, Pat Byrne ferreted in his pocket and withdrew a box of matches. In no time, a cloud of choking pipe smoke was enveloping those sitting close to him. As the pros and cons of the game were being enthusiastically discussed, Pat curled his lips away from the pipe shank.

"Be God, men. Do you know what, but I hear that Mick Mackey would go through a stone wall with the ball on his hurl." This extracted a throaty 'feck ya man' from Auld Tommy, followed by 'so would you Byrne if you thought there was a pint of porter at dudder side.'

It was getting close to match time, when my father came in with a newspaper under his arm. He half opened it and then, in an attempt at informed hurling comment, he quoted a passage from the newspaper – a passage that to his annoyance was debunked there and then. It was being heard for the first time and no one believed him, but was however subsequently to find a place in the archives of hurling folklore. Slapping the newspaper with his hand, he said, 'I see where that Limerick goalkeeper Paddy Scanlon, trained his eye by keeping swallows out of a barn'. Tommy Coakley immediately interjected 'Ho, ho, ho. God Bless you, Boss. You're soft in the head if you believe that sort of stuff. T'would be an eegit of a swallow that wud go anywhere next or near Paddy Scanlon with a hurl in his hand.' This irritated my father, who once again in an attempt at erudite hurling comment was not taken seriously, in spite of the fact that he had actually quoted from a newspaper. "Well, I can tell you it says so here," he grumbled, aggravatingly raising the newspaper, then, quickly tucked it under his arm and disappeared through the door into the parlour, a room which looked out onto the front yard.

Anyway it was now approaching match time. We could hear the Artane Boys Band as they played familiar marching airs. Sometimes on such occasions they included *Kelly, The Boy From Killanne*, and whenever that happened it was not allowed to go unnoticed. The adrenelin count in that kitchen was going up. Silence descended –

then the National Anthem, followed by the roar of the crowd. "The ball is in and the game is on" yelled a youthful Michael O'Hehir. Pat Byrne appeared to be eating the stem off his pipe. Auld Tommy was swirling the cap to and fro on his head. Pat Lynch produced a strangely coloured handkerchief from his pocket, followed by a loud blow of his nose. Mick Neill, a local carpenter, kept repeating 'Be the Mac, be the mac – that's hot stuff." Charlie Foley, whose eyes were still rivetted to the door which my father went through, was emitting a spasmodic 'Yis, yis', intermingled with blinks and grimaces.

The four of us boys sat tightly together on a form, mentally drinking in the mention of each star's name as Michael O'Hehir's unique voice added drama to their every twist and turn. At this point my mother tactfully withdrew from the kitchen, and went to join my father and sisters in the parlour. As the game progressed, it soon became evident that my brother Jim was a fanatic supporter of Limerick. His two principal heroes were Mick Mackey and Jackie Power. John, Bobby and myself sat more or less quietly, with strong leanings in the hope of a Kilkenny victory. However, the real essence of listening to the game was the inspirational effect Michael O'Hehir's shrill voice was having on our youthful hurling minds as he brought to life the names of the legendary players of that era: The great Paddy Clohessy and the young Dick Stokes of Limerick, and the Limerick sub, Tony Herbert whom we boys were to confront in latter years. Likewise, the unforgettable Kilkenny men, whose names were indelibly imprinted on our young minds; Langton, Grace, Gargan, Mulcahy, to mention a few.

The full-time whistle blew. "The game is over and Limerick are All-Ireland champions beating Kilkenny 3-7 to 1-7." The words had barely died away when Jim jumped up, went straight to the dresser, picked the ball off it, then to the side, grabbed his hurl and was out the door, with Bobby, John and myself doing the same and in close attendance. Once outside he started a solo run, hopping the ball on the hurley. I could hear his excited voice as he rounded the end of the house towards the front yard. "Mick Mackey has the ball on his stick ... He's gone five, he's gone ten, he's gone fifteen." We were closing behind Jim as we rounded the corner to the outer yard. "He's gone twenty." He had barely uttered the word "twenty" when there was an almighty crash of broken glass. Jim, who under normal circumstances, was a very accurate striker had, in the excitement of the moment totally misjudged and sent the sliothar like a rocket through the parlour window. Seated inside, availing of the light, was

Father reading. His tranquillity was explosively disrupted as the ball, in the midst of a shower of glass, landed in his open newspaper. The four of us stood like statues, surveying the damage. The enraged countenance of the Boss quickly appeared, framed by the broken window.

"I'll burn those bloody hurls!" he bellowed, "That's all there is to it."

Body building

1940, was a memorable year for the Rathnure Hurling Club, winning its first title alone was enough to see to that. The sap was rising and in more ways than one, the club team had now moved up into senior grade and naturally the further challenge of a breakthrough lay ahead. Willing helpers were in abundance; solid committees were formed with the club deciding to enter more teams, eventually ending up with teams in all grades; minor, junior and senior.

Sadly, the year 1940 also left a dark cloud behind. The hurling fever was so infectious then that even after the Christmas dinner of that year, the practice field in Rathnure was noticeably filled with young men, pucking the ball about. One of them, a fine young player, approximately eighteen years of age, collapsed as he was leaving the pitch, and in spite of having a doctor quickly in attendance, he passed away in a short time. Tommy Ryan, a strapping six-footer, had been suffering from a severe bout of pleurisy which he had just put behind him. He looked in fine form that day, but inexplicably fell to the ground and died.

It was not until 1948, and after a lot of disappointments that Rathnure finally managed to win a senior hurling title. However, the minor teams were quickly on the mark, winning in '41, '42 and '45. Some interesting names appeared on these teams, such as Paddy English, a forerunner to his dynamic brother Jim English and Mark Codd, a brother of Martin's, whose vital role in the 1956 All-Ireland final will always be remembered, specially by Wexford followers. Two other names appeared that were also to have a bearing on the future of the game in Wexford, but one in particular was to make a shuddering impact and that, of course, was Bobby Rackard. The other one – Jimmy Rackard – was also a very promising minor. Some believed that he was endowed with even more hurling skills than any of his brothers. He was, in fact, to play Senior County in the half-forward line and also in goal, in which position he was to win a Senior Leinster medal on the Wexford team that finally made the breakthrough in 1951. He also gave sterling service to his club Rathnure as goalkeeper and in the process, at this level, again won senior honours. The odds, however, were against him remaining in the game at senior grade. His most apparent drawback was a lack of physique. Nonetheless, had other essential components been in place, that may not have mattered, and the missing ones were concentration and dedication. From an early age, Jim developed a dependency on the hard stuff. He became a closet drinker and had such a capacity that at times it was hard to tell whether he was drunk or sober. He had little regard for money. It was there to be spent, and as for responsibility – it was not on his agenda. Jim, easily the most popular of the Rackard boys, refused to take life seriously. He was born to hang out with the lads. Needless to say, his hurling career was not programmed for success.

At this stage in my life, it was generally accepted that, based on my age and existing build, I would probably grow to Jim's stature or smaller. I had developed a deep love of hurling, and was satisfied with the progress of my skills, but haunted by the feeling that I would be too small. Although most people were kind and considerate about it, I still sensed it, and the vibes were, "This fellow will not grow sufficiently to make a senior hurler." On the contrary, it's strange how an unconsidered remark by someone you respect can unintentionally affect your attitude and give you hope. It was during my very early teens. I had cut my arm which needed bathing and a bandage. My mother was attending to the injury, she flexed my forearm back, then in a soft voice she said: "Do you know, one day you will have very strong arms." The manner in which she said so was to remain with me and prove to be a great morale booster.

As a family we divided into peer groups. The oldest two of the family, my sisters Sally and Essie, were at this stage independent young women with jobs and boyfriends. The youngest two, Molly and Rita, played together, neither being robust enough to participate in our energetic activities. However, it must be said that none of my sisters came into the tomboy category. As brothers, the older two, Nickey and Jim were close, whilst Bobby, John and I ran about together. Bobby, the eldest of our trio, was the natural ring leader.

My father, with the advent of Jim and Bobby as prominent hurlers in the minor grade, was noticeably taking more interest in his sons' prowess. Apart from attending some minor hurling games to watch his sons, he made a point of rounding us up before bedtime, where, on the kitchen floor he showed us how to do various muscle-building exercises, the principal one being press-ups. He counted these each night, always insisting on one more until we could finally go no further. Nickey, who looked a more powerful youth than his brothers, was now in Dublin University Veterinary College and not involved in this.

Bossman Rackard, about five foot eight inches in height, was himself exceptionally strong in his younger days, a time when strength was a necessary ingredient for any young man in a rural society that was devoid of present technological farming assistance. It was also a time when tests of strength were commonplace. In his prime, he was almost unbeatable at hoisting the four stone weights up and down above his head. He was also reputed to be an accomplished swimmer, unlike any of his sons, and during his days in Dublin was a regular at the Forty Foot in Sandycove. An avid reader, with excellent general knowledge, he kept abreast of topical affairs both at home and abroad. His main sporting interests were cricket, horse racing and boxing.

His insistence on his sons doing press-ups almost every night, unquestionably had an affect particularly on Bobby, who was a very gangly youth with knock knees. The result was that in time Bobby became obsessional with the development of his strength; a desire that compelled him to write for relevant booklets pertaining to the subject, such as Charles Atlas' *Body Builder*. He quietly adhered to the recommendations in the booklets and with good constancy of purpose he kept at it. His appearance didn't alter, but he did acquire phenomenal power which totally belied his physique. This strength or power he combined with his hurling technique – a combination that was to become an irresistible force, eventually culminating in one of the finest individual performances ever seen in an All-Ireland hurling final in the year of 1954.

Embarrassment for Essie

One summer Sunday in the early forties, my second oldest sister Essie, father and myself were outside the GAA grounds in Bellfield, Enniscorthy. It was about half-an-hour before the Rathnure minor hurlers were due to play. My sister and myself walked behind him as he approached the gate. There was an official with a satchel around his shoulder taking money and handing out tickets. When it came to our turn, my father just put out his hand, brushed the official to one side with the words, "I want you to know that I have two sons providing part of the entertainment here today, and it's not my intention to pay the GAA for the privilege of watching my own sons." I was taken by surprise, but didn't mind, whereas my sister Essie was not alone furious with him but very embarrassed and told him so. "Daddy! That's awful," she cried, but it fell on deaf ears. Luckily, and to my delight, the official recognised my father and with a gushing, "Ah, Mr Rackard – sure it's you. That's alright. Go ahead," and in we went without paying. After the game, Essie went off to visit some friends, whilst I tagged along behind my father, eventually ending up in a pub full of Rathnure supporters. I had my favourite red lemonade and he had a whiskey as we both stood together listening to the ever-increasing din of voices as the liquor slowly loosened the tongues of eager customers. My father was not a man who stood out in a crowd, but we quietly downed our drink and had more of the same (my thirst for red lemonade was insatiable), then almost out of nowhere, a large arm stretched across my head, extending a big paw which came to rest on my father's shoulder. This was followed by a gravelly voice:

"Be God, Bob," the voice said. "Dem's right chaps of yours." It was a farmer from our parish who was seeing my father in a totally different light for the first time. It was the age-old moment of reflected glory and my father's first dose. Looking up at him, it was easy to see, by the expression on his face, that he was enjoying it, which was only natural. "Do you think so Tom?" he parried.

"Oh be God, Bob, I do. We all know that older lad of yours is going to be a star, but so are these chaps we saw today." My father's face was a study. He was fumbling for a reply and then to my astonishment he said, "I have two more you know, just you wait until this fella here grows up, placing a hand on my head." "He's going to be the best one of the lot of them." I was astounded, and before I got the opportunity to savour my father's unexpected compliment, the farmer's big hand was outstretched, supported by the descent of two large friendly eyes. My little hand was just about big enough as we engaged in a warm hand shake, followed by the question "... And your name is?" "Billy," I answered, gently withdrawing my hand. But my father's words were ringing in my ears. As a family, compliments to each other were something that were not indulged in. Praise, no matter what was achieved, was a scarce commodity. I found it hard to believe what my father had said about me and repeatedly tossed it about in my mind, asking myself had he really meant it? Anyway, I rationalised, he did say it so I would take a degree of comfort from it.

However inside twelve months or so I was to find out the real reason behind his praise. The fact that he was now the father of sons who were now looked upon as excellent hurlers was having its effect on him, and nowhere more so than on his ego. It was this, allied to behaving like the fictional Irishman who, when complimented about his outstanding son, horse or greyhound usually brushed it to one side with the blasé comment, "That's nothin'. Sure you should see the one I have back at home."

As his sons became more prominent at the game there were certain occasions when this attitude of my father's took a grip on him; and sometimes with comical effect, although at the time he wasn't aware of it. On arrival back home that evening, my sister, informed my mother about the incident as we made our way in to see the game. Mother was not pleased and she forcibly made her feelings known to him. "You are not to do that again" she scolded in strong wifely tones. "It's alright for you but the fact is that it's not just you. It's your family, you should also bear them in mind on such occasions. It's all so very embarrassing." This corrosive assessment of his behaviour had my father shifting uneasily in his chair. "I don't care" he grunted huffily. "A lot of those fellas I wouldn't trust when it comes to handling money and furthermore, I would like to know what the GAA does with all that cash." It was a weak defence and he knew it.

CHAPTER TWELVE

1940 was to leave its destructive mark on the county of Wexford, not to mention the rest of the country. War raged off our coasts and in the air above. The German Luftwaffe brought tragedy to Campile in South Wexford when they bombed the creamery during the early afternoon of August 26th. Three girls working there were killed. Rumours abounded that butter from the creamery had been discovered on British troops at Dunkirk and that this was the cause of the inexplicable raid. In order to preserve neutrality, the Irish Government accepted the apologies of the German Legation and their offer of compensation.

Two days previously four bombs had fallen near Duncormick, again near the Wexford coastline; this time causing no casualties. Then in December, the 'Isolda' was bombed by the Germans as it brought supplies to Connibeg lighthouse killing twenty-six of its twenty-eight man crew. This was an horrific assault on defenceless men from a neutral country.

January 1st, 1941 heralded further bombing on land. The Shannon family lost three members when their farm at Knockroe, Kiltealy, on the boundary of North Wexford/Carlow, took the brunt of another miscalculation as an aircraft returned to base. The German plane, believed to have been losing altitude, decided to jettison its load upon this lonely mountain region – such was the explanation offered by the German diplomats – this did not excuse the disaster as a bomb made a direct hit on the Shannon household. On the following Sunday I can recall riding Bill the cob along with other horsemen and a multiplicity of bicycles through Scallogh Gap to see the devastation of the Shannon farmstead. Then ten bombs were similarly released over the townlands of Ballinstraw and Glenbrien, frightening the daylights out of the locals, none of whom fortunately were injured. Some of these bombs dropped ominously close to Balinakeele House, the lovely home belonging to the Maher family who had years before bred the famous mare *Frigate* ridden by H.B. Beasley to win the Aintree Grand National.

People were mesmerised by the sight of the Luftwaffe and the RAF accidentally invading Wexford's airspace and engaging in dog fights overhead. This was at the height of the Battle of the Atlantic. Some planes appeared to have lost direction on their return flights from bombing the convoys; others crashed, and their pilots were interned if they survived or were buried locally if they did not. The dead were disinterred at the end of the war and reburied at Glencree, Co. Wicklow.

A mysterious figure called Herr Thomsen, who was a councillor at the German Legation in Dublin, came down to preside at these funerals, complete with a swastica armband and Nazi salute. As he spoke in German over the flag-draped coffins, few understood what he was saying. After the war it is said that he went to live in Rathmines.

Crash!

It was almost ten o'clock. My mother had made several unsuccessful attempts to put her two younger daughters and three youngest sons to bed. We had heard rumours that the Crabbe children down at the cross were allowed to stay up to 11 p.m. We were harassing our mother with this information in order to gain extra time. Usually we went to bed not later than nine o'clock, but now that it was well after ten o'clock, and going by the expression on our mother's face, then it was time to go, we felt, so off we went. I had just put my head on the pillow, easing into a gentle sleep, when there was an almighty bang. I had never previously heard anything like it. It was followed by a huge rumble, which felt like it was coming down the mountain. Simultaneously, John and I jumped from our beds and peered out the window. It was dark outside. A German plane, fully loaded with bombs and mines, presumably on an outward journey to the Atlantic, had crashed into the Blackstairs killing both occupants instantly.

The Red Cross unit in Enniscorthy, who were under almost continual standby were alerted as quickly as was possible, driving up the hillside as far as the terrain would allow. The next stage was a considerable climb on foot to the crash site. George Ryan, the first member of the field ambulance unit to reach it, recently told me of his recollections. The smell of burning flesh is still vivid in his mind, but there was nothing anyone could do as they watched the burning bodies of the dead airmen draped halfway out of the dismembered remains of the cockpit. A rim of searing heat kept everyone well back. Finally, when the heat subsided, they managed to retrieve the remains of the two Germans.

The field ambulance members were not the only people who climbed up the Blackstairs on that very night of the crash. The crash naturally aroused a lot of curiosity and even though it was late at night, a number of locals, whose motivation was mainly and understandably mere curiosity, also decided to make the ascent. Armed with flash lights, up they went, assembling in twos and threes around the carnage. During the ascent there were small explosions indicating the activating of light incendiary devices. These explosions were not alarming. However, it was not until weeks later, when the Irish army detonated the plane's main cargo, that they discovered a formidable collection of huge bombs and mines all destined for the waters of the North Atlantic. Massive death-carrying devices used to prevent merchant shipping bringing much needed supplies to a half-starved Europe. It was only after hearing the terrifying explosions they caused, did the locals realise that through their curiosity, some might have lost their lives that night.

Our local hackneyman, Tom Skelton, also went up the mountain that night. Tom was born further North on that very mountain, but at a lower level from where the plane crashed. He came down to Killanne, and he worked for my father for a while, then fell in love with and married the local schoolteacher, Mary Byrne. A nice house was built and they lived in fine surroundings. There were no children. Mary was a good provider and so was her husband, when his taxi ran. But Tom had something else going for him, something that was to give him an entrée to certain elements in society. He was an acknowledged expert on gun dogs and grouse shooting and was also adept at preparing a greyhound for the track. There were monied people in Dublin and elsewhere who liked gun dogs and shooting on the mountain, and Tom was the expert on both. A good-looking man, he discovered how to exercise social skills appropriately, and sink whiskies. The local GAA was not on his list of charities. He had a pal who also travelled up the mountain with him on that historic night. His name was Jim Rackard. Their almost first glance at the burning aircraft was distracted by some movement close by in the heather. Tommy investigated, swooped down, and turned about to his friend, ecstatically cradling a fully grown hare in his arms. It had been disorientated by the big bang and was just lying there. The pair immediately forgot about the horrific crash, setting off down the mountain gleefully with the hare. Skelton had a promising greyhound, almost ready for a gamble, but in need of sharpening up, and this hare from heaven was just the ticket.

Waste not, want not

The crash of the German aircraft on the Blackstair mountain directly behind our house at Killanne was in time to support the old adage of "It's an ill wind that blows no good." Some small artifacts were quickly recovered from the debris. A lucky local lad was the proud finder of a flick knife, a fascinating object much envied by his contempories.

But the biggest and most beneficial item was a wheel of the aircraft. One had stayed intact but one had broken loose. Some young men raised it up, setting it off down the hillside and apparently it was quite a sight as it hurtled downhill, obstacles in its path causing it to make gigantic leaps into the air. It eventually came to rest behind a farmhouse high up on the mountainside. It was in time spotted by an enterprising local cobbler who managed to saw off hunks of the large tyre, the subsequent salvage leading to the resoling of many pairs of shoes in the parish of Rathnure. With the existing leather shortage, word quickly spread, resulting in other cobblers climbing the hill and availing of the plunder. By the time I saw the wheel it was almost denuded of its entire rubber.

Wexford's troubles paled proportionately when news reached us that Dublin had been bombed during the early hours of Saturday, 31st May. Three bombs fell on the North Strand and North Circular Road; a fourth near the dog pond in the Phoenix Park. The latter did no damage, but the first three brought tragedy and wide-spread destruction. Twenty-seven people were killed that night and forty-five wounded. Twenty-five houses were flattened and no less than three hundred more rendered uninhabitable. The sound of the explosions radiated as far afield as Mullingar.

After this appaling calamity, everyone was urged to join the Red Cross or the Civil Defence. My sister Essie volunteered for the Red Cross. Earlier, across the border, there was devastating destruction in Belfast, with five hundred killed and fifteen hundred injured in April. It is warming to remember the 'hands across the border' spirit as fire brigades from Eire rushed North to give assistance.

The merchant navy were to take a pounding. Their plucky crews took a terrible risk each time they put to sea – yet this country depended on them to do so. In June 1941, the Rosslare-Fishguard boat, the *St Patrick* sank with the loss of twenty-three lives. This was the fourth attack by dive bombers on her, and her sistership had been sunk with heavy casualties the previous summer. Her master was Commodore James Faraday. The Wexford Steamship Company's motor vessel, the Kerlogue was attacked by an unidentified plane. Eleven of her crew were injured.

On the night of Tuesday, 2nd December, the village of Rosslare and Wexford town were woken by a blast described as like an earthquake. This was the effect of a floating mine being washed up at Tuskar Rock lighthouse. Of the three keepers, one was killed, one injured and one escaped. The latter bravely returned immediately to his post.

Washed up mines were an occasional hazard on beaches, with, on one dreadful day, several soldiers being killed as they attempted to dismantle a mine which had floated ashore.

No way lay Mr Forristal

In Wexford's win over Cork in the All-Ireland Final of 1956, five of the team were from Rathnure. During my years in Rathnure National School, I was to sit alongside Martin Codd. Ahead of us, by a couple of years, was my brother Bobby, whilst about one-and-a-half miles away at the Curacy School in Templeudigan was Jim English. Nickey, of course, was not at the National School during my time. Anyway, in our win over Cork in the All-Ireland final of 1956, Bobby, as we know, was at right corner-back marking the incomparable Christy Ring. Jim English versus Mick Regan at half-back, alongside myself at centre-back, confronted by Josie Hartnett; whilst up the middle of the Wexford forward line on that famous occasion was Martin Codd at centre-forward up against Willie John Daly, with Nickey at full-forward against John Lyons.

However, back in 1942 or thereabouts it would have been a very courageous clairvoyant who would have dared to make such a prediction especially if he had seen the old schoolhouse and its facilities. Partitioned in the centre, with a door into each section, at each outside gable end were dry closet toilets; one for the boys and another for the girls. Neither could boast of running water.

During lunch break we sometimes played rounders in the small triangular-shaped yard that fronted the school building which had a clay perimeter fence running by the roadside, carrying a nice growth of mature beech trees. On the other side was a stone face ditch that looked out on an open field. It was here, on the rough surfaced yard, that we spent the lunch-time break. Marbles or as some called it taw in the hole was a popular game. Next was rounders. The best 'taw in the hole' or marble player in Rathnure was academic-looking Dominic Fenelon, whose boney knuckles, after a few preliminary prods at the ground, released the marble with astonishing speed and accuracy.

As well as his expertise at that sport, he was also good at repartee and noted for producing some appealing-looking gadgets from his pocket, to dazzle the onlookers. A pencil-peeler was a common everyday object, but on this occasion, Dominic produced one that had everyone entranced. It was shaped like a light bulb, only smaller and at the obvious end it sharpened the pencil, but the bulbous section sported nothing less than a map of the world. We gathered round him admiring it as he held it aloft for all to see. One hypnotised onlooker asked where Ireland was on it. Dominic eventually got fed up answering questions about where this and that was. But the last straw was when a simple lad inquired about the pink area at the top. Dominic, who was tall, simply put his hand on the lad's head, twisted it about towards the field, from which came a loud murmuring of starlings (always referred to locally as Jack Stabbers). "Do you see all them Jack Stabbers out there?" he asked.

"Yes," replied the puzzled lad.

"Well, that pink spot. That's where they all come from." I still have a vision in my mind of the lad scratching his head in between glancing towards the field of starlings and Fenelon.

Most boys at that school were keen to bring hurleys with them, but without ground to play on it was pointless. Consequently a plot was hatched. The field across the road facing the school was owned by a Mr John Forristal. Mr Forristal, with the prime of youth well behind him, cut a solitary figure as he walked the roads. He and his wife had suffered the tragic loss of their only child, a little girl who died at the age of four. He always wore a hat, and keeping great custody of his eyes he never appeared to glance left or right. With his hands sometimes clasped behind his back as he walked, he just stared at the piece of road directly in front of him. Not a community man, he and his wife lived near Rathnure village in a splendid residence that boasted of very large acreage. There was a distant aloofness about him, but nonetheless, John Forristal was looked on with great respect.

The plan was that two boys would be nominated to intercept Mr Forristal on a day when he walked past the school yard. Filled with trepidation, they would need sufficient nerve to confront him and ask straight out if it would be okay if some boys did a bit of hurling in his field. The two selected were Bobby Rackard and Martin Codd. The rest were ordered to keep a constant lookout for a day, when Mr Forristal was passing. And so it happened. "He's coming this way," they shouted. The skirmishing stopped amongst the boys and everyone went quiet. Out marched the two nominees to confront the austere-looking Mr Forristal. The rest, clinging lizardlike to the trees, on the perimeter fence held their breath. Out on the road Mr Forristal and the two lads appeared to be just staring at each other. Then, as if a starting gun had been fired, the two boys quickly turned, came back at full speed, jumping the school yard fence in a single leap. There was no need to ask what Mr Forristal had said. We looked back towards the road and there was Mr Forristal walking abstractedly past, gazing straight ahead as usual and appearing totally oblivious to the resulting delirium caused by his magnanimity.

Later on that year, just before the Christmas holidays, all the boys made a collection for Mr Forristal. The lookout again took up position, and eventually the shout came. "He's on his way." Once more the same two boys marched stiffly out to again confront Mr Forristal. They lifted up a little brown parcel towards him. "This, Sir, is for you with a Happy Christmas from all of us."

Rafferty goes up in smoke

Hugh O'Reilly, the schoolmaster was a Cavan man. Although a rather serious individual and very seldom seen in a flippant mood, he was still well-liked. He was viewed as an excellent teacher, but lacked the ability to teach Irish. This was reflected afterwards by pupils from the school who went for secondary education, an unusual occurence at that time. O'Reilly, who married a local girl, showed no real interest in gaelic games. Nonetheless when asked to help out with the club administration after its foundation during early legislative teething problems, he was a willing adviser. During my time he was getting on in years and appeared to be afflicted by a spasmodic drink problem. Little did he realise that the entire school was always aware of his wet periods. It was publicly signalled to all and sundry by the incessant popping of lozenges into his mouth. Whilst our school principal had minimal interest in hurling, the parish priest, Father Hore, had absolutely none. This was much to the chagrin of the Rathnure team who envied the neighbouring parish and strong rivals Caim/Kiltealy, as their priest Father Murphy was a fanatical supporter of that team.

One evening after school, Rafferty and myself were cycling home. About halfway on the journey, Rafferty put his boot to the ground, bringing the bike to a standstill. Sitting on the saddle, he rummaged in one of his many waistcoat pockets and produced the old fashioned packet of five Woodbines, the ones that stood upright in a little paper jacket. Rafferty's waistcoats were always a source of envy and admiration for me. I think they were hand-me-downs and seemed to have endless little pockets. He shook the packet coaxing out one of the Woodbines, then fingered another pocket. Out came a box of matches. The end of the Woodbine was suddenly a bright red as he took a long drag out of it. For quite a time there was no sign of any smoke, then all at once it came billowing out through his nostrils and mouth. At no time in my life could I inhale cigarette smoke. I looked on in amazement as he did this; then he would take another pull at the Woodbine, shape his mouth like a duck's backside and with his cheeks working as if he was getting something in place, his mouth would pop open now and then like a fish and out came varying sizes of smoke rings. I begged him to teach me how to do it, but I never succeeded.

Anyway we pushed off and after some distance, Rafferty took another long drag. Then out of the blue, we heard the whirring of bicycle wheels and lo and behold, who sailed in between us only the schoolmaster, O'Reilly. For a change, he was full of chat. After absorbing the shock, I looked across at Rafferty who was still holding the smoke. The schoolteacher, for whatever reason was full of bonhomie and throwing conversation about. I looked across again. Nature at birth bestowed a permanent state of blush on Rafferty but now his face had turned purple, and he looked like a football with two green eyes. Somehow, he managed to release the smoke without the schoolteacher knowing, but there was no sign of the Woodbine as we sailed down the hill on the bikes. Approaching the bottom, the schoolmaster suddenly looked at Rafferty and shouted: "You're on fire!" O'Reilly eyed Rafferty's indian war dance as he stamped on his jacket with a mixture of amazement and suspicion. Finally the teacher just hopped on his bike and with a shake of his head, pedalled out of sight.

CHAPTER THIRTEEN

My favourite cycling trip was the one home from school on the day we got our summer holidays. I cradled the delightful knowledge that for a long time to come, I would not have to go back there.

Of all the activities I looked forward to during that long break, my favourite was being part of the hay-saving team. It brought my hunter-gatherer instincts to the fore, from seeing it cut to the final pleasure of watching it all being tucked away securely for the winter under cover in the hayshed. My father sensed when the time for cutting was near. Bill, the chestnut cob was yoked under the spring cart, although not as elegant looking as the trap or back-to-back, it was still my favourite method of travelling. With both of us sitting one each side, legs dangling down, we set off. Shep loved that spring cart. He would leap in, standing straight up on all fours. He looked the very picture of contentment with his hairy tail held high. A turnabout by him and that tail brushed the back of your head. At the other end a large red tongue flopped out, especially if the weather was hot. Sometimes a little terrier we had would make a fuss. He wanted to go too. Eventually he was hoisted in. On arrival my father trudged out a distance into the meadow to have a closer look, pulling a few strands here and there of the long sweet stems as he went. One of my favourite vistas is watching a mature meadow being buffeted by a brisk wind as it creates a convulsive movement in the long grass. Intermittent sunshine and shadow manufactured by fast-moving clouds far above it, give the illusion of an ocean swell as the mature meadow undulates in one direction then another.

I spent many magical moments lying on my back in the long grass, just staring up at the blue sky watching clouds going over, lazing there, listening to a buzzing jungle of little sounds which seemed to be everywhere but sometimes interrupted by the leathery flutter of pigeons' wings as they quickly passed on their journey overhead.

I eventually saw my father wending his way back to the gate where Bill was tethered on the road outside. I followed suit, and on reaching the gate, I placed my fingers in my mouth and emitted a loud whistle. It didn't take long before the two happy dogs came charging through the long grass, ears flopping and each sporting a red tongue. When we reached home my father hopped off. "Untackle that fella and put him in his stall. When you have that done see if you can find Joe Hogan and tell him I want him," he said.

I knew then that the meadow was forward enough for cutting. The mowing machine and the binder had kept each other company in a state of redundancy now for many months. Looking at them pushed in tight together in a large lean-to off the main hay shed, they sometimes appeared a sorry sight. Wisps of hay had fallen on them; hens had climbed over them; dust had settled; all adding up to a picture of inactivity and unkemptness. Now, for the mowing machine, it was action stations once more. Next morning Joe Hogan deftly manoeuvred some of the common carts that also shared the cover of that shed to protect them from unfavourable weather conditions. With help he made space to pull out the mowing machine from behind its winter companion, the binder, the wheels making a clicking noise as it was dragged out into the sunlight.

Joe Hogan was a careful man. He moved about it quietly with a large oil can, peering here and there. He knew exactly where the oil was needed. When it went into hibernation, Joe had secured the long blade in a safe place wrapped in oily rags and now remembered where it was located. He was a master with the sharpening stone as he meticulously resharpened each diamond shaped blade that was attached to the cutting bar. When in use, this bar lay flat in its housing on the ground, but for transportation reasons it was levered into a perpendicular position, giving the impression of an upstretched arm. With two horses, one at each side of a single shaft and the driver holding long reins back to the raised seat, it gave off the appearance of an ancient Roman chariot of war.

A day or so later, weather permitting, it was all systems go. The machine was now ready for action with two horses yoked and Joe having a last minute check as he walked quietly around looking closely at both the machinery and horses. Bill, the cob, was ready to move out again with the spring cart, only this time there was an extra passenger and extra baggage. The extra passenger was Jim Blackburn, and in the well of the spring cart was a scythe, a sharpening stone and a couple of hay forks. Finally, my father would send me into the dairy for a can full of fresh buttermilk and a mug. Both were tucked in the corner of the cart and shielded from the sun by a few wads of cool, hand-pulled fresh grass.

We set off in front at a brisk pace, this time with the dogs trotting alongside. On reaching the meadow, Blackburn quickly got to work, his sinewy arms acting like pistons as he went up and down the scythe blade with the sharpening stone. In a matter of minutes, what looked a disorderly overgrown scene was changed into a neat trim picture as Blackburn, with mighty swipes, wielded the scythe outside and inside the gate, changing it into a state of orderliness. Then the gate was pulled back, with the area immediately cleared for the mowing machine to take over. My father's advice of 'Keep their heads out still' was totally unnecessary to a man of Joe Hogan's experience. The horses slowly halted and shuffled on all fours in unison, making the perfect angle for the machine to enter the field. A few circuits of the field, and, the air was heavy with a scented sweet-smelling aroma that only comes from new-mown hay. The mowing machine continued on an ever diminishing circuit of the meadow, laying flat each and every long stem of grass that came into its lethal path. Joe Hogan appeared a silent, lonely figure as, aboard the machine, he was steadfastly and irrevocably pulled along by the two willing horses.

A moving mowing bar, concealed so close to the ground is a dangerous piece of machinery, so at all times, Joe was keeping a close look-out for fear of an impending accident. The two dogs were the most likely to come in contact, but should they come close, he would pull the horses to a halt and warn them off. By now Shep and the terrier were fully aware that there was a rabbit or two trapped in the remaining hay left standing. A few had already made a successful dash for freedom, but the growing prospect of another chase was making the dogs excited. The rabbits need not have worried, because Shep, who in his younger days was capable of nabbing one, was no longer fast on his feet. The terrier yelped more than was necessary, but whilst his enthusiasm was admirable, he was even more incapable of out-running or outwitting two smart bunnies who showed both dogs their white little scuts as they disappeared at full speed into the boundary ditch.

"Whoa boys," as Joe Hogan brought the horses to a halt. My father handed him a mug of fresh buttermilk. Blackburn and myself had already delved into it earlier, replacing it carefully in the shade in a corner of the meadow. When it came to dinner time, both horses were unyoked and tied separately, near the gate where there was a patch of lush grazing. The collars and hames were taken off each one so that when the horse lowered his head, he had complete freedom of movement. Joe Hogan, an excellent horse man, was also a horse lover. Before he tied them up, he meandered a short distance with them down the road where there was a little stream. They drank their fill of fresh spring water and after returning and tethering them, he went and scooped up an armful of freshly mown hay, dropping a bundle in front of each one.

At this stage my father, Blackburn and myself and the two dogs were aboard the spring cart waiting for him. Bill, the cob, was a fast mover, going in any direction, but once his head was turned for home he seemed to find an extra gear. Sparks were flying as his shoes made explosive contact with the road. My father never left Bill tied up like the heavier working horses. He was always put in his stall with a measure of golden corn laid in his feed bowl. Watching him tucking into it, his pleasure was signalled by the jerking of a knee as he rapped it noisily off the manger in sheer delight as he masticated the energy-giving oats.

After the dinner, my father did not go back to the meadow. Instead I was given the job of bringing the two men back there. Being left in charge of the cob and the spring cart was sheer joy. I quickly delivered the two men back to the field and returned before four o'clock to bring them each a large bottle of hot tea and a couple of slices of brown bread and jam. Heading back to the meadow on my own with just the basket in one corner of the cart, I stood up and jammed my feet at opposite sides. Approaching the crossroads at Killanne, I would turn left, a nice sweeping turn. Bill knew I was going that way. Nearing the turn, I lolloped the reins along his back. Doing that always brought an immediate response, one of increased speed. He was fairly flying as he swept left. I moved my weight about and then it happened. I had heard about this from my older brothers; now I was achieving it myself. One wheel left the ground and with the speed of movement and distribution of the driver's weight, it was possible to keep that balance and to round the corner on one wheel.

Yippee! I had done it. Fantastic! I did not brag about it to my father. I left that to my doubting Thomas brothers.

When the hay was ready for making into cocks, the scene in the meadow changed dramatically. The place became a hive of activity. Everyone and anyone that could was rounded up, with some released from normal duties to also give a hand. The men who worked on the farm were naturally the backbone of the team, which included all of us boys. A neighbouring farmer would send a helper, a reciprocal practice amongst farmers. There were two assistants in the shop and one of them, Fintan Coogan, was usually directed from his duties behind the counter to show his prowess with the hayfork. His attempts at pitching hay were generally the butt of derisory looks and comments by Blackburn and Co.

"Look at 'im. He doesn't even know how to catch the bloody pitchfork and he hasn't any knee action either. He's hopeless." Soon Coogan was displaying beginner's blisters much to the derision of the others.

Blackburn was the star of the show. He was in charge of a small grey horse yolked to the hay rake, and the whole operation depended on his expertise. This horse-drawn rake collected up a monstrous bundle of hay, growing in size so that eventually Blackburn could scarcely see the horse's backside. With a wooden arm attached to the rake held in his hand, he tumbled the rake, releasing all the hay, but this demanded agility as the driver then had to quickly hop over the partially flattened hay to keep in touch with the horse who was marching steadily on. A few round ups like this and there was a large ring of hay ready to be cocked, and this is where the amateur helpers, led by Tom Dreelan, came in. Tim Breen, Joe Hogan and the neighbours then usually designed and saw to the making of the cocks, the rest merely pitched the hay in their direction, until the cock was deemed to be sufficiently large. It was then slapped conditionally with a hayfork and the sides neatly raked. If the field was exposed excessively, it was common practice for a pair of stones to be slung across, each attached to a piece of string that didn't reach the ground. Another pair of stones hanging similarly meant the twines crossing the top prevented it blowing off until it settled.

There were two aspects to hay-making I did not like. One was the hayseed, always a source of irritation as it inevitably made its way down the back of your neck. The other was the perpetual thirst. My father made periodic visits, just checking on progress ensuring that there was still some buttermilk left or some spring water. When all the loose hay was finally rounded up and made into neat cocks, the field again took on a different appearance. A sweeping look at the haycocks scattered about the place conjured up an image of a Red Indian village of wigwams.

The next stage of the hay-saving was by far my favourite and that was when the time came for transporting the large haycocks back home to the hayshed. This meant using what was called the haylifter, a large, unwieldy looking wooden horse-drawn crane worked by pulleys, with three huge steel L-shaped prongs pushed underneath the haycock as it was hoisted up off the ground then lowered onto the cart. The cock was securely tied down to the cart. Sitting on top you could just see the horse's neck and head. I felt so proud the first time I was allowed to take one back to the haggard in sole charge. Sitting on top the haycock, surveying the countryside, I was filled with inner pride at the thought of being given such adult responsibility. On the ground, in the hayshed, were usually two of the strongest men. Ropes untied, the cock was pushed off, then sometimes in unison, the two men would dig in the forks and pitch up the hay, two more taking it from them and transferring it again to a higher bench where another packed it tightly. When that section was packed the same pattern started again at ground level. Finally the shed was well-packed with the sweet smelling hay - a happy and secure thought for any farmer when contemplating the winter that lay ahead.

Divided loyalties for Nickey

Rathnure, having won the Wexford Junior hurling title in 1940, made very little impact once they moved into the senior ranks. Nickey, who from 1941, was a student in the Dublin Veterinary College, decided to leave his old club and play for Young Irelands in the Dublin Championship. This was a difficult decision for him and was brought about by a combination of factors. Firstly, it would be virtually impossible for the present generation to comprehend the difficulties of regular travel in those times. Leaving Dublin and returning the same day was out of the question. Nonetheless, forsaking his old club was to prove emotionally debilitating for Nickey; but it was helped somewhat by the fact that his team-mates in Rathnure were anxious that he should play a few years in the Dublin Championship. He would then be rubbing shoulders with the best, finding out in the process what the game was like at the top club level, and in time return to his old club and county benefiting in every way from such an invaluable experience. This he did.

He played in his first Dublin Championship in 1941 with Young Irelands. His absence naturally weakened the Rathnure team, and they were subsequently beaten in their first year in senior ranks. This made very little difference to the rank and file hurlers of the time in Rathnure. The Barrack field and the pitch in Rathnure were as full as ever with vibrant youth. The air reverberated with the sound of the excited voices, interrupted only by the constant 'clash of the ash'.

'A stopper'

Apart from hurling, all of us boys had a deep love of horses. My father occasionally had some nice-looking horses. He would sell them unbroken or just broken and riding. He did not then ride much himself, and whilst he liked hunting and took pride in seeing his sons doing a little, he never kept horses specifically for that purpose. Most of the working horses, mainly Irish Draft, were capable hunters, not to mention the chestnut cob. He did, however, once buy a black fourteen-two especially with Nickey in mind for the purpose of hunter trials.

I recall a young girl riding into the yard one morning to join Nickey in a school for both animals over a specially made water fence, a de rigeur obstacle in all hunter trials then. As they jumped the bushes fronting it, both merely landed in the shallow water. They tried again with the same results. My father was furious about this, telling the two teenagers to stay put whilst he went quickly back home on the spring cart. He returned with some rusty sheets of galvanise which he placed underneath the water. "Come on now," he shouted. Both animals again did the same thing, only this time they landed on the galvanise which frightened the wits out of them. "Come on again," shouted my father "and push 'em out." This time both ponies sailed way above the water. My father was well known for his impatience and quick resort to some idiosyncratic method. This time he was delighted with the result.

The girl in question was a Miss Orpen, who lived in the local manor house at Monksgrange, later in life to become a household name in Ireland and England as Mrs Charmain Hill, the owner of the legendary race mare, *Dawn Run*.

A day out with the local Bree hunt meant asking permission from Father, which was granted only if the horse was idle and not needed for more important farm work. There was one fine big chestnut Irish draft called Phelan, whose easy technique, ability and sheer love of jumping was well known by huntsmen in the area. Davy Crane, a local farmer 'whipped in' now and then for the hunt. He borrowed Phelan one day for this purpose and the horse gave such an exhibition of jumping that his name was on everyone's lips. No matter what the obstacle, he made it look simple and easy, and refusal was just not part of his nature. He was a natural. Like all farm horses of that time he was fit, full of oats and trace-clipped. My father was pleased at being the owner of such an animal – until a few days later that is – when Phelan was put between the shafts of a dray cart to do his normal work. The horse refused point blank to move! Hunting, his real love in life, had triggered off a change in his attitude and brought about the use of the ugliest word in a horseman's dictionary – 'a stopper.' Phelan had become one. Subsequently, when alongside another horse pulling a plough, the mere sound of a huntsman's horn in the distance would have his ears twitching, with Joe Hogan terrified that the horse would decide to down tools! He was such an excellent hunter that in time it was decided to exonerate him from farm-work for most of the hunting season. The Whipper-in, Crane, helped the situation by substituting one of his own work horses. When the hunting season was finished, Phelan after a couple of weeks would resort to becoming once again a willing helper with the rest of his equine brethren.

Nickey, Jim, Bobby and myself were adequate riders, capable of even riding in a point-to-point. John, however, was not. His hurling resembled his horsemanship, displaying an essential lack of quick reflexes. He did eventually learn to ride quite well, but he was not fussed or phased by his lack of proficiency at either. John, an amiable easy-going type, was to grow into the biggest man of the family, quite a formidable size even in his teens, ending up about six foot three as a grown man and built proportionately. Another Rackard, he cut quite an image when togged off, complete with hurley stick. His career was to be short-lived. He liked sport, but knowing his deficiencies, was too philosophical to decide to take it seriously or compete with his razor-sharp brothers.

None of my sisters chose horse-riding as a sporting outlet, although, there would be a burst of enthusiasm now and then, like in the aftermath of the film *National Velvet*. In retrospect, however, things might have been different had suitable animals been provided for them. This and more encouragement could have made the difference, but I am afraid our house and precincts was very male-dominated. Another factor was that, in spite of his wonderful qualities, Bill, the chestnut cob was not an animal for beginners. Show him a bank and you were delivered to the far side swiftly. Whilst he was never known to fall, his contact with the bank was brief – you had to sit tight!

CHAPTER FOURTEEN

One Saturday morning, I was in the haggard doing nothing in particular. I noticed the six span hayshed had two spans still full. What a wondrous hide and seek area a hayshed is! All of us boys spent happy hours playing in it, as well as burrowing a tunnel right through at ground level. It was a perfect hide-out, but in time was usually commandeered by the dogs. Shep would appear, stretching his every limb as he sniffed the open air. Then Topsy, a brown cocker, yawning as he came out and finally the small head of the terrier, Sparks, would protrude. As I walked about, I observed the fine rick of straw that was still there, and two large pits; one of mangolds; another of turnips and beet. They were well-covered and secured from frost and rain. Tim Breen had just left with a load of turnips to feed the cattle which were in the fields above the house, a usual task for him, only this time there was something different. He had Bill, the chestnut cob, with common tack on him and between the shafts of a common cart. Although Bill was well-capable of such work and was incapable of refusing any request, it saddened me to see him being downgraded and demeaned in such a manner. He looked so smart with a driving harness or better still, with just a saddle and bridle, but there was a reason why he was now being used for this purpose. Most of the horses were in harness, putting out dung whilst Joe Hogan had another pair doing some early ploughing.

I was still poking about the haggard when I heard the singing sound of a bouncing football. Just seconds later, Nickey appeared doing a toe to hand. The local doctor had been to Dublin on Friday and had made him an unexpected offer of a lift home for the weekend. As he approached, he immediately started drop-kicking the ball against the full span of hay. Nickey never bothered with football until he went to Dublin. In view of that it comes as a surprise that, although not a natural, he was quite successful at it. Not alone did he play for the county for many seasons, which included winning a Leinster title in 1945, but he was also selected at inter-provincial level. In fact, on one St Patrick's day he was to play in both hurling and football railway cup finals. As the ball came back off the hay he sometimes kicked it as it rolled, other times he picked it up. This time, as he picked it up, he just stood quietly turning his head sideways. "Can you hear anything?" he called out to me. At that moment I couldn't. "Come up here to the top of the haggard and listen" he said. Then I knew what he meant. I could hear it plainly. It was the sound of foxhounds giving tongue and it seemed not too far away. He dropped the football from his hands and jumped up on the haggard ditch. "There", he said, "just over behind the Rectory." He jumped down and went as fast as his legs would take him down to the yard, disappearing through the stable door. He had no sooner gone through the door than he was back out. "Where are all the horses?" he yelled as he strode back up.

"They're all working" I shouted.

"And the cob — where's he?" he asked.

"Tim Breen is putting out turnips to cattle with him – just over there".

"In which field?"

"The Iron Gate field," I replied.

He took off again at breakneck speed in its direction, slipping and falling to the ground once as he charged along. I went after him as fast as I could, and when I arrived at the gate I could see Tim Breen as he started dropping the turnips out one by one; the cob walking straight on of his own accord. Tim was surprised as Nickey arrived at the cob's head, panting and looking out of breath. As I walked up the argument had begun.

"Pull the lever and tip out them turnips," ordered Nickey, "I want that fella."

"Nickey, you know I can't do that – your father would kill me if he found out."

"But he won't find out," went on Nickey, "just tip out the bloody turnips."

"Look" said Tim "You know how fussy your father can be. If he finds them turnips in a heap and the cattle walking on 'em, he'll sack me, that's all."

At this point, Nickey went to the front of the cart and pulled back the lever. Putting his shoulder under the front of the cart, he shouted, 'You'd better jump off, cos I'm jacking this yoke up.'

He had no sooner said so than up went the cart, Tim, turnips and all. He then pulled the body of the cart back on its frame and leading the cob, set off back down towards the haggard at a trot. None the worse, Tim picked himself up and shaking his head in dismay, made his way back down toward the farmyard. I ran on in front of him. When I arrived in the haggard, Nickey had unyoked the cob and was throwing the heavy tackle onto the cart.

"Come here and hold this fella" he shouted as I came in sight. He then went like the clappers again towards the stable, this time re-appearing with a saddle and bridle. He slapped the saddle on, instructing me to take the winkers off and put the bridle on. In a matter of seconds, he had tightened the girth, lengthened the stirrup leathers, pushed the legs of his trousers down into his socks, jumped into the saddle and like the proverbial bat out of hell disappeared back up through the open gate and across the field at a furious gallop. I again ran up and about three fields away I could see a number of horses cantering, one rider easily distinguishable by the pink coat. Nickey was a fearless horseman, and God help a horse that would attempt to refuse when he was in the saddle. Although Bill the cob was not quite up to the weight, it made no difference as the pair of them barely checked at the few formidable fences that separated them from the rest of the hunting field. In a matter of minutes he had joined them and they all disappeared out of sight. I turned and went back home going down through the haggard into the farmyard. I could see Tim had started cleaning out manure from the cowshed. Everything was fine until my father appeared through the kitchen door. He always had the habit of now and then leaving the shop and having a look in the farmyard to see what was going on. Tim was tidying the manure heap as my father walked towards him. "Yoke that cob under the trap," he ordered, "I need to go down to Caim."

Caim was about two-and-a-half miles away and where my father had a similar business to Killanne with farm attached. None of the family lived there, but he had a manager in charge of the business. As he gave him the instructions, my father more or less turned about, walking back towards the kitchen half door. Closing the half door behind him, he looked about and saw that Tim hadn't moved. He changed his mind and marched back.

"I thought I told you to yoke that cob – well, go and do it immediately", he ordered, almost belligerently. Tim just stared at him as he held the sprong in his hands. My father became irritated. "What's the matter with you?" he asked.

"The cob's not here, sir" said Tim, giving him a baleful look as he spoke.

"Not here!" echoed my father with an air of disbelief and stomped off towards the stable door. He was about a minute inside when he reappeared, walking towards the middle of the yard, stopped and more or less muttered to himself; 'I see, yes, I see. So that's where he is. Just wait till that son of mine gets back."

My father kept a sharp look out for Nickey's return and guessed correctly that, when it occurred, it would not be through the front yard where he could be easily spotted. He intercepted him neatly as he made his way down from a different entrance via the haggard. Stepping out in front of the cob, he laid his hand on the rein. Straightening himself up and putting on his angriest face, he started. "It's bad enough having to pay for your upkeep, give you pocket money and see to your college fees as well, but it's the bloody limit that when you come home, instead of giving a hand, you can find nothing better to do than interfere with the work that goes on around the place." As my father was speaking, his eyes started roaming over the cob who looked an equine picture; his neck nicely arched, the tail held out attractively, his coat looking sleek with a shine showing through. Nickey kept silent. He was waiting his chance for a question which would give him the opportunity to side-step his father's anger. Horsey men are renowned for indulging in visual enjoyment when they see a well-formed animal. This was what my father was doing right then, only more so because this animal was his. Furthermore the pleasure he was deriving from staring at it standing there looking so magnificent, was vindicating his judgement of the moment he had first set eyes on it as a scrawny three-year-old at the fair in New Ross. My father shifted his feet, coughed as he looked up and then came the opportunity which his son was desperately waiting for. Instead of pressing home the disciplinary attack, he made the fatal mistake of asking, 'Well, how did he go?'

"How did he go?" repeated Nickey. "I'll tell you this much – there was nothing out there today that would stay with or outjump this lad. We were up in front all the way." A large smile fought hard to cross my father's face, but he staved it off as he strained at maintaining his angry countenance.

"Ha, ha! I thought that" he said almost triumphantly. "The first time I saw that fella in the fair in New Ross I knew immediately that he was the making of a right one."

But Nickey wasn't finished yet.

"Oh, by the way – there's a man wanting to buy him. (That was the clincher.)

"You bet there would be no bother selling that fella! Who was it?" asked my father.

"Matty Parle" said Nickey, now showing the sanguine appearance of a man who had escaped a jail sentence.

"Matty Parle," repeated my father. "The shrewdest man in the business. It wouldn't take Matty long to pass that fella on and in the process make a nice profit. He's not for sale and that's all – and you should know that."

Nickey was by now in command of the situation, his father's anger well diluted after such a gratifying account of the cob's performance. A final, albeit weak attempt at reprimand was made, when with a withering look, Nickey was ordered to put that cob in the stall. "And don't just throw him there. Clean him off properly, put his rug on and make sure he gets a hot bran mash, but don't let me catch you doing this again when there's work to be done."

Nickey's yarn about Bill the chestnut cob's performance was probably reasonably accurate, but his father's angry reaction to an animal being used for pleasure when instead it should be doing vital work on the farm, was a relic of the nuances of those days. Work usually went before pleasure. Nickey's reputation in the area for his courage and ability to back an unbroken horse was well known and a great source of pride to his father, a factor that was occasionally a great help to him in a tricky situation.

"Bring that horse down here Eddie," said my father, cheek to jowl in the bar with a neighbour, "my young lad will soon put manners on him." It may appear from this story that Nickey went rough shod over Tim's feelings, and to an extent he did, but not as you might imagine. When doing so he had about him an air of roguery that put him above normal convention, with the result that both he and Tim Breen looked back on the incident as enormous fun.

Nicky nicks a twinset

When it came to getting what he wanted, Nickey usually took a short cut. He would count the consequences afterwards. An incident of a similar nature took place concerning another horse belonging to father, which he was to prepare and ride in a local point-to-point. We all went as a family. I, being considerably younger, was with my mother in the parade ring, full of family pride. I watched as the riders came out. Suddenly my mother exploded. "My God, I'll kill him when I get him home!"

For his racing colours Nickey was wearing the inner part of her most prized twinset, which was now considerably stretched. The evidence was conclusive. It was obvious to her that he had rummaged through her private chest of drawers without her permission and she was not pleased, but that was Nickey — he would get away with it. The horse gave us all a good run, finishing second, and later on that evening, Nickey switched on his broad grin which had the desired effect on his by now calm mother.

For a long time point-to-points, more especially during the war years, were a big local sporting and social occasion. In those days they were run over a single line course stretching the full three-and-a-half-miles and presenting a variety of fearsome banks and ditches. It was a day out not to be missed. Almost everyone looked forward to the races. This traditional unique occasion had an Irish flavour all of its own. It incorporated a lot more than horses and jockeys. Faced with the unsophisticated and limited menu of entertainment in the forties, it was an event to be savoured, transversing all age groups from little lads like myself to giggly teenagers, right up to sharp-eyed grannies.

In between were those who were seriously implicated – the real players, the three-card-trick man, and Billy Fairplay with his 'money that just can't pass you by.' Believe it or not he wants you to have it; the roll-em-into-win man and the roll-bowl-em-pitch-em-or-lob-em man who categorically emphasises 'you may have come here in your bare feet, but I will give you the chance to drive home in a motor car.' A perennial sight too, was the doyen of fairground gurus, Micky Donnelly from Enniscorthy. A tall mournful looking character, sporting a permanent drip on the tip of his nose, Micky offered you five six-inch nails for twopence. Drive one down in three strokes of the hammer into a thick circular piece of wood and you were entitled to the lordly sum of one shilling. The problem was the piece of wood was positioned on a springy tea chest. If Micky wasn't in attendance, the pitch was usually in command of his aide-de-camp, another universally-known Enniscorthy man, by the appropriate name of Stumps Larkin.

Then there were the owners, the jockeys and of course, the bookmakers. Apart from the actual racing there was an unrivalled carnival atmosphere. The very appearance of some bookmakers looking so sublimely confident in their expensive clothes as they stood perched on high, fronted by a leather satchel full of money, evoked in me a reverence that was tinged with fear. I looked up in awe at an enormous ruddy-faced man whose stratum of stomach was expertly concealed behind a well-cut fawn crombie overcoat. In a deep husky voice, he repeatedly bellowed; 'I lay four-to-one the field.' All of us lads looked forward to the point-to-point, travelling there by pony and trap or bicycle. On this occasion I cycled with Nickey, who was burdened with my mother's explicit instructions to look after me. There was an eight-year gap between us but, in spite of that, the mutual love of horses made us kindred spirits. On that morning of the races my mother had given Nickey more than instructions about me, she had also given him some money.

"Look Mammy, give me a fiver and I'll bring you back forty pounds."

"I will not," she said "You must think I'm mad to give you that much money. It would be scandalous."

Two pounds was a farm labourer's weekly wage then.

"Honest," said Nickey "I know what I'm talking about. Sure Airgead Suas and Biddy's Knock are certainties."

The battle raged. Finally my mother conceded, handing him two pounds and stating that she didn't care what he did with it. She wanted no bookmaker's money – all she wanted was the two quid back.

As we jumped on the bikes and set off for Boolabawn, the Bree Point-to-Point, Nickey shouted back to her, 'Don't worry, I know exactly what I'm doing.'

Five shillings then would be today's equivalent of a tenner, with a prospect of eight such bets and a bit of luck, we had a chance to make some money – that is if everything went according to plan. After the first two races I watched as Nickey disconsolately tore up the bookmakers tickets. I rambled off amongst the crowd. Back-to-backs and traps were everywhere, their occupants standing about with some animals still between the shafts, some munching from a feed bag.

The third race started. No loudspeakers. No binoculars, just people scanning the far-off fields, watching what looked like toy horses as they started out on their hazardous single journey to the finish. Standing there in the midst of a fraternity of horse-drawn carriages, my attention was taken by a sound that was incomprehensively out of context. It couldn't be, but it was definitely happening. I moved closer. A handful of people were saying the Rosary. No mistake as I moved even nearer.   'Holy Mary, Mother of God. Pray for us sinners, etc.' One of the group who held his hand shield-like above his eyes suddenly stopped praying. "She's down. She's fallen" he barked.

The Rosary came to a halt as his eyes searched the far-off fields again.

"No, she's not," he blurted, "she's alright," whereupon the Rosary restarted with renewed vigour. The group consisted of the owner, his wife and friends. As I moved away in search of Nickey I could hear melodramatic screams floating above me. It was Billy Fairplay, screeching his proclamation of a big pay-out. With five and ten pound notes pinned to his fairground hat, he moved about offering you a paper straw in return for a mere sixpence. You could win up to ten pounds if the slip inside said so. His decoy-croney had just moved in and purchased that very straw! Billy's fractured condition attracted a fresh audience, as he screamed, "Get the fire brigade, the milkman, the guards. Anybody, but see that this man gets his ten pounds." There was an immediate pressing demand for the straws, which a revived Billy Fairplay energetically handed out in return for the hard-earned sixpence.

Double crossed at the Point-to-Point

It was starting to drizzle as we approached the last race. Nickey's spirits were as damp as the weather. Five races over and not a winner. This was his last chance. It was all or nothing on a horse called Bendigo. I watched as privileged information about the well-being of this horse was imparted to Nickey, by a friend in a huddled discussion that lasted nearly ten minutes. As the horses left the paddock, cantering away towards the starting point, they gradually disappeared from sight as they were enveloped by the drizzle. All was quiet for what appeared hours, when there was a shout of 'they are approaching the last.' Two horses appeared like phantoms out of the mist, and neck and neck they pounded towards the finish. We strained our eyes to see. It was Bendigo in front as they approached the winning post.

"Get up you little daisy," roared Nickey as good old Bendigo held on by a neck. He turned to me clutching the bookmaker's ticket. "Three quid to collect here, ya know. We're in the clear."

At that moment I happened to glance in the direction of the line of bookies. Considerable gaps had appeared in their ranks. "Nickey," I said, "That bookmaker seems to have moved."

We ran up towards the ring. No sign of him. Nickey scanned the place in desperation, then took off down to the bottom of the hill where horse-drawn carts were disgorging onto a narrow lane. I ran after him. Passing each cart, he looked closely at the occupants. Then he stopped. The drizzle had turned to pouring rain as he held up the ticket to a scrawny-looking individual perched on a side car with a brown Derby hat pulled right down over his ears.

"I want my money," Nickey loudly demanded. "I'm broke," retorted the bookie "I'll see you another time." "You will like Hell," reposted Nickey, jumping up and hauling the unfortunate soaked bookmaker from his seat. "But I don't have any money," he protested.

Nickey had him by the lapels, and in between shaking the poor man, he kept asking where his money bag was. He finally retrieved it from the jaunting car, opened and shook it empty. It was all silver and it came to just thirty-two shillings. Twenty-eight short. Drenched and feeling miserable for the bicycle journey home, Nickey's concern was not about the weather. He was more worried about how he would explain this to his mother. He had a strong feeling that she might not believe him.

CHAPTER FIFTEEN

It was a cold winter's Saturday night. My mother and the two youngest of the family, Molly and Rita, plus Bobby, John and myself were huddled around a roaring open kitchen fire. Mother was an industrious person, always doing something; in fact, she looked happiest when she was working. Not that she was unhappy – she never appeared that way, it was just so unusual to see her sitting in an armchair doing nothing more then putting her feet up and resting. If she were sitting down, she would be either reading or knitting. Right now she was knitting. "Come here, you," she called to John "and turn your back to me". She held up the knitting to his shoulders taking a line on how much more needed doing. This pullover was for John, but she left no one out when it came to knitting warm, woolly pullovers.

It was just then that I heard the words of a song, words that I had never really listened to, up to now. The door from the lower end of the kitchen was open. It had led up a stairway which went to the main landing, but midway up it diverted separately down to a hallway which had a door into the bar. Both doors were open, making sounds from the bar audible. The bar was full, and whilst Killanne was not noted for its songsters, on some Saturday nights there would be an occasional spillover of levity leading to inevitable rebel songs from the past, a hurling song or an emigrant lamentation. Mick Dunne, a popular local warbler, was in full throttle:

> Tell me who is the giant with the gold curling hair
> He who rides at the head of your band
> Seven feet is his height, with some inches to spare,
> And he looks like a king in command . . .

> Ah my lads, that's the pride to the bold Shelmaliers
> amongst heroes the greatest of man
> Fling your beavers aloft, and give three rousing cheers
> for John Kelly, the boy from Killanne.

The clicking of the knitting needles momentarily stopped as my mother ordered one of us to run and shut both doors. I had heard those words about John Kelly on many previous occasions but they seemed to carry no meaning for me. Now suddenly, it had all changed.

> "John Kelly, the boy from Killanne
> amongst heroes the greatest of man."

I turned to my mother. "Mammy," I asked. "Was John Kelly real and is it true that he was born in this house?" My mother threw her head back against the armchair, turning in my direction as she dropped the knitting on her lap. She gave a big sigh.

"Oh, that was all so long ago; but this house was looked upon as the house where he was born and grew up in. Historians wrote little enough about him, but all you have to do is talk to old Johnny Byrne across the road. He was born in 1855, not so many years after the rebellion, and old Johnny is full of stories about John Kelly, told to him by his father." My mother turned to me again.

"Seeing that you're so interested, you should know that in the old store adjoining the road is where the United Irishmen in this area held their meetings."

The words of the song that evening had stirred my interest in John Kelly, and as the years progressed, that interest never abated; but for the moment as a starry-eyed youngster growing up in the same house, I was becoming afflicted with pseudo-ancestral ties. As I climbed the stairs to my bedroom that night, the thought crossed my mind. Had John Kelly at my age perhaps, climbed the very same stairs?

Johnny Byrne lived to the age of 103. I have treasured memories of an extraordinarily lucid conversation I had with him shortly before he died. He was, in fact, related to the Kellys and was an exceptionally tall man. One of my questions, when we talked of John Kelly, was about his height. Did P.J. McCall, the writer of the song *Kelly, the boy from Killanne* exaggerate when referring to Kelly's size? Seven feet was his height with some inches to spare. According to Johnny Byrne's father, Kelly was indeed supernaturally tall. Kelly also wore his hair down to his shoulders and it curled as stated in the song. The sight of John Kelly astride his horse as he led his men up Vinegar Hill to join up with Father John Murphy for the first time was a sight never to be forgotten.

I will never forget the day I found a more visible reminder of John Kelly's existence. On exceptionally wet days when roads were flooded and the rain pelted down like stair rods, school was called off. This meant that we boys were confined to the house. After a bit of horseplay in the kitchen, my mother would eventually lose her patience.

"I want all of you out from under my feet and out of the kitchen. Go outside to the hayshed or one of the lofts and you can jump about all you want – but just get out of here," she would say. "I can't take any more."

Apart from the hayshed, there were several old stone buildings with lofts approached by stone steps. Over the stables was one always containing oats, but the favourite was the one above the cow house. It was usually filled with hay. There were openings in its floor at one side, where the hay could be pushed down for handiness onto a passage running parallel behind the cows feeding racks. Playing games, hiding and jumping about in that loft, listening to the rain as it beat a steady patter against the slates was exulting entertainment for young lads. As we jumped about with not a care in the world, we had the additional secure comfort of looking through a large opening onto the yard and seeing our mother moving about the kitchen as she started preparations for the dinner.

It was on a day such as this that I first caught sight of the letters and date. Sliding down the hay, it caught my eye. I went over and with my hand, rubbed at the dust which was considerable and there – easily detectable, carved in the stone was J.K. 1788. I held my breath as I stared at it. Without looking around I called out. "Anybody know who carved this thing on the wall?" I looked behind and there was no one to be seen, but then came a muffled shout from somewhere underneath a hideaway in the hay. "Did you not know that? Sure, John Kelly himself is supposed to have carved them." Look over a bit to the left and you'll see more . . ."

I searched about, looking up and down the old stone wall, and after a little while again made out more lettering, and there sure enough, unmistakably was N.R. 1936. No prizes for guessing who that might be. Both carvings were the work of fourteen-year-old boys.

Biddy's fat bacon

Father and mother, the two youngest Molly and Rita, Jim, Bobby, John and myself were seated around the breakfast table. We had just finished some delicious porridge which had been simmering all night, over to the remains of the open hearth fire. We were now tucking into and relishing the flavour of a tasty fry-up. There was no conversation, just the increasing sound of knives and forks as they made noisy contact with the emptying plates. Finally the silence was broken by my mother. As she finished her meal and pushed the plate slightly towards the centre of the table, she sat upright in her chair, looked about her. "Did any of you hear someone whistling in the back yard at all hours this morning." she asked.

There was no answer, forcing her to repeat the question. My father rubbed his chin and looking across with a face that hinted at mental suffering. "Do you mean to tell me that you don't know who that was?" he said.

This brought an expression of exasperation from my mother. Straightening herself again in her chair, she threw her husband a stern glance. "You must think I'm psychic – expecting me to know who's walking about in the dark whistling."

My mother's annoyance was not helped by my father's reply. "You don't know what's going on around here at all."

She quickly realised that she was being teased, and quicker still knew that a further show of impatience would only serve to make her look silly. "It doesn't matter - forget it," she said. My father was chuckling by now. "Jim, you tell your mother who that was whistling at all hours in the yard this morning." Jim, with his face yearning to break into an all-over smile, said "Mammy, that was Mike O'Brien looking for Sparks."

"Mike O'Brien looking for Sparks – at that hour of the morning? Dare I ask what Mike O'Brien was doing in our yard looking for a terrier at that hour of the morning?"

"For God's sake" said my father. "Today's Biddy Leary's thrashing, and Mike calls here every year for a terrier."

"For God's sake, you!" interjected my mother, "What does the terrier have to do with Biddy's thrashing?"

"You know woman, you're slow," replied my father.

"So I'm slow am I?" There was fire in my mother's eyes. My father sensed he had gone too far. Quickly changing his tone of voice, he calmly explained. "Everybody knows that Biddy doesn't boil the bacon enough for the men to eat, and surely you can guess the rest. Mike brings the terrier, and, when called into the dinner, ties the dog to his leg under the table, and if Mike can't eat the bacon, the dog gets it. Now do you understand?"

"So that's it," said my mother. "Poor Biddy Leary. Men are cruel to say such things."

"Okay," answered my father quickly. "But that's what they will tell you after a day working for Biddy." My mother was slowly beginning to see the funny side. "Yes, of course," she said. "It would just take Mike to do a thing like that."

Approximately four weeks later, as my mother presided over a similar breakfast scene, her face took on a curiously mischievous look as she again broke the silence. Stroking her chin and looking blankly into space, followed by a couple of little coughs, she asked if anyone had heard what Tom Dreelan said to Biddy Leary.

My father was midway through his fry-up. "What was that? What did Dreelan say to Biddy?"

There was no answer. He swallowed what food was in his mouth, and cleared his throat. "What was that you were saying Dreelan said to Biddy Leary?" After a long pause my mother replied, "Do you mean to tell me that you don't know what Dreelan said to Biddy? My goodness, you're slow if you don't know that. Sure everyone's talking about it."

My mother put on her matter-of-fact face, cupping her hand and vaguely peering at her fingernails as she spoke. She was getting her own back as she continued to play on her husband's impatience.

"Sure, you don't know what's going on around here half the time." After that remark my father twigged what she was up to. Feeling she had more than levelled the score, she finally gave in, after watching him as lay down his knife and fork, and irreverently raise his eyes to the ceiling.

"Alright then, I'll tell all of you," she conceded.

Biddy asked him had he sugar in his tea. "Begor, I have Biddy," replied Tom. "Sure I can see it in the bottom of the mug." My father gave a loud laugh.

"Do you know what, but that Dreelan can be a bit of a comic," said my father, "But he can be an idler too. You have to watch him all the time."

A common expression of my father's was 'I know them men are idling.'

"Did he say any more?" queried Jim.

"Oh yes, he did and to Mrs Hennessy over in Milltown." Mrs Hennessy was another parsimonious farmer's wife where man power was reciprocated.

"Go on Mammy" urged Jim. "Tell us."

"Apparently Biddy overheard Tom, as he stared at a plateful of mainly fat bacon, and it's likely he intended her to overhear what he said. Anyway he addressed the fat bacon with the words 'you needn't shiver. I'm not going to touch you".

"What did she say to him?" asked by father, now with a smile the full width of his face.

"It appears," continued my mother "that she put a plate in front of him containing one herring swimming in gravy. Tom sat on his chair transfixed. "Why aren't you eating up, Tom?" asked Mrs Hennessy.

"I can't" said Tom "Not until the tide goes out."

My father burst out laughing again. "Well. Do you know what, but that Dreelan can be quick. He's a born comic, that's all."

He had hardly said so when a frown again crossed his face.

"But he can be an idler too. I still say you have to watch him all the time."

'Achtung, Heil Hitler, Vere am I?'

During 1942 and 1943 shortages and rationing had become an accepted part of peoples' existence. Having enough clothing coupons to purchase a new suit was a problem for many, a factor which resulted in making the donation of such coupons a most desirable wedding present. Many a time I heard my mother as she let it be known that there was a round up on spare coupons which she needed as part of her present on the occasion of a forthcoming wedding. Following the news of the war was another huge factor in people's lives. Ireland of today is not a multi-racial society, and certainly in the forties and in a sleepy little village like Killanne, knowledge of other cultures or contact with foreigners, apart from the odd Englishman, was non-existent. Therefore when we gathered around the wireless to absorb the latest atrocities committed by the Germans, or to listen to Herr Hitler ranting and raving, we were not kindly disposed toward the Germans as a people. We know now, of course, that in every country there is good and evil and there were, of course, people in Germany who were opposed to, but unable to do anything to undermine the dreadful Nazi tyranny. At any rate in Killanne at that time, if you walked out to your back garden and were confronted by a giant five foot high poisonous tarrantula spider, you would deem it more desirable than to run into someone who told you he was a German.

Lord Haw-Haw is on the wireless tonight. This unfortunate man, a William Joyce originally from Galway but now employed by the German propaganda agents, was always sure of a big audience in our kitchen as he poured out venomous threats about the invincibility of the great German war machine. The programme usually started with 'Lord Haw-Haw calling, Lord Haw-Haw calling.' and the subsequent ridicule and jeering at the inept Allied armies inability to stop the superior German soldiers was always guaranteed to get listeners' hackles up. At the end of the war and Nuremburg trials, his neck was considerably stretched, and the fact that he was known to be Irish did not invoke any sympathy from those who for the most of four years had listened to his insufferable propaganda on behalf of the Nazis. On the other hand, there was a train of thought that felt he had really committed no personal atrocity other than being a radio propagandist and his death by hanging was a sentence that did not befit his crime.

At around this time, my brother Jim, having finished at the Enniscorthy Technical School, came home to work full-time in the business in Killanne. His outgoing personality, popularity and alacrity behind the counter made him look the perfect young recruit to the business. The shop and pub was always busy when Jim was about and my father was delighted with him. However, subsequent events were to prove different, as Jim, the obvious inheritor of Killanne, and ostensibly a promising young business man was, in fairness to him, not ready to shoulder responsibility. There was no tomorrow where he was concerned, and unfortunately growing older did not alter him. Facing up to the real facts of the situation was not for Jim. Likewise in those days of monthly credit, Jim was too soft-centred. He just could not say no, and collecting outstanding credit was something totally beyond him. A successful prank meant more to him than collecting debts. Even so, it broke my father's heart when in time he had to let him go his own way. This did not seem to bother Jim, who remained as happy and contented as ever.

One night in the bar he was engrossed in rather a longer than usual chat with Tom Dreelan. Tom, who with a few Guinnesses inside him was prone to telling implausible stories about how he had hurled the legs off everyone over in the field in Rathnure, they were all afraid of him over there. Jim had him well stoked up as Dreelan continued explaining now about his prowess at riding bucking horses.

"You seem to be afraid of nothing then, Tom," said Jim as he poured him out another Guinness.

"That's right" said Dreelan.

"Well, what about Mrs Molloy then?"

At the mention of her name Dreelan picked up his drink, threw it down in one gulp, banging the empty glass against the counter.

"That auld bitch. I'd love to frighten the shite out of her – that's for sure."

Mrs Molloy was a formidable-looking widow woman with a threatening appearance, and her awkward big frame contained the strength of any man. She was one of many helpers who worked for my father during the picking of potatoes. Her tongue was as threatening as her appearance. I witnessed her and Dreelan in violent verbal exchanges in the potato field. He was not a match for her.

"There, Tom," said Jim "Cool down. Get that into you." Placing another bottle in front of Dreelan. Jim's face creased into a knowing look. He snapped his fingers. Dreelan threw him a liquid glance.

"Tell you what, Tom. I have a great idea." He then lifted up a hinged piece of the counter, went outside, put his hand on Dreelan's shoulder and whispered in his ear.

"We'll dress you up as a crashed German pilot. You knock on Mrs Molloy's door, and if anything, that'll surely frighten the shite out of her."

This suggestion was instantly and vociferously endorsed by Dreelan.

"We'll frighten the shite out of her, that's what we'll do," he repeated with drunken assertiveness as he banged his fist off the counter. Jim knew that I had overheard what he was planning, came across, grabbed me by the ear.

"You keep your mouth shut."

"Look, Jim," I said, "I know what you're up to and I want to go too, but I bet he won't do it when the time comes." "Wait and see, and just do as I said, keep your mouth shut," as he sidled back behind the counter to serve another customer.

"Psst Psst – I want to talk to you." It was Jim about a week later beckoning me into the privacy of the bottling shed.

"Say nothing and okay you can come with us, but first of all I want you to do a few things for me. After your supper tonight, go over to

Tom Skelton (the hackney man). He will give you a parcel for me. On your way back call to the Barracks and ask for Garda Kane. He'll give you another parcel. Bring both of them to the store loft – I'll be there before you."

Skelton opened the door, and on seeing me his rascally eyes instantly showed a knowing gleam. He pulled the door after him, pointing to the shed where he kept his hackney car. He went to a corner and opened up a trunk, pulling out a magnificent rich-looking leather jacket. It had a big collar which was lined with what appeared to be lambswool.

"Got it from an English fella I sold a dog to," he chortled. On the way back, I called to the barracks and when Garda Kane arrived, he just handed me a smallish brown parcel.

"Give that to Jim," he told me, shutting the door almost immediately. In the dark I could not make out what was inside. The store loft, which was mainly for animal feed stuff, had a gas light which was on when I arrived. I immediately looked to see what Garda Kane had given me. They were motor bike goggles. I had no sooner climbed the steps than the two arrived. Dreelan's confidence of the previous week was non-existent. He appeared wan and looked at me with hunted eyes. Jim quickly got to work.

"Here Tom. Wrap yourself around that," he said, as he handed him an uncorked bottle of Guinness. ". . . And there's plenty more there."

After about half-an-hour, Dreelan was dressed up in riding breeches, leather riding boots, the fancy leather jacket, goggles, augmented with a smack of polish here and there on his face. He looked unrecognisable, and after downing about five more Guinnesses, his confidence had made a welcome return.

"Now Tom. Listen and repeat this after me." went Jim. "Achtung. Heil Hitler. Vere am I?"

The look of Dreelan as he uttered and re-uttered the words on Jim's instructions was knicker-wettingly comical. I could hardly wait for the action. Before we left, Tom downed another Guinness. His confidence appeared just right. Off we set on the short journey to Mrs Molloy's. It was pitch black, but Jim had a flash lamp. An oil light was lit in her kitchen. We crept around the house and peered through the curtain. She had two blocks of timber positioned on a larger solid timber base. As we looked in, she wielded a hatchet with terrifying impact through the top blocks, splitting them both with one stroke. Jim pulled at Dreelan's jacket.

"Now Tom. Go on, knock on the door. Remember – 'Acthung, Heil Hitler, Vere am I'?" We both withdrew to the shadows and to the kitchen door went Tom and knocked. I can still see Mrs Molloy's large frame silhouetted as the door opened, with the hatchet dangling from her right hand. "Acthung." Dreelan had barely said the word when she interrupted with a loud, "Ask what?" That was enough for Dreelan. He turned, did a flyer over the yard fence and up the road as fast as he could go, with Jim after him.

"Come back, come back," he beseeched, but all to no avail.

CHAPTER SIXTEEN

Mother often recalled that Jim was the most mischievous and carefree one of her family. I forget what the reason was, but as a little lad he kept on doing something that was a source of annoyance. If he did not stop, she threatened to dress him up in girl's clothes. She eventually was forced into doing so, hoping that he would break down and cry under such humiliation, when she could then bargain with him. He wasn't at all bothered. On the contrary, he disappeared out the kitchen door and straight down the road to the Garda barracks, where there were at least four gardaí who were my mother's contemporaries and who thought she was a fine, well-balanced mature woman. She had to run after him at full speed, nabbing him as he was about to knock on the Garda Barracks door. My mother would finish by saying, "What must those men have thought of me", she said, "dressing my son in girls' clothes!"

Whenever I was at home from school and left to my own devices, I would inevitably, at some stage, indulge in a bit of ball practice against the wall of the old storehouse which ran parallel to the road. As usual, I derived great satisfaction from doing so as well as enjoying a brief chat with the locals as they passed. From a distance I knew who was approaching, but on this occasion as I looked down the road, the figure slowly coming towards me looked familiar but I was still unsure who it was. Gradually the individual came near enough for me to recognise. It was Auld Tommy, but there was something radically wrong with him. The happy walk was replaced by a shuffle. His head was dropped with his chin almost resting on his chest, whilst his arms, noted for swinging expressively, were now hanging limply at his side. As he approached, I stopped hurling and holding the ball in my hand, I gaped at him. As he came closer there was no familiar, 'Pull on that ball young fella. You're lifting it too much.' He silently turned left, heading towards a door beside the shop where my father had his office. Just as he turned left I was distracted by a scraping sound from behind. It was a local lad coming to a halt on a bicycle. He was substituting dragging feet for a braking system. "Poor Auld Tommy," he said. "His wife died this morning. He's making arrangements for the funeral."

Watching Auld Tommy walking towards the office door, I felt a wave of sadness sweep over me. Everyone knew that Auld Tommy and his wife were an extremely devoted couple. Mrs White, a quiet gentle lady completely understood her husband's unconventionality. He was not a man bound by fixed rules and no matter what time he arrived home, he was always welcomed with a hot meal. They were blessed with mutual understanding and enjoyment. Theirs was a happy existence.

Further dilemmas for Nickey

In 1942, Nickey was picked as a sub on the Leinster hurling team, the beginning of his many appearances on such a prestigious selection. 1943 also saw him win a Dublin Senior title with Young Irelands. Such achievements were closely monitored in his native county. Rathnure, after their Junior title breakthrough in 1940 had now won the Wexford Minor Championship in 1941, an honour that the club regained in 1943. My brothers Jim and Bobby played both years.

The following may, at first, seem irrelevant, but was in a way to concern Nickey's future. In 1942, Dublin appeared in both All-Ireland finals, winning the football title and giving Cork a close call in the hurling decider. What is generally unknown is that, at this stage in his career, Nickey was not only proving himself as a top class inter-county hurler, but was also catching the eye with his senior football displays for UCD. Wexford hurling and football was at a low ebb then compared to Dublin. It inevitably happened – a very tasty carrot was dangled at him. Declare for Dublin. There was no question of his place on the hurling team, but he was also led to believe that he would be given strong consideration for a position on the football team, the then reigning All-Ireland champions. For a twenty-one-year-old fanatic of both codes, it was a dazzling opportunity. Meanwhile, he was more than aware of the growing hurling fever back in his native parish, allied to the prowess of his two younger brothers and the possible appearance of two more. Dublin GAA officials and friends in the city brought a lot of pressure to bear pleading with him to don the All Blue Dublin jersey. What was he to do? A grinding decision-making struggle took place. He finally decided that he would renege on his native county for at least one year. His decision remained intact – that is until he came back home to Killanne after the Easter holidays.

At that time amongst the Garda in residence in Killanne barracks, was Garda Tom O'Rourke. A former Clare hurler of renown, he was also a member of the famous 1927 Garda hurling team, looked upon by some experts as the greatest hurling combination that ever walked onto a pitch, containing such stars as Garrett Howard, Fowler McInerney, Matty Power and Jim Walshe, the builder. The bulk of this Garda team made up the Dublin county side that defeated the then All-Ireland champions and favourites, Cork, in the 1927 hurling final. Tom O'Rourke was at centre back on that team – a team devoid of even one Dublin-born player. To the locals in Killanne, O'Rourke appeared a serious man, with little to say about hurling, but he was an acknowledged master of the game and spoken about in hushed tones by aspiring young stars in our parish. He was unquestionably a 'rara avis' in our midst. Not a legislator, he offered no ostensible help or advice to the fledgling club or hurlers around him. Although it was difficult to set him in motion about the game, he still concealed a deep, sincere interest in the progress of hurling in our parish. He was respected and his rare opinions were prized. It transpired that his opinion was the one that altered Nickey's mind, causing him to rescind his decision to play for Dublin. Nickey was always grateful to him for doing so.

At this time in their hurling history, Wexford's last victory over Kilkenny in the senior All-Ireland Championship went back to 1908. Although they won a Leinster Junior title in 1926 and 1940, the Wexford Senior hurlers during that period, especially during the twenties and early thirties had difficulty at times even fielding a senior team. Up to the early 1940s, they were more or less fodder for the likes of Kilkenny and Dublin, but a change was slowly taking place. The result of the Junior Leinster 1940 success was bearing fruit, with some fine players coming on stream, such as John Foley (Adamstown), Mickey Redmond (father figure of Rathnure hurling) the Boggan brothers, Billy Kielty, Paddy Kehoe, Tom Butler, Joe

Bailey and of course Nickey, who in those days was a strapping midfielder or half-forward, a totally different player to the later burly full-forward. The challenge to Kilkenny's supremacy had gathered momentum, when to everyone's surprise in 1942, it almost happened. In that championship game at New Ross, Wexford, to the delight of their supporters and to the horror of the Kilkenny followers, were in front when the final whistle should have sounded. In a bizarre ending the ref continued the game (some reckon fourteen minutes overtime) until Kilkenny went in front! It appeared that he was an unwilling official who just could not preside over such a break in tradition or status quo. He then blew the final whistle, looked at the justifiably angry Wexford following and prudently decided that, instead of going to the dressing room, he would sidle off to one side of the grounds, and make a quick dash across the nearby fields to the safety of the town of New Ross. Some Wexford followers who saw what was happening took action which resulted in a ludicrous chase across the fields in pursuit of the referee. Fortunately for him he arrived safely in the town, where he subsequently kept a very low profile!

In 1943, Wexford were once again to exit in the Championship. During one or possibly two of those years, I happened to find myself in the Wexford dressing room when the team was getting ready. The reason for my being allowed in was the fact that I was Nickey's younger brother. Prior to leaving the rooms, a well-known GAA official of the day gave the team a pre-match pep talk. Even at my tender age, I was shocked at the gist of what he said. During the course of his spif, he exhorted the Wexford players not to give up, no matter how much they were being beaten. Another old chestnut, deep rooted in Wexford hurling at that time, he directed at the Wexford corner-back, who had the onerous task of marking the slippery and classy Jimmy Langton. He advised him to stay behind Langton and, to quote his exact words: 'Whatever you do, don't let him in on the goalman.'

This last piece of advice reflected the ills of Wexford hurling at that time. Anyone with an ounce of knowledge about the game will tell you that allowing a forward like Langton first choice of possession would be a disastrous policy. Your only hope which is applicable to playing any such great forward, is break in front, reverse roles, or make him mark you. Accomplishing that demands full confidence, a positive attitude, and a belief in your skill to take the ball with you should you get in front, which is often easier said than done. With regard to the latter part of that advice, Jimmy Langton was a class forward who had no interest in clobbering goalmen. All in all, it was fairly astounding counsel, even to my young ears. It is my belief that around the late thirties and early forties, Wexford had top class players, capable of taking on the best, but who unfortunately had the wrong attitude and 'stay behind your man' was one.

Another was the physical attention they paid to their immediate opponent. Lack of priority in gaining possession was replaced in some instances by what can only be construed as the village hero ethos of 'clobber your opponent no matter what' even if it meant losing the game. However, the growing change in attitude and approach was gently taking place, as an exciting new generation of young Wexford men, in the space of the next five to six years, came on stream, one by one, to bring about the dawn of a glorious new era for hurling in the county.

Off to St Kieran's

The autumn of 1943 saw a big change in my life. I was packed off to St Kieran's College in Kilkenny as a boarder. During my time in Rathnure national school, I was looked upon as a little above average scholar, and I know my parents had high hopes for me in secondary education. The college entrance exam placed me as as average student, but even at that, I had difficulty keeping up. I felt I was a bit of a disappointment to them, which I certainly was to myself. However, St Kieran's college staff and students were collectively crazed about the game of hurling, and this naturally was right up my street. Nickey's exploits and achievements in the college colours were well remembered. During his years there, he won a Leinster College Junior title, two Leinster Senior titles, and one All-Ireland Senior title. He was also a member of the inter-provincial college team. In 1940, that team beat a star-packed Munster side after extra time, in what some critics felt was the greatest game of college hurling ever witnessed. An extraordinary aspect of the extra time was in that period the Leinster lads chalked up thirteen points without reply from Munster. Midfield on that Leinster team was Eamon Young of Cork and Tommy Maher, later to become president of St Kieran's and manager of successful Kilkenny All-Ireland winning teams. The Munster team boasted such men as Con Murphy, Harry Goldsboro and Din Joe Buckley. Having an older brother who carved such a niche in college folklore was understandably to my benefit. The first time I togged off (and no matter what the conditions, there were no half measures) I was closely watched; but I wasn't worried. On the contrary, I was bubbling with confidence and all the skills I had honed in the Barrack field and against the old storehouse wall were put to instant use. I knew immediately, by the reaction of my contemporaries and peers, that I was not a disappointment as far as hurling was concerned. "He's small," they said, "but this young fella knows a bit about the game."

Life as a boarder in any college during the war years of endless shortages was not a nice experience. In St. Kieran's, breakfast was mainly porridge – no fry-up – followed by just tea and bread and butter. There was a minimum of meat for the midday meal, whilst supper or evening meal consisted of just two small pats of butter, combined with more slices of bread that had that strange indistinct colour and texture, washed down with more tea, which resembled boiling water with milk added. You looked enviously at students who opened and delved into well-stocked tuck boxes. In spite of all that, everybody seemed healthy and contented. Personally, I wasn't upset or worried. I just accepted the situation, but I can tell you it was a joyous moment for me whenever I was handed a sizable brown parcel with the address written in my mother's handwriting. That initial college term was my first time away from home for such a long period. Unlike today, there was no break of any description for boarders. If your parents arrived, you might be let out with them for an hour or so.

For a lad of approximately thirteen and a half years, who had never been previously away from home for such a long period, I felt a desperate need to re-enter the atmosphere of such a strong family environment as existed at home in Killanne, so it was a joyous day when the break-up for Christmas finally arrived. Bus or train services even today between Kilkenny and our nearest town Enniscorthy, are non-existent, so my parents were left with no option but to hire the local hackney man, Tom Skelton, to fetch me. My mother travelled with him. I was waiting for them with my suitcases all ready long before they arrived. At last I could see the car entering the college grounds and in no time, the cases were put in the boot and the three of us set off on the return journey to Killanne. As the car climbed each hill and turned each corner, my mother kept bringing me up-to-date on all the happenings back home. With the passing of each mile, I could perceive a delightful glow of growing contentment. Home at last for Christmas. I suppose we all feel that our own house is somewhat special at Christmas time. For me the magic of all the happy Christmases I had spent in our old house, especially as an impassioned advocate of Santa Claus, even beyond a credible age, undoubtedly made the place for me a treasure trove of warm and happy memories.

Although Christmas fairy lights didn't exist then, the old house, once dressed in seasonal trappings of paper bells, paper chains, streamers, holly and Christmas tree, gave out a pervading influence of Yuletide celebration, augmented by the two plum puddings that dangled from the ceiling just inside the kitchen door. My mother, with the expert help of Maggie, had as usual achieved an excellent decorative festive feeling. Reciprocal presents, at least in our family, were non-existent then. The later day culture of our social welfare society, of father's day, mother's day, birthdays was light years away in 1943. Santa Claus however, made sure that no one was left out. My two elder sisters Sally and Essie, who were then working, were very generous to their young brothers. They went to a lot of bother and expense to provide us all with a little present. Those presents were the first for me (apart from Santa) as an individual, and I can still remember being covered in bashful confusion when I tried to say thank you, strongly prodded on by my mother. Having spent the last month or so living in such a spartan manner, I looked in amazement at our huge Christmas table, as it groaned under such an abundance of food. In those years we were all at home for Christmas, but just like all families as the years passed the numbers around the table dwindled. The first two to go were my sisters Sally and Essie, both married in the forties. Nickey was always home for Christmas day, but whilst the rest of us played records on the gramophone or had a go at the piano, or perhaps settled in a sulk corner with the latest comic, Nickey did not stay around – only for Christmas day. The age gap was having its effect, but of course he was now a young man, with different company on his mind. He was definitely his mother's favourite, and what was totally beyond us younger brothers was the fact that he knew how to lay his charm on her. "Nickey," she'd say, "are you sure you have had enough? You'll eat another plateful." And he usually did. I often wondered where he put it all. He seemed to be stocking up for the week ahead, which pleased his mother no end.

The chat during Christmas dinner usually got around to discussing what happened in the bar the night before. Christmas

Eve drinking in an Irish pub in those days meant that if you didn't go several over the top, you weren't normal. Songs that hadn't been aired for twelve months were laboriously dragged out. As the glasses were topped up and the mood changed into a discernible surge of exhilaration, the balladeer would show his hand, but only just and with a certain amount of cunning and purpose. The extra Guinness swirling about his innards was a strong mood changer, propelling an irresistible urge to sing but, adept at cloaking his exhibitionist nature, he had to be asked. His modus operandi was to pressurise someone else into singing, especially someone who couldn't and was terrified at even being asked to do so. He would keep that pressure up with a few "Go ons" and "sure we know you can do it". Finally he extracted what he wanted, which was to force the other person into turning on him and asking him to sing himself.

A few more exchanges would eventually bring the balladeer to his feet and at the end of the night, when all modesty and shyness had escaped him, you would have trouble shutting him up. Those sort of sing-songs, minus a voice that set too high a standard and gave the rest a complex, were my favourite. It usually resulted in a spontaneous spillover of merriment that saw everybody having a go and a stone floor which made for good acoustics. I've always felt the quality of singing in an Irish pub doesn't matter.

All the regular customers who drank in our pub at that time seemed to me to be almost an extension of the family. Killanne may not have been noted for harmonised music or tuneful melodious voices but there were still some worthwhile performances that could bring silence to the room. Dancing a jig on the stone floor of the bar whilst someone jigged or lilted also brought whispers of awe, especially when performed by local carpenter, Mick Neill, an expert on Irish dancing and folklore. Even late in his seventies, Mick with the right quota of half-ones on board, was still as good as the best. Seeing people who had witnessed your tender years, unwinding and enjoying themselves brought a warm glow to all of us. My two older sisters, who were no longer living at home, were always keen to know how the locals were keeping. Did Charlie Foley still recite *Dangerous Dan McGrue*? Did we still flatten our ears against the door when Mick Dunne, another long-standing customer, was exhorted to give a rendering of *The Springmount Hurlers*?

The advent of the New Year did not witness any unusual celebration, except that New Year's Eve was a sure night for a full house when it came to dancing in a local hall but generally there was no special emphasis at the old Year's departure to make way for the new. However, next morning around our breakfast table the conversation always took on a similar pattern to the previous year. "Did you hear him last night?" some would say.

My father would jerk his head backwards in an exasperated gesture. "Indeed I did – the blithering auld fool and his bell." As long as he was in Killanne, Fred Crabbe walked up the village starting right on the stroke of midnight, ding-donging a welcome to the New Year. For us it was another strange custom Fred brought with him to Killanne, and with his demise it stopped, and a little bit of colour disappeared from our lives.

CHAPTER SEVENTEEN

I was in the last term of my first year in St Kieran's and eagerly looking forward to the college sports, which were to start the following Sunday, three days away. The morning rising bell rang out across the dormitory. I tried to lift my head from the pillow, but was unable to do so. It felt as if there was a heavy weight bearing down across my forehead, pinning me against the pillow. My entire being felt most peculiar. I just lay there whilst all about me the other students washed, dressed, made up their beds and disappeared off to the refectory for breakfast. About an hour or so later the sister, a nun in all-white flowing garments, who cared for sick students, arrived at my bedside. She gave me a cursory look and having asked me a few questions, I was given some tablets which I swallowed. I think it was the following day that the Dean, Fr Lowry, arrived in the dormitory, pulled a chair up to the bedside and leaned in close to me. He fixed a stern gaze on me.

"Have you been smoking cigarettes?" he asked. Feeling dreadful as I did, the question made me, if possible, feel even worse. Smoking was going on in the college and was looked upon by the Dean and prefects as a strong breach of college rules. I had heard stories of students who were caught, getting four or six of the best. I had prided myself on my non-desire to smoke. There was no self-denial involved, my system merely rejected the habit. I looked back at the Dean as best I could.

"Father," I said, "I'm not interested. I just can't smoke."

His stern gaze rested on me again.

"Why don't you tell me the truth?" he asked.

A type of anger welled up in me. "But Father" I said "That is the truth."

He sprang up from the chair and with his long soutane sweeping the floor, he marched out of the dormitory. The Sunday of the sports day turned out to be a bright sunny day. Most of the dormitory windows were opened to allow in fresh air and sunshine. Just outside one of the large windows was situated the finishing line for the various races. Loud cheers and more loud cheers as the participants raced for it. I had been eagerly and excitedly looking forward to taking part. Now as a solitary sick student in that dormitory, my disappointment at being unable to do so was acute. It was, however, well overshadowed by my condition. I was now feeling extremely feverish, but worst of all the pain and pressure in my head was symptomatic, if one can imagine that of a hatchet being imbedded in your skull. The spasmodic cheers entering the room via the large windows were a huge measure of aggravation to my condition. My memory of what happened afterwards is somewhat hazy and can only connect with that of someone leaning over the bed, and endeavouring to engage me in conversation. My eyelids were heavy as I tried to look and focus, but the voice was unmistakable. It was my mother and standing beside her was our family doctor of that time, Dr P.J. Daly. Fr Lowry and the sister were also present and even in my condition, I could detect a heated exchange of words. In the end the sister put forward the suggestion that I should be brought to a local hospital, a suggestion that was firmly rejected by my mother. "I am taking him back home," she said curtly. Dr Daly disappeared for a short period, reappearing with two large blankets. He proceeded to spread them out on the dormitory floor. The pillow from behind my head he then placed on the blankets. He then gestured to someone (I think it was the Dean). They both picked up the sheet, hammock-style with me inside, placing it gently on the blanket on the floor. I was rolled up in the lot, carted out and placed on the back seat of the doctor's car for the journey back home. I had contracted meningitis and again double pneumonia and was destined to spend not weeks but months recovering, a period during which once again the Parish Priest administered to me the last rites. My last day at St Kieran's had indeed been a dramatic one.

Convalescing was a long slow process. My bedroom was adjacent to the bathroom, three sizable steps down; steps that demanded careful negotiation. Consequently, in view of my weakened condition, it was necessary to place the old-fashioned highly useful and essential commode in my room. A long period elapsed before I was strong enough to make a trip to the bathroom. As I lay in bed making my recovery, I was more than aware that my dodgy chest or wheezing had made its return. It was a most unwelcome thought, invoking the prospect of more red flannel! I felt so weak, I hadn't the strength to lift a kitten. Without realising it, at my age hormonal changes were, of course, taking place. But there was something else. And lying there in bed, I couldn't quite identify what it was until I made my first trip down to the bathroom. I felt light as a feather, as I carefully and gently transferred my feet to each step. It was a biggish bathroom with the washhand basin and mirror at the furthest corner. I stood gazing through the large window overlooking the garden. For a few moments I remained staring out and looking across towards the mountains. It was such a nice day but I had this odd feeling. I shuffled across the bathroom towards the washhand basin, placing my hands on the tap, turning it and simultaneously lifting my head to look in the mirror. It was then I realised what the odd feeling was. Disbelievingly I peered into the mirror, but I was so delighted I felt like shouting out loud. The last time I looked in this mirror, I could only see the top half of my face, now I was looking not up but down into the mirror. Without realising it, I had, during my convalescence, stretched to quite an extraordinary degree. I stayed there enraptured, surveying my new height and taking stock of my gaunt pale features, which about the cheeks were now displaying a previously unseen light fluffy growth.

I made a slow and tedious recovery. Fortunately this time, unlike with my previous bout of pneumonia, there were antibiotics available to counteract the fever. When I was well enough, various people came to visit me, including the local school teacher, Hugh O'Reilly, who was anxious that I should continue with a secondary education. He made his feelings forcibly known to my parents who agreed. Looking back now I must have been very debilitated as a result of it all, because even by the following autumn, I wasn't looked upon as strong enough to return to any college as a boarder, which was the only option for me. It was not until the autumn twelve months later that I returned to college. I was offered the choice of Blackrock in Dublin or the Good Counsel in New Ross. I opted for the latter.

He was seven feet tall

When Hugh O'Reilly visited me during the time of my illness, I made known to him my interest in John Kelly and how I wished to find out more about him. Although there was no mention in our National school history curriculum about *The boy from Killanne*, I was delighted to discover that O'Reilly was a keen historian and had some years previously been collecting what oral folklore there was available from reliable sources. His compilation was to be regarded by historians as one of the most important and successful folk memory research projects of this century. I had made an unexpected, gratifying discovery and O'Reilly, although getting on in years, was more than pleased to enlighten me on the subject of John Kelly.

Still, time hung heavy during my long convalescence. Being a boy of outdoor interests which I could no longer indulge, I retreated more and more into a world of the imagination. John Kelly was beginning to obsess me. This romantic giant of a man who came to such a terrible end had been born in 1776 and had been reared right here in this house, maybe even slept in my room. Here was a role-model, though I knew I could never grow up to be such a brave and charismatic man.

In my mind, I followed him through his boyhood in Killanne; an only son playing with his two sisters in the yard around the house. His father, also named John, like mine, had been a farmer and a shop owner. Killanne in those days had been an important staging post between the big, deep water port of New Ross and Bunclody. His mother, who had been born Mary Redmond, also came from Killanne, so maybe there would have been cousins as well. Nothing was known of his education, but educated he must have been because he was 'the son of a man of respectability in this neighbourhood ... had been in Dublin and had been sworn.' Also according to Dr John Colclough, another leader of the ninety-eight rebellion, he was 'one of the better sort and a well-conducted man and one who could have a considerable influence.' Thomas Cloney years later in his *Narrative of 1798* refers to him amongst others as 'a gentleman of rank who was executed after the mere shadow of a trial.' Local lore had it he also taught at the hedgerow school in Rathnure, but there is little evidence for that. We do know, however, from an existing letter to Mr Colclough of Duffry Hall, now in a neighbour's possession, that his handwriting and fluency with words were those of an erudite man.

I was hugely impressed with the physical appearance of Herculean proportions attributed to Kelly. What an asset he must have been to the United Irishmen whom he, an untried officer, was to lead in battle after months of drilling and preparation. I would wonder if there had ever been a portrait painted of him, but thought probably not as he would only have been just twenty-three when he died. As I was later to understand, a pall of silence fell over the county concerning the ill-fated rising of '98, particularly amongst the family survivors of the rebels. It would be over a hundred years before it could be taken out publicly, mourned over, and finally celebrated for the brave act of defiance it was.

Our barn was supposed to have been a secret meeting place for the leaders. Whether John Kelly's father knew and approved is not known, but from the said letter, it seemed he tried to prevent his son from visiting some unidentified man to warn him he was in danger.

Anyway, in my mind I embroidered and embellished the historical facts my kind teacher had given me. I followed my hero through his campaigns during the glorious month of revolution; the capture of Enniscorthy, when cattle were stampeded through the streets; the first battle of Vinegar Hill when he fought beside Father John Murphy; then on to Forth Mountain just outside Wexford town; where they established a camp at the 'Three Rocks'; then ambushed and killed some seventy men of the Meath Militia and the Royal Irish Artillery Regiment.

I marched behind him during the triumphant entry through St John's gate in Wexford town, where the rebel army were feted, wined and dined in the streets after releasing Bagnel Harvey from the town jail, who was then appointed their leader. The triumph turned to disaster when the army then marched on New Ross, which they needed to take to clear a path to Waterford. With five hundred of the fifteen hundred men under his command (Thomas Cloney commanded the other half of the three thousand Bantry men), Kelly drove in the outposts of the King's troops between the rebel camp and the town. It seems that Kelly either misunderstood his orders not to attack the Three Bullet gate at New Ross before the other leaders had positioned their men at the other gates, or, more likely, they were forced into premature action. After the initial successful entry into the town amidst fierce fighting, he was wounded in the thigh and as he lay in the street, his demoralised men were scattered in disarray, no match for the cannon fire in the narrow streets. As Cloney recalled, 'This was a great loss to us at such a moment, as his men were greatly attached to him.' I wondered how they had managed to return him to his sister's house in the middle of Wexford town (coincidentally the site of a property I would one day own). It must have been a horrendous journey for a sorely wounded man, but take him there they did.

A postman, called James Forrestal, my teacher went on to tell me, claimed to be a collateral descendant of the Kellys of Killanne. The story had passed down in his family that John Kelly had been engaged to a Miss Molly Doyle of Castleboro, Clonroche, and had fought with a scythe by his side at New Ross. This rang bells in both our minds. The ballad *The Heroine of Ross* goes like this:

> On to Ross! our pulses quickened
> as the word from man to man passed along,
> and bold John Kelly forward stepped to head to van . . .
> and again
> but a figure rose before us. T'was a girl's fragile frame
> and among the fallen soldiers there she walked with eyes aflame
> and her voice rang o'er the clamour, like a trumpet o'er the sea
> Who so dares to die for Ireland, let him come and follow me.
> Then against the line of soldiers,
> with a gleaming scythe on high lo she strode . . . .

There certainly was a Miss Doyle at the battle of New Ross. She was described as a woodcutter's daughter from Castleboro. The rebel army had a huge following of women and children, which must have been a great hindrance to them, but Molly Doyle was one of those who fought beside the men. With her faggot-cutting scythe, she cut the crossbelts and cartridge cases from the dead and wounded Dragoons to supply her friends. For some reason she was named 'The point of war.' She was last seen sitting astride a howitzer which had been captured at the Three Rocks, and haranguing the retreating rebels not to 'Leave our dear little cannon behind which had cost us the lives of some heroes to obtain', and threatening to remain to be shot if they did not help her drag it away.

She sounded like a somewhat Amazonian lady for the gentlemanly Kelly to have been engaged to, I thought, but no doubt hard times bring out the fighting spirit in all of us. Anyway our source, the postman, tells of her love for him and how she visited him in Wexford as he lay badly wounded in hiding. How I would have loved to know if she escaped capture and how she lived out the rest of her days if she did. Cloney, who was clearly fascinated by her, said he was ashamed 'this warlike woman' was neglected and allowed to disappear after the action was over.

The end came abruptly and cruelly after the retaking of Wexford by General Lake. They discovered Kelly's whereabouts, hauled him from his sister's house for a summary court martial, where a man called Mr Whitney of Gurrawn, near Killanne gave evidence against him in spite of the fact he already owed Kelly his life from an incident earlier that month.

I lay in bed and shuddered in horror as I visualised the execution. A wounded man, brought by cart to the centre of the new wooden bridge over the Slaney, hanged then decapitated. His body flung into the river below to be borne out to sea. His head, like all the other executed leaders, adorned a spike in the market place, having first been used as a football by the vengeful mob.

His sister somehow managed to retrieve the head and, I think, the body as well, and made the agonising journey to Killanne to bury him in the graveyard there.

I was always puzzled as to why Thomas Cloney, alone amongst the leaders, except for Myles Byrne who escaped to France, managed to escape execution. He had lived at Moneyhore, which would one day be my Granny Doran's home. Her husband's ancestor, Myles Doran, had distinguished himself in action during the rising. It seems that, after hiding under the bed of a woman who had just given birth in a house in Wexford town, Cloney was captured, courtmarshalled, and condemned to death. This sentence was commuted to transportation, and eventually reprieved by Lord Cornwallis. A year later he was a free man. He claimed he had joined the rebels under pressure, and clearly had friends at court.

The Tinker's baby

With the gradual improvement in my health, I was eventually allowed up, but ordered to stay indoors. This ultimately led to my occasionally helping out in the shop, especially behind the bar. On this particular evening, about 6 p.m., there were a few locals there enjoying a drink and a bit of banter. Amongst them was our local doctor, P.J. Daly (later to become medical adviser to the fifties

Wexford hurling team). Daly was in ways a strange man. Despite being a prominent doctor, he was nonetheless a social maverick, and not interested in mixing with the genteel classes. He was at times a heavy drinker and whenever he was known to be 'on it', his preference was for local pubs and local people. Not for him the golf club society or newest hotel lounge. There was nothing false about him. His austere look and sometimes harsh bearing concealed a heart of gold. Money and medicine, where he was concerned, did not mix. Charity was high on his list. He was relaxed and part of the scene as he sat back and enjoyed the craic and the company of the local wags. That was what he was savouring right now when the door partially opened and the anxious face of a tinker lad pushed itself around. In true Gerry vernacular and solicitous fashion, he inquired if the doctor was amongst us. The room we were in had a separate entrance from the main pub door. From it there was access to behind the counter and also a door leading to the private hallway of the house. Nobody spoke and eventually the tinker lad, with a very troubled look on his face, pulled the door closed. The term continued for about ten minutes when I heard sounds that were totally unfamiliar and they were coming from the private hallway. It was just seconds later that the door from the hallway opened and there stood my mother wearing a very grim expression, and when she looked like that it was wise to take notice. Her eyes fixed on the doctor, instead of speaking, she put her hand up and beckoned me. Daly had been drinking, I would say, most of the day and was in no mood for medical matters. The unfamiliar loud screams started again. They frightened the wits out of me and put an end to the levity. All were now wearing serious faces. My mother was still staring at Daly.

"This baby is coming. You had better follow me," she said, then she pulled the door closed. "Well, blast that auld bitch anyway," said Daly. "She had nine months to get as far as Wexford Hospital. Now here she is under my nose." He turned to Tom Dreelan, who was the only one who appeared to be getting some fun out of it all. "Go out there and get that black bag from the car." A wicked grin crossed over Dreelan's face as he made for the door. He wasn't long gone when the door barely re-opened, and all we could see was a hand stretching in, which was holding a car spanner. There were guffaws all round, then Dreelan pushed open the door holding the bag. Daly disappeared through the door towards the hallway. The tinker woman meanwhile had been carried down to the kitchen table where the baby was delivered. As soon as I knew this I ran around the back with Dreelan in support and still wearing the wicked grin. We listened at the window. At the height of the drama on the kitchen table, my father, semi-somnolent after a customary nap, appeared on the landing that looked down into the kitchen. It was a relatively easy birth and in no time she was sitting up holding her baby. I can still remember overhearing Daly saying to the woman: "Listen here you. I know bloody well you're not finished at this game yet, but don't do this to me again. Get your arse down to Wexford Hospital next time."

In my furniture business in Wexford I occasionally sell old mattresses to travelling people. By virtue of their life style they are inclined to barter. Their pursuance of discount, in spite of negative answers, can be a source of annoyance. The year was 1993, I was displaying short-fuse symptoms with a rotund middle-aged travelling lady when suddenly she said, "Sure, we know the Rackards well." Actually I am on first name terms with a lot of such folk, but when I was dismissive of this woman's claim, she looked me in the eye and in the nicest possible way stuck me to the floor with the words, 'Sure, wasn't I born on the kitchen table in Rackards' Killanne.'

CHAPTER EIGHTEEN

Some time later when the birth of the tinker baby was being recalled, Maggie turned to my mother, "Surely Mrs Rackard, that must be one of the strangest things that ever happened to you?" My mother's face creased into an uneven smile.

"No, actually" she said, "something more bizarre than that happened to me. It happened, not at the beginning, but at the end of a life. A good few years ago the local Protestant vicar died. Myself and a neighbour put on our best and called to the vicar's residence to pay our respects. The door was opened by a maid. She never spoke, just ushered us to a bedroom where the deceased vicar lay very dead, eyes open staring at the ceiling. There was no one else there, nor did anyone appear. After saying a few prayers in support of the dead clergyman, we sat down and stayed for about fifteen minutes. We then decided to leave, and made for the bedroom door, turned the handle but couldn't get out. It was locked! Almost two hours elapsed, during which time we made several unsuccessful attempts to open the door. There we were, prisoners in the room with the dead vicar staring at the ceiling, and a feeling of panic beginning to envelope us. At last we heard a click and sure enough the door opened and there stood the wacky maid, still tongue-tied as she turned and led us towards the hall door. We had hoped to render our condolences to the vicar's wife, but she never appeared. Anyway . . ." said my mother as she laughed heartily, "we were so relieved at making our escape, that any sympathy we may have had for the vicar's wife had by then completely evaporated."

John makes his hurling debut

The year 1944 was a bench mark in the history of Wexford Senior hurling. Their last win over Kilkenny in a championship game went back an incredible period of time to 1908. Now the impossible had happened. The Wexford senior hurlers set the heather blazing with a fine victory over their talented neighbours in an exciting game played in the then Barrett's Park, New Ross. The dormant hurling fever in the county was ignited to its fullest and there were high hopes for the purple and gold as they faced Dublin in Nowlan Park in the Leinster final. I was lucky that I witnessed those games. My frail condition was a constant source of concern to my mother. However, seeing the agony I would suffer if I were not allowed to go, made her believe she might do more harm by keeping me at home. It transpired that Dublin were far too wiley a combination for Wexford in the final. Whilst the win over Kilkenny was a much needed tonic for the game in Wexford; Dublin, with a team that included such crafty and talented players as Harry Gray, Tony Herbert and Ned Wade, cruelly exposed the deficiencies that still afflicted Wexford. When the final whistle sounded I was crestfallen with the disappointment of that defeat. However, back home the hurling fever raged on unabated, in spite of championship defeats by all club teams. As for myself, with the gradual improvement in my health, I was by the end of summer, allowed to play a little hurling against the store wall adjoining the road. Meanwhile the practice fields in Killanne and Rathnure were filled on Sundays and bright summer evenings with strapping youth and older men pucking the sliothar about for just sheer pleasure.

> Who says our country's soul has fled?
> Who says our country's heart is dead?
> Come let them hear the marching tread
> Of twice five thousand hurling men
> They hold the hope of bygone years
> They love its past; its smiles and tears
> But wavering doubts and shrinking fears
> Are far from Ireland's hurling men.
>
> *Brian na Banban*

It was 1944 and my brother John was making his debut with the Rathnure minors. I was sitting with my father on the sideline when the team came on the field, but John wasn't amongst them. Due to a breakdown in transport he was late. The match started without him, but before half-time the player that replaced him was taken off and he was sent on. As John strode across the field to take up his position, there were almost audible gasps of admiration from the onlookers. Another Rackard and just look at the size of him and he's still only a minor. No doubt for an underage player he was a formidable sight as he walked across to take up his position. All of six foot three and well over thirteen stone, the mere sight of him embued foreboding amongst the opposition. The crowd looked on in a mood of elevated expectancy.

"Look," observed one critic from behind, "He's a citóg (left-handed). They are even better and impossible to handle."

All opinions remained intact until the ball eventually landed between John and his opponent. I'm not sure what he was attempting, but he turned one way, abruptly changed his mind, turned the other way and lashed out with the hurley stick. He connected alright, but not with the ball. The flat boss of the stick made resounding contact with the backside of his opponent, who, at this stage, had the ball in his hand. He was completely taken by surprise at being whacked across the arse, jumped about a foot off the ground and in the process dropped the ball. The crowd didn't react angrily because John's strange movements looked completely devoid of malevolence. The whistle blew, a free puck in favour of his opponent. Fine, until the next ball landed between the two. They squared off again as the ball was falling. John, who was not athletically inclined, seemed to re-enact his earlier stratagem, deciding to do something, but at the last second changing course. The clash of the ash or the clash of the arse. Whatever way he moved this time, he was the recipient of a strong whack on the rear end. His opponent again looked bewildered at such a happening. The onlookers were more than baffled, but before he was taken off the pitch my father put his hand on his forehead in dismay and clicked his fingers in the direction of the Rathnure selectors who were sitting near us. "For Christ's sake" growled my father "Take him off before he kills somebody or gets killed himself."

John's hurling career, before it could even start, had spluttered to a premature stop. Before penning this I phoned him, asking why he didn't do better. Was it because he wasn't interested or what? There was a long silence and then, in his usual philosophical way, he said:

"Oh, I was interested enough. That wasn't the case. Sure I was no bloody good. It was as simple as that."

Rosaries and missions

Staying holy was almost a fulltime occupation back in the Forties. First the family rosary, later on followed by individual bedtime prayers, Mass of course, on Sundays, adherence sometimes to the seven first Fridays, weekly or monthly confession, Sunday afternoon prayers or Benediction, and maybe the stations of the cross during the week and finally the year of the mission. A week, usually during the summer, that included Mass every morning said by one of the specially trained fathers from a religious order, followed by a light religious soliloquy given from the church pulpit and lasting about ten to fifteen minutes. The major sermon was in the evening followed by Benediction. It was a week that amounted to a general spiritual whip round on everybody and anybody, ensuring that all transgression of God's Commandments were put in order. It culminated sometimes in general absolution that saw all citizens (except a few hard chaws) leave the church on the final night with a contrite soul as pure as the driven snow, and cherishing a divine clean slate. My mother was insistent that as often as was possible we all knelt down together for the family Rosary. She tried her best to make a particular time for it, but was often heard to say, "You know, it amazes me how everyone manages to disappear around Rosary time."

My father although not intending to, gave the impression that he was not as concerned as she was. When it came to the time for giving out the Rosary, it was always her who started. My father now and then made what appeared an unselfish gesture, suggesting that he would relieve Peter Byrne from the bar to take his place. He was eyed suspiciously by his wife when he nobly stated that Peter "was a religious man and most anxious to join in and should not be denied the opportunity to do so." A well-known expression at that time, certainly in rural Ireland was 'don't go there now. You'll get caught for the Rosary.' Many an individual about to press down on the kitchen door latch quickly and softly u-turned when he heard the drone of prayers coming from inside. I often heard it in the bar during conversations

"Jesus. Do you know what? I got caught for the Rosary dudder night. I thought that auld Mrs Quigley would never stop, the trimmings on their own must have lasted a full ten minutes."

One night, in our kitchen, we had all just knelt down when there was a loud whistling and footsteps coming around the house. The door burst open, and before he could back out, glances were fixed on him. It was too late – he was caught. Cap off and down on bended knee was his only option. When the normal Rosary time had expired, I was surprised to hear my mother continuing on. I thought she would never stop evoking blessings from saint after saint. Finally it ended. She stood up with a very gratified look and when the 'victim' did his business and left, her gratified look was transformed into one of accomplishment.

"I was delighted to catch him" she said, "and for plenty of trimmings as well." Normally she didn't drag them out.

No doubt, had he been more careful and known the Rosary was in session, he would have u-turned quickly and quietly – and she knew it. It was Skelton, the wiley hackney man.

The parish priest of Rathnure at that time was a man who placed money high on his list of priorities. During a break in the Mass, he would discard his outer vestments and with that well-known, long-handled collection box, there was no escape. Having dealt with the main body of the congregation he sought out even the most torpid individual, let him be lurking in a corner at the back. No relief for him either as the wooden collection box was placed before him putting the most unresponsive side of his nature to the test. Then there were the annual dues read out from the pulpit. On such a Sunday it meant spending over an hour in church as every householder in every townsland heard their name called out, coupled with their financial offering. A public declaration of your fiscal well-being. At the top of the list were the well-to-do, usually starting at one pound ten shillings down to one shilling subscribers. Strangely, no one seemed to be adversely affected by such exposure and no one showed any obvious symptom of humiliation. Nonetheless it made people cringe.

"That doddery auld man should never have been a priest. All he ever thinks about is money." said my father expressing his sentiments driving home from Mass one Sunday.

"Will you whist?" spat my mother. "Those chaps will hear you in the back."

"I don't care," said my father "and what I'm saying is true and you know it."

She was the archetypal Catholic mother who just would not tolerate criticism of a priest. "I wish you lads would refrain from using that foul-smelling embrocation when you know you are going to Mass." We had just come back from Mass this Sunday, and most of us were seated in the kitchen as our mother and Maggie Clince prepared the dinner. "I hate the smell of that stuff and honestly it seemed to be everywhere in the church this morning" she continued. Nickey had introduced his younger brothers to this ache-relieving white substance which did smell unpleasant, but had an excellent soothing effect on tired legs. There was usually a bottle of it in a bathroom cupboard. Bobby looked across with a perplexed shoulder hunch.

"Not me," he said.

Jim and John looked at each other, shaking their heads in unison. "I certainly didn't use it," I said, as I endeavoured to float my words towards mother who had her back to all of us. "Well, somebody used it." The four of us were exchanging puzzled glances when the door opened and Father came striding through with a newspaper tucked under his arm. He was going towards the parlour for a quiet read. As he marched past, everyone looked at him, noses twitching. He had opened the parlour door and was about to go through when Mother, who was standing at the cooker, turned around.

"Come here, you" she said in an assertive manner, "and closer."

She went up to him sniffing. He was bald with a growth of hair on one side which he feverishly encouraged by brushing relentlessly across the top.

"Well honestly!" she gasped, "What do you think you're up to - putting that stuff on your head?" Strangely he hadn't noticed, and if he did get the smell of embrocation, he was sure that his sons were the cause of it.

"What stuff?" he asked, showing mingled surprise at the question. "Sure, that's Brylcream – I put a little on every Sunday morning!"

'I'll never ride her again'

When I took my seat the interior of the church was reverberating with the sound of footsteps. The minutes passed, the sound of walking lessened as the church quickly filled to capacity. The place was crammed and everyone seemed to have arrived that bit earlier, making sure of a seat. A bigger than usual congregation as all space was filled and there was a reason for it. Tonight that charismatic preacher Father Ryan from the Enniscorthy Mission house was giving the sermon, and everyone knew that the theme would be company-keeping — a euphemism for sex or sins of the flesh, the fight against carnal pleasure a topic that was then, always has been and always will be, an irresistible drawing card. The silence was broken only the sound of harmonised coughing in the midst of which came the echo of light footsteps. It was Mrs Flynn, a frail elderly little lady, who lived very close to the church. Her fragile frame meandered up the aisle and then stopped, plonking down on a bony little knee. She had picked her spot carefully, as she wavered about in exaggerated discomfort. The chivalrous looking gentleman seated at the edge of the pew couldn't help but notice her. A victim, he was totally oblivious to the fact that she was putting the bite on him. He looked at her one more time and quickly succumbed. In a matter of a few seconds, Mrs Flynn, who had no distance to travel, had made a last minute entry and literally got the best seat in the house. From behind I could not help but overhear a truculent whisper. "She's done it again," came the woman's voice.

No more footsteps. The odd nose was blown, then the vestry door beside the altar opened and Father Ryan, a man of impressive physique, appeared. As he walked slowly towards the pulpit the coughing, nose blowing, in fact all noises subsided. Slowly he appeared at the top of the pulpit, taking his first glance over the congregation. There was now absolute silence. You could hear a pin drop. He placed a slip of paper in front of him, straightened himself up, at the same time lifting both hands to adjust the shoulder cape of his soutane. He emitted a few light coughs, stood quietly for a short while, just staring out over the congregation, then to everyone's surprise he produced a box of matches. He took a match from the box, struck it against its side. It instantly ignited, the little flame taking immediate hold and burning brightly. He started to count. Some in the congregation exchanged puzzled glances. The counting reached ten and he continued to look at the little flame. At fifteen he shook the match as the flame reached his fingers. It went out. He straightened up, again adjusting the cape of his soutane, again he coughed lightly; this time placing both hands on the rim of the pulpit and looking deep into the congregation. Slowly and quietly he spoke:

"That was a very small flame. It lasted just fifteen seconds." he said "If I were to light another match, is there anyone here tonight who would place his or her finger in such a little flame for as long as it burns – a mere fifteen seconds? I expect not. And why?" he asked "Because the pain inflicted by that little flame would be insufferable." He straightened up again, still speaking softly. "Now let's try to imagine a bigger flame, a much bigger flame, say as large as this church, even larger. Now let us contemplate fifteen seconds as opposed to fifteen minutes, hours or days or years." His voice rose to a crescendo.

". . . forever and ever – Eternity"

He straightened up again and nervously fingered the black cape of his soutane. He placed his hands on the pulpit one more time, looking deep into the congregation and asked, "Is there anyone here tonight in mortal sin?" He paused, his eyes searching the crowd, some people shifted uneasily in their seats. The tone of his voice gathered impetus, finally swelling to above its previous crescendo as he asked, "Is there anyone here indulging in sinful company keeping? Because if there is," his voice now resounding loudly throughout the church, "He or she, unless they give it up and seek repentance, will end up in the flames of Hell for ever and ever, for all eternity."

Silence. There was a long pause. Father Ryan was about to begin again, but refrained from doing so as a scuffling of feet caught his attention. It was near the door and he could see two men helping another man, taking him outside. Vickham (nickname) Tompkins was a hard drinking Lothario, whose nerves were frayed. Even in Rathnure at that time there was the odd menage à trois. He was part of one, but the pressure had been getting to him. He was on a slippery slope and he knew it. Father Ryan's sermon on perdition piercingly clarified what his destiny could be. The monologue depicting Hell-fire proved too much. His present state of mind couldn't take it. There and then he had a nervous breakdown.

"I'll never ride her again." he sobbed as his friends brought him outside.

"Calm down, Vickham. You'll be alright."

"You'll be alright," they assured him, "Stop worrying."

Father Ryan continued with his sermon. In a corner, at the back of the church, stood a strongly built middle-aged man. His face was creased into a knowing smirk as he listened. Jim Phelan had fathered nine children, all outside wedlock. The asperity of Father Ryan's sermon, devoid of any theological niceties as it was, had no effect on him. The grin on his face looked permanent as he whispered to the man beside him. "That poor priest will never get sense. Sure if they don't take fellows like us in heaven who are they going to get?"

CHAPTER NINETEEN

Jim Phelan was surely one of the most remarkable individuals that ever lived in rural Ireland. A man who had the benefit of a college education, he scorned convention, and was before his time – a drop-out, a hippy, a new age traveller. In the Catholic dominated culture of that time, he was totally impervious to the utterances of priests, bishops, or anybody. He owned a fine farm, but was too indolent to work it anywhere near its full capacity, preferring instead to extract from it a mere subsistence. He fell in love with an attractive tinker woman and between them they produced nine children. Jim and his lover finally decided to tie the knot, embracing the sacrament of matrimony at the same time as their youngest was confirmed. Jim had good connections, even two nephews who became prominent medical men, but nothing bothered him.

The travelling people, much to Jim's pleasure, eventually invaded the precincts of his farm. Everything was for sale and there was constant selling and replacing of animals. It ended with his place becoming a menagerie. It became a sort of stud farm, with all species represented from a top class Irish draft stallion down to a dog fox, which was even possible as foxes were well-known Phelan pets. Call to the homestead and you might be startled at a badger casually walking about. Although Jim Phelan and his wife are now a long time gone and the remaining members of the family all live in England, his penchant for a practical joke and his legendary repartee still live on.

His sons and daughters were extremely popular, being very gentle and inoffensive. We Rackards were contemporaries with some of them and attended Rathnure school together. Even though O'Reilly, the teacher was married to their father's sister, they showed little interest in learning – nor were they interested in sport. Now and then young Jim, Dan and Miley came to the Barrack field to join in some hurling, but their hearts weren't in it. Their minds were elsewhere and much closer to nature. They seemed to be endowed with bush souls. Likewise at a tender age they had an unexpected ability for impassive adult comment, sometimes to startling effect. I was of similar age as Miley, maybe only eight at the time. We were both strolling home together from Rathnure school when a well-to-do farmer reined up his stylish horse and trap. We turned and looked at him.

"Are you young Phelan?" he asked directing his words towards little Miley.

"Yes sir," said Miley.

In retrospect, I know that this man had a nanny-goat running with his cattle. He wanted to breed her but didn't want to make an idle trip.

"Tell me," he asked. "Does your father still have that puck-goat?"

I had become aware of the word but had never heard anyone of my age use it before. I was in for a shock as little Miley quickly and without the flicker of an eyelid replied, "Yes sir. Yes sir. A right one sir. Fuck goats like chain lightening, sir . . . "

One of my favourite tasks was taking Bill, the cob, to the forge for a new set of shoes. There were two blacksmiths in our area, but we usually did business with Big Mick Cullen, who lived on the mountain side of the village about a mile-and-a-half away. It was an exhilarating ride up there with plenty of sod margin on the road's side, which County Council men had spiked with little drains for water flow. My boyhood imagination used to run riot. On a magical summer morning, with the cuckoo, the gangster of the bird kingdom, trumpeting his repetitive message, and the wind singing in my ears, I would kick Bill and with his neck arched, we popped at top speed over the little drains. "Valentine's Brook second time round – come on Bill – we can do it."

The slightest movement of encouragement meant more speed. Bill and I had won many Grand Nationals going to and from the forge. Big Mick Cullen was the very epitome of the village blacksmith. A large, taciturn man, with soulful eyes and pendulous cheeks, over-developed from a lifetime of blowing away the white fumes that billow up when a red hot shoe is pressed onto the horse's hoof. The burn is essential for proper shaping. As I entered the forge, neither Mick nor his son, a youthful facsimile of his father, spoke. We merely exchanged glances. Mick Cullen earned his living from the obvious sweat of his brow. A careful but honest man, and straight as the pieces of iron he and his son were now going to chop into four sections and with their craft make into four horse shoes. It was hard work as they pounded, hammering in turn. After a short while Mick came across, put his hand on the cob's neck who was tied to a ring in the wall. He must have said something, because I could detect Bill's eye swivelling towards him as he stooped down gently. Picking up and looking at each hoof, he emitted a soft flow of inaudible words, all directed at the cob. There was predilection in his every movement, an innate safety measure inherent in all blacksmiths, soothing the animal against any latent desire to kick out. Mick Cullen, having looked at the last shoe, straightened up, mild pain showing on his face as he put his hand around his back. He looked at me, uttering his first words and he was a man of few. "Your father must think I'm a magician, but I'll do the best I can."

Bill, the chestnut cob was wearing shoes out so quickly that there was no time for fresh hoof growth. Insufficient renewal of hoof horn meant no new nail holding areas. It was nearing the end of the shoeing and I was beginning to savour the prospect of the trip home when I heard singing coming from outside the forge. "But come ye back when summer's in the meadow or when the valleys hushed and white with snow . . ." I looked out through the little forge window. It was Jim Phelan walking towards the door leading a rather weary looking nag. Big Mick had his hand on a horizontal wooden arm which, when pulled down, activated a bellows blowing air to the forge fire. It sprang up automatically. In a matter of seconds, Phelan had walked through the door and proceeded to tie the nag up to another ring in the wall. All the while he kept up a constant flow of chat, asking questions and answering them himself.

"That's a fine morn there now Mick. Begob it sure is, I think this weather is going to last. Looks good anyway." On and on he went. Mick looked across at him. He was using the wooden arm, up and down, up and down, making the fire burn brighter and hotter, but not a single word did he utter.

Phelan continued, "De di dum, de dum, that fella is a bit bare on the front there Mick. Ah sure, when you're at it you might as well put on the full set. De di dum - de dum . . ."

It was a verbal one way street as Mick guardedly eyed Phelan. He knew in his heart that if he shod this horse he would not be paid. Phelan was a man of low credit worthiness. Suddenly Mick released the arm of the bellows. It sprang up into position as he turned and looked across at Phelan.

"That'll do you now, Jim. Sure you always goes to Ned Ryan (the other blacksmith)." Phelan, who was now perched on a work bench, his legs dangling, hopped down, went across, untied the nag and made towards the door, but he hadn't quite shot his conversational bolt. He was not a man to pass up such an opportunity, no matter what the consequences. He stalled just before his exit, turned and looked across at the lugubrious blacksmith.

"Be God, Mick, sure you're dead right, but do you know what? The fucker has started to charge me!" He was barely outside when the singing started again, "But come ye back when summer's in the meadow . . ." and he slowly wandered off with the nag plodding behind.

Almost everyone of the older generation in Killanne has their very own Jim Phelan anecdote. This easy-going man, endowed with such biting wit and lightning quick observance of a humourous situation will always be a folklore figure in our village.

Jim Phelan's Irish draft stallion was, I believe, one animal that was not for sale. He was outstanding of the breed and a reliable source of income. Mares came long distances even from the Carlow side of the mountain. A long time after the breeding season, when mares were known to be in foal, Phelan would occasionally hire the local hackney man, Tom Skelton, and go on a round-up of outstanding stud fees. It inevitably resulted in a rather liquid return journey. On this occasion, they had parked the car in a Carlow farmyard. The avenue into the yard on each side was stone-faced, packed tightly with the odd quarry slate here and there. The farmer acknowledged his commitment and, in fact, had the money right there in his possession. He produced it and was about to hand it over to Phelan when he withdrew it. He was a non drinker and a very correct and careful sort. A fastidious man, especially when it came to money and more importantly his own money. Another factor alerted him. He could smell drink off the two. His mind was becoming active. He had heard stories about both of them. A pair of rapscallions, he thought.

"Sorry Jim, you can have your money when you show me a receipt."

"God damn it," said Phelan "What do you need a receipt for? You surely to God know I'm not going to charge you again. I'm not that type."

The farmer was not impressed. Phelan and Skelton looked at each other, ferreting in their pockets. No pencil, pen or paper – and nothing in the car either. A demanding thirst was taking its grip on both of them. They looked at the farmer.

"Now don't ask me, there's nothing like that up at the house."

Strapped for cash, Phelan could see the tip of the two pound notes (the stud fee) protruding from the farmer's fist. A desire for more drink was intensifying. He suddenly turned eyeing the stone fence, took a couple of steps, extracting a large piece of slate. He then stooped down, selected a sharp edged stone, placed the slate against the fence and with the stone he scratched out the receipt then thrust the slate at the farmer.

"There you are – there's your bloody receipt. That satisfy you? Now give me the money."

"Oh be God, Jim. That won't do," went the farmer, tightening his grip on the two quid. Phelan rounded on him.

"What the hell do you expect? Didn't our Lord give the ten commandments to Moses on a slate, and it's not good enough for you . . ."

The Phelan homestead was located on the very border of the Rathnure parish. It touched on the next parish, Caim/Kiltealy, whose hurlers at that time were a threat to rising Rathnure dominance. Although he was only mildly interested in the game of hurling, it would appear that in a crunch against Caim/Kiltealy, Phelan was anti-Rathnure and that belief is born from just one word uttered by him. He was standing on the crossroads close to his home, the border between the parishes. On this Sunday, Rathnure were playing Caim/Kiltealy in Enniscorthy and approximately twenty Rathnure players cycling almost en bloc, approached the cross on their journey to Enniscorthy. As they floated past, complete with gear and hurley sticks, Phelan was heard to utter just one word.

"Murderers."

My mother had her own special Jim Phelan story. It concerned a rare occurence, when Jim Phelan was outwitted. A fair day in Enniscorthy back in the twenties, as Phelan rambled about having a few drinks and just killing time, he spotted a garish-looking billboard outside a hall door. 'Have your eyes tested,' it stated, 'you could need spectacles.' 'Fine,' thought Jim, an enterprising way to pass the time. 'I will test this fella myself.' The unfortunate oculist had exhausted all his talent and equipment. No matter what strength of lens he equipped this man with, he couldn't even make out the largest letter on the test board across the room. The penny dropped. He took the spectacle frame off his patient's face and started pacing to and fro. Phelan was in his element. He had the poor man frustrated out of his mind, or so he thought. The harmless looking oculist suddenly stopped, whipped about and stared at Phelan. "I'm very sorry sir," he said. "I very much regret my inability to be of help to you."

"Be God, that's terrible" interjected Phelan, faking deep concern.

"However," continued the oculist "I could make a suggestion."

Phelan's passive exterior concealed a belly full of mirth.

"What's that sir?" he asked.

"A few yards of stout string and an intelligent dog!" Phelan was minutes standing out on the street before the full caustic content of the suggestion dawned on him.

In that rustic era of the thirties and forties, every village in the country seemed to have more than its quota of colourful local characters with distinctive humourous traits, and rapier wit. Such was the case whenever Auld Tommy and Jim Phelan got together in Rackards, Killanne. Sometimes, when a couple of them were holding the scene in the local pub and the right topic came along, you were in for a night of rare entertainment.

Granny wields a hatchet

Wexford senior hurlers, after their defeat by Dublin in the Leinster final of 1944, were once again onlookers in 1945, as the old order in the Final, that of Kilkenny versus Dublin, was reinstated. Kilkenny were victorious over Dublin five-twelve to three-four. However, the gloom cast by the downward spiral of hurling in the county was alleviated of its usual measure of disappointment. There was huge compensation for G.A.A. enthusiasts provided by the footballers who regained the Leinster senior football title after a twenty-year lapse. The purely hurling parish of Rathnure and the little village of Killanne were immensely proud of the fact that they provided one player on that team. It was, of course, Nickey.

1944 was a difficult year for me. My illness had prevented me from returning to college in the Autumn. Christmas came and went and by the Spring of 1945, I was apart from my wheezy chest, almost

The Rackard pub, grocery store and adjoining farmhouse with thatched roof, Killanne 1904.
(L to R): Nicholas Curry, Mary and Sarah Rackard, Youth unknown.

Rackard's, Killane, as it is today. To the right is the old store where the United Irishmen met.

No hurling at the dairy door! The dairy door is to the extreme left of the building facing us, while the kitchen door is on the building to the right.

John Kelly, United Irishman, etched his initials in stone in the old loft.

Bob Rackard Senior

Anastasia Rackard

The Rackard family:
L to R: Back row: John, Nicky; 2nd row: Myself, Sally & Bobby; Middle row: Rita, Jim, Essie & Molly;
Seated: Father & Mother.

My sister Essie and I in the front yard, Killanne, 1937.

Nan Wheelan, a devoted hurling fan.

Good Counsel College New Ross, 1945. I'm in the centre of the back row.

National Velvet fever! (L to R): Myself, Sr. Taracisius,
Molly, and Rita on Bill, the chestnut cob, 1946.

One of my hunters 1953.

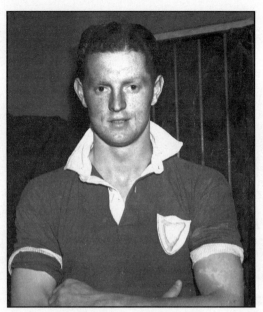

Billy Rackard — Rising young star, 1950.

The Rackard brothers before the final of the Century, Wexford v Tipperary, 1954.
(L to R): Bobby, Nickey, & Billy.

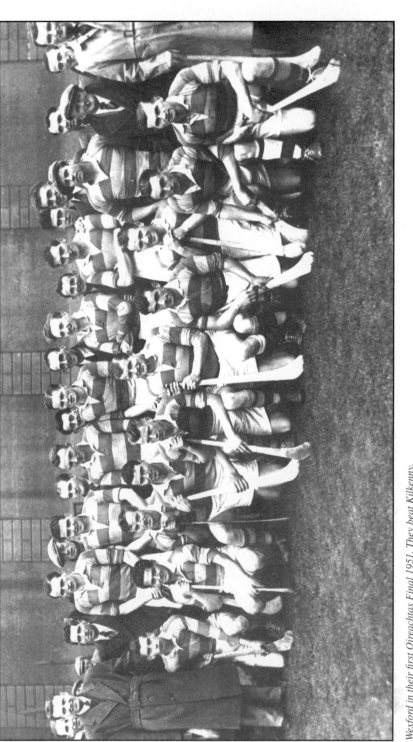

Wexford in their first Oireachtas Final 1951. They beat Kilkenny.
Back Row (L to R): E. Cullen (selector), W. Kielty (selector), Dr P.J. Daly, J. Bailey (selector), R. Rackard, M. Redmond (selector), Padge Kehoe, T. Kehoe (county secretary), M. O'Hanlon, M. Flood (subhead), W. Rackard, J. Walshe (selector), T. Russell (unknown), N. O'Donnell, M. Codd (sub), W. Esmonde (trainer), Wilkie Thorpe, S. Browne (county chairman), J. 'Crocks' Leary (bottleman), D. O'Neill (sub), J. Canavan (selector).
Front Row (L to R): P. Kelly (sub), T. Flood, J. Cummins, J. Morrissey, E. Wheeler, A. Foley, M. Byrne, S. Hearn, D. Ahearne.

Legendary hurlers in the 1952 Leinster Championship, Wexford v Kilkenny.
(L to R): M. Marnell, J. Hogan, P. (Diamond) Haydon, Padge Keogh, W. Walshe, T. Flood, N. Rackard.

All-Ireland final. Wexford v Cork, 1954. I tackle the famous Christy Ring, whilst behind, Bobby tries to grab the ball on bended knee. Bobby played the best game of defence ever witnessed.

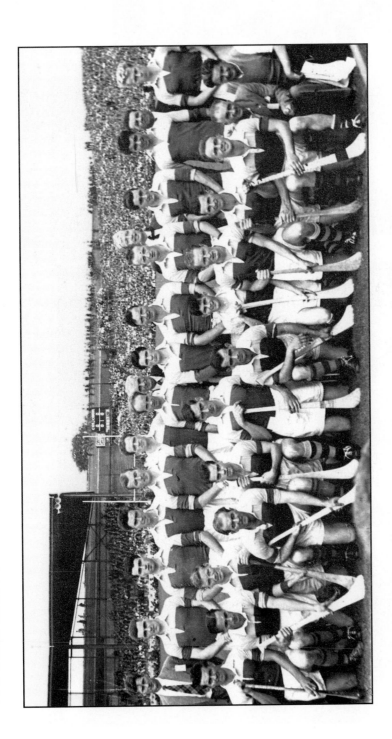

The first breakthrough in forty-five years for Wexford as they reach the 1955 All-Ireland Final to beat Galway:

Back Row (L to R): K. Sheehan (trainer), Padge Kehoe, J. Morrissey, M. Codd, N. Rackard, T. Ryan, T. Bolger (sub), N. Bowe (selector), O. Gough (sub),
W. Wickham (sub), M. O'Hanlon, T. Dixon, H. O'Connor (sub), Dr P.J. Daly (team doctor).

Front row (L to R): T. Flood, R. Rackard, J. English, Paddy Kehoe, M. Morrissey, N. O'Donnell, A. Foley, C. Casey (sub), W. Rackard, D. Ahearne,
S. Hearne, Syd Bluet (masseur), P. Hayes (selector).

J. English and Nickey Rackard with the McCarthy Cup 1955.

The heroes homecoming 1955.
(L to R): Michael Murray (photographer), Nickey Rackard,
Nick O'Donnell, Paddy Kehoe, and Art Foley.

The jubilant county welcomes their team home. Wexford 1955.

Celebrating the 1955 victory with friends:
(L to R): Members of Wexford Brass Band, myself, Johnny Murphy, Bill Goggin
and Chris Casey.

Billy Rackard accepts the Sportsman of the Year award from Michael O'Hehir 1955.

The All-Ireland Final 1956, Wexford v Cork.
Back Row (L to R): Myself, N. O'Donnell, N. Wheeler, J. Morrissey, M. Codd, N. Rackard, P. Keogh, R. Rackard.
Front Row (L to R): T. Ryan, M. Morrissey, J. English, A. Foley, T. Flood, T. Dixon, S. Hearne.

The Rackards in New York 1957, prior to one of the last big matches to be played in the Polo grounds. (L to R): Billy, Nickey & Bobby Rackard.

The All-Ireland Final 1962, Tipperary v Wexford.
J. Doyle and I lead our teams onto the pitch. I broke my hand
at the start of the match but had to continue playing.

Captain Billy Rackard accepts the Bob O'Keefe cup on behalf of his team in June 1962.

Billy Rackard accepts the 1992 All-Star Hall of Fame trophy.

back to my usual health. During that year at home I tried to pull my weight by becoming a general factotum about the place, from helping in the shop, or on the farm, or merely running messages. My grandmother (on my mother's side), was still alive and for a while she resided in a caretaker capacity in Caim. I often cycled there in the evening time, bringing her milk and staying overnight. I found her a very interesting person who had absolutely no fear of anyone or anything living or dead, or of being in the house on her own. A devout, intensely religious old lady, she said seven Rosaries per day. This didn't alter the fact that she was as tough as old boots.

"Granny," I once asked her, "If someone tried to break in, what would you do?"

She got up and brought me to her bedroom. "What would I do?" she repeated as she lifted up the pillow. "If I heard him he would be in for a shock." There beneath the pillow lay a hatchet and a revolver. My eyes almost popped out of my head at the sight of the gun.

"It's alright" she said, "You can pick it up – it's only a toy." But it looked the real thing.

The business in Caim was usually opened after second Mass on a Sunday. My father often went to Mass in Caim church instead of Rathnure. Granny was collected on the way. She would get in the front of the old Model Ford whilst my father ran in for a quick look about. She was terrified of motor cars, and during his brief absence, we lads in the back were warned to be perfectly still.

"Don't fiddle with anything," she would say. "Any wrong movement and this contraption might take off."

CHAPTER TWENTY

The little roads around Killanne had never previously seen anything like it. Farmers' heads turned and stared as she peddled past. "Who is that woman?"

On a splendid bicycle with a carrier and front basket, and dressed in a smart bluish uniform, with white collar, Nurse O'Shea, a Kerry woman, cut an elegant picture as she cycled to see her patients. I believe she was the first district nurse the area had seen. Her presence, not alone lit up the countryside, but every kitchen, parlour or bedroom she entered. She gave everyone who came in contact with her, a feeling of warmth and well being. Not alone was she excellent at her profession, but one would be forgiven for thinking that whoever wrote the song 'when Irish eyes are smiling' must surely have seen her first. A bachelor lady, a status, I felt she intended keeping, she rented a newly-built bungalow, and to everyone's delight she loved giving a 'dance.' Many's the night there, the locals pranced to the early hours, hoofing it out on half-sets, jigs, reels, the 'Stack of Barley', not to mention the latest hit, the old-time waltz, *Moonlight in Mayo*.

Nurse O'Shea led all a merry dance, and if you were shy about 'getting up', her sheer exuberance and enthusiasm soon fixed that – but it wasn't all dancing. During the course of the evening, in another room, a table was set out, laden with neatly cut sandwiches, supported with a variety of sweet cakes, all to be washed down with cups of piping hot tea. Then back to the kitchen, with the local lad Hugh O'Neill picking up his accordion again. All energies renewed for another session of battering the floor. Nurse O'Shea was an excellent hostess, showing no differential treatment, everyone equally sharing the glow of her warm personality. A well-balanced, fun-loving person and the more people saw of her the more she was valued, liked and respected. She was to spend a lot of time in our house, talking privately to my mother. It was evident as time passed, that Nurse O'Shea confided in her. It was getting duskish one evening when my mother called me into the kitchen.

"Get on your bicycle," she ordered, "and bring this parcel over to Nurse O'Shea."

It was a pleasant task and a mere twenty-minute cycle. I set off in a good mood and in what seemed no time, I was free-wheeling downhill towards the bungalow where she lived. There was a short gravel path up to the house which had a deepish trench to one side, containing the run of a little stream. On the other side, was a wooden fence which led towards the gravel fronting the hall door. I stood the bicycle against the wooden fence and looking forward to seeing Nurse O'Shea, I sprightly bounded towards the hall door and banged the knocker a couple of times. After about twenty seconds, the door opened and I was all set to see Nurse O'Shea's smiling eyes. The next minute or so is a bit vague in my mind. Something happened to me that had never happened before. It was as if a tornado had flattened me. I opened my mouth and tried to speak, but no words came out. Then I heard a voice.

"My name is Eileen, I'm Nurse O'Shea's younger sister."

I stood rooted to the ground. I had never seen anyone like her before. Her brown eyes lazily held my gaze. Her flawless porcelain complexion augmented by the most attractive sensuous little mouth I had ever seen. Her shining clear hair hung down almost to her shoulders curling up in a delightful symmetry. I tried to speak again. The words came out but I didn't recognise my voice. Neither did I recognise that for the first time my youthful hormones had set off on a mad gallop. Finally I got my message across.

"I've a parcel for Nurse O'Shea," I croaked. No sooner had I said so than the lady herself appeared.

"Billy," she called, "Come on in and have a cup of tea."

We all moved to go inside when she turned. "Eileen, this is Billy Rackard, the youngest son of a very good friend and neighbour, and Billy, I want you to meet Eileen . . ." then apparently changing what she intended to say as she looked closely at her sister. "She used to be my little kid sister, but my goodness, how she's grown! Anyway . ." continued Nurse O'Shea, "I don't know exactly what age Billy is, but I do know that next birthday Eileen is sixteen."

I sat in the room off the kitchen whilst the tea was being made. Soon the two of them joined me, carrying a tray containing teapot, cups, saucers, biscuits etc. Sitting there sipping tea, I was very conscious that I should be on my best behaviour during all this. I could almost hear my heart thumping off my ribcage. Everytime I looked across at Eileen, those deep brown eyes just held my gaze. We engaged in a long mutual stare, but as young and naive as I was, I could still detect silent eloquence in those lovely eyes. I didn't stay long. Nurse O'Shea brought me to the door.

"Thank you for bringing the parcel and tell your mother I will see her soon."

I jumped on the bicycle and set off home, swamped with a previously unexperienced irrational feeling that the world was a wonderful place to live in, I burst into loud song. "Come, come beautiful Eileen, come for a drive with me, over the mountain and down the fountain, over the high road and down by the by road . . ."

I had never known the sensation of such a rapturous mood. There was still a little light in the sky as I ecstatically sailed downhill towards home. My father's land fronted a stretch of this road, and standing with his big Roman-nosed black face over a gate and half asleep, was Heavy Harry, one of our plough horses. I stopped, went over and scratched his nose. He just opened his big eyes, looked at me, and closed them again.

"Well, Harry," I asked. "How are you? Are you happy?" I then jumped back on the bicycle, started singing again, and in a matter of minutes I was slumped in a chair by the kitchen fire. Sitting there for quite a while, I was totally oblivious to the fact that I was being asked a question. My mother was sitting nearby knitting. It was only when she tapped me on the elbow I realised that I was being talked to. She dropped the knitting in her lap.

"Do you know that three times I've asked you how Nurse O'Shea was and you haven't heard one word I've said. What's the matter with you? You haven't spoken a word since you came in."

"I'm alright and Nurse O'Shea is fine Mum," I replied.

Displeased with the tone of my answer, she irritatedly shifted about in her chair.

"There's something the matter with you that's all."

Half-an-hour had elapsed, other members of the family came in and went out. There was spasmodic conversation as mother put her knitting down once more, and looking across at me, asked

"Oh, by the way, did Nurse O'Shea's sister arrive? She was expecting her yesterday . . ."

I fought hard against a rising blush as I struggled to answer. Again I scarcely recognised my own voice as I said, "Yeah. She has."

"And what's she like?"

With my mouth half-open like a fish out of water, I emitted another hoarse croak which once again sounded alien to me.

"She's alright," it said.

No longer my loquacious self, for the next week or so I walked about like someone in a dream. It was my first time experiencing such amorous feelings and I just didn't know what to do. Maybe, I told myself, I should get out the bike and head off for the bungalow again, but then I didn't have a proper excuse for doing so and in the end fought off such impulses. My mind was in a turmoil as I conjured up all types of ideas, but on closer examination, they were completely daft and ludicrous, and worse still I felt, would expose my true feelings. I had no option but to suffer on. A little more than a week later, I was coming downstairs and about to open a midway landing door. As I was doing so I couldn't help overhearing Nurse O'Shea's voice. There was a conversation going on and she was talking compellingly to my mother.

"Don't worry, Mrs Rackard. He will be alright and we will send him home around eleven o'clock."

Then I heard my mother. "He is very young to be out until that hour at a dance."

"Don't worry, Mrs Rackard" reiterated Nurse O'Shea and then lowering her voice to a hoarse whisper and to my sheer delight she said, 'I know that Eileen will be very disappointed if he is not there.'

An uncontrollable wave of pleasure swept over me.

Finally the day arrived. Tonight I would see Eileen O'Shea again, I kept telling myself. By nature I'm a sleepy head, but I hopped out of my bed that morning truly bright-eyed and bushy-tailed. During the day, I gave a chirpy greeting to everyone I met, at the same time doing my utmost to look cool and nonchalant. I must have paid a dozen visits to the kitchen to check the time. I thought the hour would never come when I should start cleaning myself up and getting ready. Finally, dressed in my Sunday suit, I carried out a careful last minute inspection of my face in the mirror and made my way to the kitchen. Bobby was sitting by the fire reading a book and when he looked up at me, his mouth fell open and then he started laughing.

"You know," he said "You won't need the bike at all. Just stand on your head and you will be able to slide down to Nurse O'Shea's."

I had a head of curls in those days, which I hated, wanting desperately to look like Gary Cooper. My mother then arrived in the kitchen. When she saw me she gasped out loud. "What in God's name have you done to your hair?".

"I've just put on a little Brylcream" I replied.

"Go upstairs this minute, she ordered, and wipe that muck off your head, it's even dripping down your ears".

At last, on leaving home, I was feeling reasonably confident but on arrival at Nurse O'Shea's, I was anything but self-assured. My pulse rate had accelerated into a wobble. Standing my bike against the wooden fence amongst several others, I could hear the strains of an accordian from inside the house. A run of a comb through my hair and I headed for the door. When I saw that it was open, I just went straight into the hallway. I stood there in a state of indecision as the vibrant notes of the accordion swirled about me. The action was in the kitchen. I turned the door handle gently and looked in, but what I saw made me close it quickly. It was my much older and socially confident brother Jim, foxtrotting past to the strains of 'You are my Sunshine, my only Sunshine' with Eileen in his arms. I almost went weak at the knees. I hadn't bargained on that! Reflecting on the idea of doing a runner, the kitchen door opened and Nurse O'Shea appeared, uttering her apologies for not seeing me in. It's my belief that she instantly spotted my teenage expression of vulnerability. She placed an affectionate hand on my shoulder, directing me towards the kitchen, and before we went through, she leaned over and whispered, 'Eileen will be delighted you're here'.

I badly needed that and in my mind I made full use of it. I knew that in such a situation I could not compete with the verbal dexterity and practiced charm of my dapper older brother. The kitchen was cleared of its main furniture pieces, with just forms along the walls which gave ample space for dancing. As I sat down my eyes were inexorably drawn towards Eileen across the room. I looked hopelessly at her. She was listening attentively to animated conversation from another young man. She appeared radiant, her hair curled softly against her cheeks, moving her head from side to side as she responded to the young man's conversation. We exchanged glances. It happened again, only this time her eyes held mine with a warm interested look. For the next two dances, the young man had her a prisoner, but then came a Paul Jones.

"Ladies on the inside. Gents on the outside," called Nurse O'Shea.

This was my opportunity and I made full use of it, as did she, we almost kept eye contact as the men circled the ladies who were circling in the opposite direction on the inside. An about perfect stop to the music brought us together. After a few stumbling remarks and a longer look into those melting brown eyes, my confidence grew in leaps and bounds. In fact, leaps and bounds were the order of the night for us, as we stayed on the floor for half-sets, Walls of Limerick, the Stack of Barley, the Rakes of Mallow – the lot. As the night progressed I felt somewhat dishevelled, whilst Eileen managed at all times to display a natural restrained elegance with her voluptuous little lips never far from a bewitching smile. It was, to date, the most blissful couple of hours I had ever lived with the joyfully physical nearness of her in the waltz, that really had me soaking up the pleasure of the evening. As a young buck of fifteen years of age it was my first time putting my arm around such a girl. My hormones were truly in an uproar.

Alas, to my dismay, I hadn't noticed how quickly time had passed. It was only when Nurse O'Shea approached did I realise it was so late. With a sympathetic smile on her face, she pointed at the clock. "Billy," she said, "It's time you set off home. Your mother will be getting anxious. Eileen will show you to the door."

During the course of the evening we were tactile only when dancing. Now that the moment had come for me to leave, I felt an urgent, irresistible desire to kiss her quickly, but I had no idea how to go about it. I could feel panic as we stood outside the door. Turning to look at Eileen, I stared dumbly as the thought once again hit me, that she was the most attractive girl of near my own age that I had ever seen. As we stood there I could smell a fragrance of moist earth about the night. The few flowers about the place were displaying an expectancy as the bright moonlight burst through the gaps in fast moving clouds taking in the little garden and patio where we were. Eileen just stood silently looking up, the lustrous energy of her brown eyes and easy smile sending my heart thumping. With mounting panic and against a sea of inner emotion, I took a deep breath and made what can only be described as a clumsy attempt at kissing her. Midway I lost my nerve, turned swiftly, picked up my bicycle and half-walking, half-running, gazing back I went down the little driveway. Slowly the door closed. I jumped on the bicycle and peddling towards the road, I looked back again. In a matter of a few seconds I was viewing the moon once more, only this time from the flat of my back in a wet trench, with the bike for company. A short time later Eileen O'Shea returned to Kerry. I never saw her again.

I blow it

Despite the rise of the Wexford football team, the parish of Rathnure remained totally loyal to the game of hurling. The idea of the club purchasing a football wasn't even considered. More and more young lads with an insatiable appetite for hurling were continually coming on stream. Apart from the game of In and Out, there was as usual, non-stop practicing going in the Barrack field and also in another field across the parish near Rathnure village. It was a healthy physical scene watching strapping young men on bright evenings and on Sundays as they belted the ball to and fro, but there was something wrong. It was eventually pinpointed at a club meeting, when a member argued that there was a distinct lack of competition, which was what these young men desired and needed. As a result, it was decided therefore, to run a parish league. About six townlands entered teams, which included Killanne. In the Final the townsland of Monksgrange faced Killanne. Nickey who had transferred to Young Irelands in Dublin, was ruled ineligible. In spite of my overt enthusiasm, I was, at fifteen deemed too young and too fragile even for the subs bench. It was torture for me as I was consigned to the realm of a spectator.

Can you imagine breaking a well-run small club up into six sections? This is more or less what happened, as new committees in each townsland for practical purposes and team selection, were hastily put together. In Killanne, there was a general delight at the fact that two serious and highly respected men in the village, who heretofore had merely shown an ambivalent interest in hurling would now backbone the organisation of the splinter club and team. They were the local sergeant, James Devoy and the legendary Clare hurler, Garda Tom O'Rourke. The feeling was that with those two men showing such interest there was little to go wrong. Every decision had to be solidly based, leaving no room for error. Long before the idea of the parish league was conceived a fabled Rathnure club hurler by the name of Jim Dorgan had migrated to another parish, Taghmon/Camross, approximately sixteen miles or so from Rathnure. Dorgan was a native of Killanne. It was agreed, just before the final, that he was eligible to play. A meeting was held, a decision was necessary. Dorgan was a thickset individual with a short neck set into massive sloping shoulders from which dangled an imposing pair of arms. His overall appearance exuded animal strength. Although he never made the county grade, he was a formidable club hurler as well as being selected on district teams.

Whilst off the field, Jim was softly spoken and by nature gentle, he could, nonetheless, be fearsome when roused in battle. I witnessed him in a fracas once and he was an awesome sight as he inspired dread in nearby opponents. Everyone connected with the Killanne team unanimously agreed that Dorgan's presence on the team would considerably enhance our winning prospects in the final. The question was, could he be brought back for the event? It would have to be by hackney car and could the fledgling club afford such an expense? Another matter, petrol was then selectively used – a hackney man might want to save it for regular customers and more important work. It was decided to ask the local man, Tom Skelton if he could collect Dorgan the day of the final. He accepted the job.

At both masses in Rathnure church on the Sunday morning of that final, there was tangible tension in the air. One could sense divided loyalties amongst the congregation: Killanne versus Monksgrange.

In a field, almost parish centre, rented from local businessman farmer, Pat Doyle, that afternoon the issue would be decided. Dorgan's appearance on the Killanne selection had them slight favourites. The Monksgrange team togged off in Doyle's cowshed, Killanne players' facilities were the stables. The pitch was situated across the road from the yard. A large crowd had gathered. There was tension as followers of each side looked forward to a hard-fought game. The Killanne contingent found comfort in the fact that today they would have Jim Dorgan at centrefield, on a team that included the youthful Rackards, Jim and Bobby. Pep talks were given, the mentors walked across the road onto the playing area – the teams would appear any moment. First, came the Monksgrange lads. Crossing the road with alacrity they arrived, on the pitch, displaying excellent artistry as they flicked hurling balls from one to the other in the preliminary warm-up.

I stood with other exuberant Killanne followers awaiting the appearance of our lads. Nearby I watched Sergeant Devoy and Garda O'Rourke. This was an important occasion – the tension showed on their faces – they had invested a lot of time and effort in preparation for the big moment. There was a shout of 'Here comes the Killanne team,' as the players collectively trotted from the farmyard and across the road to the pitch. It was easy to pick out Dorgan, a veritable buffalo of a man, as he bowled along in their midst, a cap pulled down to his ears. As the Killanne players moved across to an empty area of the pitch, more hurling craft was evident as the sliothar was again flicked to and fro. One of them lofted a ball towards Dorgan, who was a fine overhead striker. He brought the hurley stick back to start his swing, but there was no swing. Something peculiar happened. He fell backwards to the ground. More peculiar still was his attempt at getting to his feet, which resembled that of a newly-born foal. A leg here and a leg there, and over he keeled again. The altruistic policeman observed Dorgan's predicament. Sergeant Devoy turned to Garda O'Rourke and asked a question, a question that subsequently became embedded in the archives of Rathnure hurling folklore.

"Who went for Dorgan?" was the question.

O'Rourke eyed him coldly, turned and passed the question to the man standing beside him. The fella scratched his head through his cap, thought for a few seconds and replied, 'I think it was Jim Rackard who went with Skelton.'

On hearing this O'Rourke immediately took off his cap flinging it against the ground with the words, "Oh my Christ!"

Soon after the game started, Dorgan's midfield partner gained possession, but was totally befuddled when he discovered himself dispossessed by his team mate, who was now embarked on a solo run but in the wrong direction!

The outing was a disastrous one for Jim Dorgan, who not alone saw his team beaten but also had to live with the memory of a display that was very far from his true worth. Jim, now in his eighties, lives near Wexford town. I see him occasionally and of course we have the affinity of being Rathnure men. Although suffering from arthritis, his formidable physique is still in evidence. I asked him about that day so long ago.

"Oh Gawd, Willie" said Jim, "that brother of yours, Jim and Skelton were two fierce rogues. Sure they knocked up every pub door between Camross and Rathnure. Sure I had a skinful of whiskey going on the field."

Skelton never billed anyone for the hackney fare. As far as Tom was concerned, he was not afflicted by the agony of the Killanne defeat. Hurling didn't particularly interest him anyway and all told found it a fun day well worth the price. It is believed, however, that he was instilled with a strong premonition that an account for the hackney run would be quickly destined for the nearest waste paper basket. As for my brother Jim, the sight of the inebriated Dorgan careering around the field made his day and far more so than winning any medal could.

CHAPTER TWENTY-ONE

It was a pleasant summer's day as I bashed the sponge ball against the old storehouse wall that faced onto the roadway. Coakley's cows, as they passed down earlier in the morning, had a 'clear around' leaving nothing to brush away. Several people I knew went to and fro, Pat Lynch on his bicycle sailed past with his coat tails as usual ballooning up behind him, and Fred Crabbe with a white enamel bucket curled off his shoulder, had gone to the village pump for water. "Give it the cuts," advised Johnny Hetterington when he just stopped and stared for a while.

I was enjoying the control I had developed over that sponge ball, lashing it against the wall non-stop, varying from drop shots to making contact before it hit the ground and hitting off both left and right hand. Nothing unusual about the day, that is until I looked down the road and watched a familiar figure approaching. Many times since Auld Tommy's wife died, as I indulged in ball practice against the wall, I had watched him sadly as he walked up the road dejectedly and without saying a word, turned in towards my father's pub. But today, there was something different about him. It was obvious even from a distance that the cheerful walk had returned. His head was high with the arms swinging to and fro. His metamorphosis brought a warm glow to me. Indeed it was comforting to see Auld Tommy back to his old self. I stopped hurling. Holding the ball in my hand, I looked at him with mild surprise as he called out with his former élan, 'Hey young fellow! You're lifting that ball too much, you should pull on it more often.' I was pleasantly puzzled.

Helping out in the bar one evening about ten days later, I served a drink to three local men. They were exchanging bar room banter which was a common enough happening.

"Oh be God, she'll bloody kill im, that's all," one remarked.

"She's definitely not from Rathnure," another commented.

"Yeah," said the third fella, "a widow woman. She's known as 'the blest candle', but sure there's no fool like an auld fool." I didn't know for certain who they were talking about, I was beginning to have an idea.

It was some days later again, when helping out in the shop, who did I see coming towards the door only Auld Tommy accompanied by a tall, handsome but stern woman dressed in black. She displayed an inability to smile and looked at you through tenderless eyes with a fixed expression. He bounced into the grocery side of the premises. It was forenoon.

"Tell the boss I want him for a minute," he called to Peter Byrne. My father was partially concealed at one end of the counter, in what looked like a railed sentry box. He was installed on a high stool writing at a tall Dickensian desk. Over his glasses, he owlishly peered through the rails. He had heard Auld Tommy's voice and was availing of a furtive look. He put down his pen and appeared behind the counter. On seeing him, Auld Tommy beckoned across to an area just off the grocery counter where drinks were served. With great panache, he thumbed the cap back off his forehead.

"Boss, I want you to meet someone.

"Kit, this is an old friend of mine, Bob Rackard."

My father shook hands with her and smiled, but that smile was tinged with a trace of apprehension. With risible enthusiasm, Auld Tommy slapped the counter.

"Give us a drink there Boss and have one yourself. We're kinda celebrating you know." Auld Tommy slapped the counter again.

"Boss, I might as well tell you out straight. Kit and myself are goin' to do the big thing. We're gettin' married. Give me a pint and herself a small sherry and whatever your own is."

"Well! Congratulations," said my father, as he put the drinks on the counter, "and this one is on the house." As he spoke there was again a taint of unease about his facial expression, but Auld Tommy didn't notice anything. The sun was indeed shining on his heart. In short, he was in love and like most men when that happens, irrespective of age or position, there can be a clouding of judgement, with the individual becoming hopelessly irrational. Auld Tommy was no different.

About two weeks later he was remarried. Many times during the course of that summer, as I banged the ball against the wall, I watched Auld Tommy approaching. He was truly back to his old self. The merry-legged walk which characterised his approach was always followed by a final chirpy admonishment, and this day was no different as about mid-afternoon accompanied by Jim Phelan, he headed for the pub door. I continued banging the ball to and fro as usual.

I was just enjoying the measure of control I had developed as I connected with the rebound. Auld Tommy had gone into the pub about fifteen minutes now, when I looked down the road and saw a pedestrian approaching. It was someone I didn't recognise, but even so I could detect menace in every step of a sinister-looking figure. As the person came closer to me, I saw that it was Auld Tommy's new wife, the former 'Blest candle.' Silently, with an ominous step, she turned, heading towards the pub door. A cloud of foreboding descended as I gawped at her, holding the sponge ball in my hand and watching as she disappeared through the door. I didn't have long to wait. The next sighting of her was a bit odd. The door opened and her back appeared. Slowly she came into full view walking backwards. She had a grip on Auld Tommy's ear and out she dragged him towards the road. Letting go his ear she quickly went behind, giving him a forceful push in the back which sent him stumbling towards the road. The push was accompanied by some words, part of which were a reference to work that needed doing. That was the last time I saw Auld Tommy. Never again did I witness his jaunty walk as he approached, or hear his half-serious comical reproof about lifting the ball too often.

Approximately six months later, Auld Tommy died. He had made his final exit from the village stage, one that brought equal sadness to all who knew him. Our little village had suddenly become a drabber place.

Father's team spirit grows

The selection of any Rathnure team in those days was now becoming a matter of immediate interest in the Rackard household. Whilst my mother never mentioned hurling or got involved in any direct discussion on the game, she still maintained a quiet background interest. She was also always available and very efficient at dealing with 'running repairs.' Cuts and bruises of all descriptions were tended to, and in the process she never spoke negatively about the dangerous game her sons were involved in. Similarly, when hurling was being discussed around the table, my father never tried to make a direct input, but it was observed that his antipathy of previous years was disappearing. The fact that he now had a chance of perhaps one day seeing at least four of his sons playing for the Rathnure club was a great boost to his interest, not to mention his ego, and also furthering his desire to be seen as knowledgeable about the game.

Tommy Coakley, our local postman, successor to the retired Fred Crabbe, was a selector on Rathnure teams, which usually took place in the old schoolhouse in Rathnure. Directly after such a meeting, Tommy cycled back to Killanne and then into Rackards for a pint of Guinness. If Garda Tom O'Rourke was sitting at the crossroads, he would hop out and intercept him. Tommy would name the team. O'Rourke, in his playing days, was known to display reckless courage. Consequently, the mention of a player's name who was known to be a bit 'shy' would bring a sour grimace from him. Sometimes, he would be very scathing about the selection of such a player in whom he couldn't see a little of himself.

"Do'ou know Tommy, that team ish fine," he would say in his rich West of Ireland accent, "but there are two min (men) there and I'll tell ou what. Ou will get one down in Kilmore, a fisherman's nit, and the first two ou catch in the nit outside Rathnure church – it doesn't matter after which mass, are better than those two."

If he didn't like the goalkeeper his advice was, 'I tell ou what Tommy. Roll up 'ur top coat and leave it in the goal. Tish better than that fella.'

On such an evening, I noticed that my father made a point of serving Tommy Coakley.

"Give me a large bottle there Boss," said the unperturbable Coakley as he sat down, totally oblivious to the boss's new found interest and attentiveness. Unbeknownst to Coakley, he would steer the conversation around to the team. With a glass cloth in one hand, he busily polished tumblers, holding the odd one up for inspection, then lacing it with a deep breath, he vigorously put a thorough shine on it. Exuding a pretence of being only mildly interested he would casually drop the question. "Well, what's the team like Tommy?"

At one period during the rise of hurling in Rathnure, Bossman Rackard had a chance of seeing four of his sons on the team. There were times when all four were selected and there were times when there were only three. On one such latter occasion, he unintentionally lost his cool and became irate with the blissfully unaware Coakley.

"Oh be God, Boss," retorted the surprised mentor, "you've suddenly become a great expert." My father dallied for a bit with a glass cloth in his hand. He then leaned up close to the counter and in a knowing confidential whisper told Coakley, "Let me tell you and I should know, that lad of mine you left off is going to be the best of the lot of them." That was always his remark irrespective of which son it was. The absence of a fourth son on the team had hurt his ego.

By the end of Spring 1945, apart from my breathlessness, I had made a full recovery from my illness. My interest in hurling was as keen as ever, revolving from the storehouse wall to the Barrack field and an occasional trip to the practice field in Rathnure. Another year of Wexford Championships were about to begin. The club was represented in three grades; minor, junior and senior. One evening, down on my knees, I was packing Guinness bottles onto a low shelf in the bar, when Tommy Coakley peered down at me over the counter.

"I've got news for you, young fella. You've been picked on the minor team."

I stood up with my heart positively singing.

"Picked on the minor team," I repeated to myself. "Fantastic." My talent hadn't gone unnoticed but the elation was short-lived. "You're in the goal," added Coakley. "In the goal?" I gulped. My silly adolescent fantasies had led me to believe that I was another Mick Mackey in the making and conjured up images of back divisions being ripped apart as I knifed through the floundering, helpless defenders at a sizzling pace, with the ball on my stick, culminating in an unstoppable shot to the roof of the net! Many times during such mental speculation, I was intoxicated with the roar of the crowd, rising to their feet and venting their vociferous appreciation of a great score and a great centre-forward; but now I had to confront the harsh realisation of those few words 'play in the goal'. Never. That's only a place for no-hopers and crocks. Me, a rising star and all they can see in me is a goalman.

I am afraid I behaved very badly and threatened not to take part unless I was moved outfield. I was quickly and correctly put in my place and told that if I wasn't prepared to play in goal, my name would be removed from the panel. I was on the horns of a dilemma, but after a good dollop of humble pie I conceded and agreed to be a goalman. The selectors were perfectly right in their assessment. I was far too skinny and weak to play outfield, and I had forgotten that in some of those rough sessions of 'in and out', for my safety I was put in the goal where strength didn't matter. Performing well, I showed a sharp eye coupled with good ball control and in the process was advertising myself as a future goalkeeper. Without knowing it and to my dismay, the die was already cast. However, there was a bright side to it all. The Rathnure minor team, which included Martin Codd and Bobby, with myself in goal, swept all before us in 1945. At fifteen, I collected my first medal. Every young player remembers and cherishes the proud moment when he holds that first medal in his hand. I nurtured the memory of that one, for a long time keeping it warm as I slept with it under my pillow.

Off to Good Counsel College

In the autumn of that year I was packed off as a boarder to the Good Counsel College at New Ross. Whilst academically I wasn't up to much, nonetheless it quickly became apparent that any chance I may have had of succeeding was destined for failure because of compulsory Irish. Translation into English was difficult enough – into Irish, impossible. I was rapidly going nowhere, ending up feeling totally inadequate and inferior to the other students, who were mainly from Cork and Kerry, all with an excellent knowledge of Irish. When it came to learning I had become hopelessly defeatist. However, I was not a failure when it came to playing games and especially hurling. I quickly made my mark and even though I say so myself, I was one of the stars in what I think was the college's first ever victory in a hurling game. It was Junior. Admittedly the standard wasn't great, but in that victory over Kilkenny CBS. I had the glorious feeling, which every player savours and longingly looks back on, knowing that you were the 'man of the match', and it happened from the unlikely position of midfield. It was to take quite a while before I would feel such an egotistical sporting glow again. That college victory may have been the catalyst, but Fr Veale, the college rector who appeared to have no interest in games suddenly had his enthusiasm ignited.

In those days, the playing pitches were about fifteen minutes walk from the college. He stipulated that no student should go or be seen there unless he were togged off and taking an active part. I usually led the charge to the playing pitches, but on this occasion, when I went to the college infirmary showing symptoms of a sore throat, Sister Rose, the infirmary sister, advised me to wrap up well, but under no circumstances to tog off. It was during cold early spring. I wrapped up well and went along with the rest just to watch. After a short time, Fr Veale, who was a rare sight near the playing pitches, came marching in. He spotted me and called me over. I explained to him my plight and what Sister Rose had said. That evening I was instructed to visit his study. I got four of the best. Poor Sister Rose, when informed, was more shocked than I was.

At the end of my first year in Good Counsel, it was decided in conjunction with my parents' wishes that there was no future for me in College, and that instead I should serve my time to a business. The mens' outfitters trade was the one earmarked. Before finishing with Good Counsel, I must mention that during my time there, a popular young Augustinian Father joined the college staff. A former Waterford hurler and a staunch supporter of Gaelic games, after a number of years he left and returned as Rector of the college. Putting in a nine-year stint in that responsible position, he left once more, but now to the delight of the people of New Ross and in particular the Geraldine O'Hanrahans hurling club, he is back with them again. I am, of course, referring to the amiable Fr Jack Power OSA.

A short time after seeing through the last term at Good Counsel college, I found myself standing behind the gents outfitting counter of a well-known general drapers, J.A. Bolgers and Co. Ltd., of Enniscorthy, known as the Hibernian house. It was a traditional old drapery emporium, with long heavy mahogany counters fronting the shelved wall space of each department. A minimum of display, the counter was strictly for utility purposes, the inside pregnant with well-made drawers of all sizes and the odd shelf here and there. The emphasis was on quality, customer satisfaction and comfort. A chair was always offered to an elderly person. Each transaction was highly personalised by well-skilled assistants who were properly trained during their three years apprenticeship – a sharp contrast to today's shopping anonymity. It was a high-class old outfit selling only the best merchandise, a large percentage of which was on credit to deemably solvent customers who settled their accounts, sometimes after months. My parents had an account there and I could recall as little more than a toddler, holding onto my mother's coat as I watched in awe as dockets and cash, stuffed into a little canister were sent whizzing along on an overhead wire to and fro from all corners to the office. It was the era of messenger boys on the firm's bicycles and endless approbation.

My immediate boss, Jim Higgins, was a Rathnure man. One Sunday, we went together to see a junior hurling match, played in the local park, Bellfield. On the Saturday before, a selection of sports jackets and gaberdine slacks were collected on approval, going to a household in a parish whose team was involved in the hurling game next day. Whenever Higgins made a good sale, it was always heralded by a characteristic bout of light staccato coughing, never heard outside his workplace. Now to my surprise, he was doing it as we sat waiting for the game to start. The coughing stopped when he directed my gaze to a group of men walking up the sideline displaying sartorial splendour. "There now," said Higgins, as he again started the coughing, "is a great beginning to Monday morning." Monday morning arrived and at about twelve o'clock, an unknown van-driver came in and dumped a huge parcel in front of Higgins, all the jackets and slacks were returned!

During my three years apprenticeship, my wages weren't even sufficient pocket money, not to mention the cost of keeping me in digs which my parents had to pay on my behalf.

However, at the end of my three years under Mr Higgins' tutorage, I looked upon myself as an expert in the bespoke tailoring business. During that period, my weekends were spent back in Killanne. I either got a lift by car or cycled home each Saturday night and returned Sunday evening or early Monday morning.

Enniscorthy is an average provincial town situated in a valley on both sides of the river Slaney. It is approximately seven miles from there to Killanne, a road that is a series of little hills and valleys, unsuspectingly fooling the traveller. He doesn't realise it but as he goes, he is climbing higher and higher. Leaving Enniscorthy, he catches only a glimpse of the blue Blackstairs, but by mid-journey it is looming large. It is a journey that has never ceased to enthrall me. Climbing to the plateau of upper Caim, for a good stretch away to his right, the traveller is offered a stunning panorama of the rich productive land of North Wexford; an endless spread of green fields invaded by large patches of brown fertility streaming the foothills and running to the horizon towards the Northern town of Bunclody.

Looking back in daytime, Enniscorthy town tucked down in the valley is barely noticeable, apart from three unmistakable features. The most distinctive is hallowed Vinegar Hill, squatting above the east bank of the river Slaney, the name revered down the generations and consecrated to historical immortality by the brave men who fought and there gave their lives in the cause of Irish freedom.

Next, poking their sharp spiritual fingers towards the heavens, are the twin spires of the Enniscorthy cathedral and the Protestant church. Before finally reaching Killanne, the Blackstair mountain range presents its full physical splendour. Regulated cultivation resembling a gargantuan patchwork quilt of agriculture running way up the mountain side. You are now looking at about half the parish of Rathnure. Prosperous, well-kept farmhouses with attendant sheds huddled against the hillside reflecting the energy and expertise of a thriving farming community. Winter and summer for those few years, I was to cycle this road, even when the hills were looking their coldest. Muffled in heavy clothes and scarf, with my bicycle, I braved the icy gusts. Months later, on serene sunny days I enjoyed the scented warm breeze coming from nearby meadows. My love of the outdoors was tested to the full during those bicycle trips home and back to Enniscorthy. I enjoyed it irrespective of conditions and particularly so, when the roads were only passable and everywhere was a wonderland of white, with familiar landmarks smoothed out in a blanket of snow.

CHAPTER TWENTY-TWO

One Sunday dinner at the end of autumn, as we pulled our chairs up to the table, the question was asked. "Anybody know the time?" The kitchen clock had stopped. My mother turned to Nickey, still a veterinary student and home for the weekend. "What time is it?" she asked him.

Nickey looked covered in confusion and wearing a worried expression replied, 'I don't have a watch. I lost it.'

Her eyes narrowed as she gave him an icy glance. "Do you mean to tell me that you lost that gold watch I gave you for your birthday?"

"Yes," said Nickey "I lost it helping during the harvest – it must be still in the grove field."

My mother quickly stood up from the table, exhaled loudly and stomped out of the kitchen. There was an uncomfortable silence around the table. Nickey was his mother's favourite son and he had quietly set his sights on this lovely watch, which was precious to her. She found great joy in giving it to him on his birthday, but now, unfortunately for Nickey, old sins were casting long shadows. University students, certainly in those days, were renowned for their many impecunious moments during their time at college, and like a lot of his contemporaries and predecessors, Nickey had resorted to the age-old method of pawning some personal effect as a means of raising emergency funds. His mother had accidentally made this discovery, and although disconcerted by such behaviour, she still remained philosophical – but this lovely watch was quite a different kettle of fish.

About five minutes elapsed when mother reappeared in the kitchen. She gave Nickey a despairing look, sat down at the table and continued with her meal. From then on the watch became a taboo subject.

On Sunday morning, approximately eighteen months later during early Spring, I had been to first Mass, and having finished my breakfast, I wandered up to the haggard. It was a bright cold day. Bill Clince had pulled a horse and common cart in close to a bench of hay. It was Sunday, but cattle still needed feeding. I watched as he sharpened the hay knife and proceeded to cut down into the hay. He then pushed the hayknife back into the upper cut section, reached for a pitch fork, which he thrust vigorously into the loose hay. As he did so something hopped up, glinting in the bright sunlight. As it fell back to the hay, he picked up the object, jumping down with it in his hand. I instantly recognised it. The grove field rotated from being a cornfield to a first crop meadow, which accounted for its re-appearance amongst the hay.

We both walked down to the kitchen door. Bill, who knew the story of the watch, looked into the kitchen.

"Mrs Rackard," he called. "I have something to show you."

As my mother walked towards him he held the watch up high. I can still see her face as recognition set in, transforming her expression into a warm smile, almost like a glow of sunshine as she looked at Bill's outstretched hand holding the watch.

One medal I regret winning

Wexford's Leinster senior football win of 1945 and subsequent narrow defeat by Cavan in the All-Ireland semi-final, gave GAA followers in the county that feeling of inhabiting the periphery of All-Ireland success. If an All-Ireland title came to the county, the general feeling and one which prevailed up to the late forties, was that the footballers were most likely to achieve it. Simultaneously around the mid-forties, the domestic hurling scene within the county was dramatically changing, and the old order was disappearing. Dominant parish teams like Adamstown, and New Ross O'Hanrahan's, two clubs that between them had won the championship from 1940 to 1946, were swept aside. Traditional hurling areas like Blackwater, Crossabeg and Shelmaliers and St Fintan's in South Wexford faded into the background. Whilst this was the case in the aforementioned clubs, the exact opposite was happening elsewhere. Enniscorthy town and a half-circle radius of approximately seven to twelve miles taking in the parishes of Rathnure and Cloughbawn was a veritable rumbling hurling volcano, almost ready to erupt. Rathnure had won their junior title in 1940; St Aidan's, Enniscorthy achieved that distinction in 1945, and in the same decade, Cloughbawn became junior champions. This meant that you now had the top three senior hurling teams in the county contained in a small geographical pocket, more or less in sight of the Blackstair range of mountains. Wexford's hurling landscape was immutably changed.

1946 saw Rathnure senior hurlers reach the county final only to suffer defeat at the hands of Enniscorthy St Aidans. It was the Enniscorthy team's first year in senior ranks and their win in that final over a fancied Rathnure side was a big surprise. There were three Rackards on the Rathnure team; Nickey, Bobby, and Jim in goal.

In 1946, I was again selected on the Rathnure minor hurling team, but this time in my yearned for position at centre-forward. We were well-beaten and like the seniors, by an Enniscorthy team called P.H. Pearses, a side that contained future Wexford stars such as Art Foley, Tom Dixon, Ted Bolger and Bob Slater. 1947 was more or less a repeat of 1946. Rathnure and St. Aidan's met again in the senior final, and after a replay, the Enniscorthy team won their second title. The Rathnure minor hurlers once more suffered defeat at the hands of P.H. Pearses. However, where I was concerned, it was a year of hectic activity. I played as expected for the Rathnure minors, but was also selected for the county minor team, playing against Leix at Croke Park. This game marked the first appearance of a Wexford hurling team at headquarters after a lapse of decades. It turned out to be an inauspicious occasion for me. Not only were we beaten, but I suffered the ignominy of being moved from outfield, again, back into the goal. However, later on in that year, my faith in myself was restored and when, to my surprise and still a minor, I was selected to play left half-forward for the Rathnure seniors in the drawn county final and subsequent replay.

As a minor or underage player, I had an active career in the grade playing both codes for club and county, club hurling with Rathnure and club football with a neighbouring team, Ballyhogue. I was selected on the county minor hurling team for three years and on the county minor football team for two years. In all these games, I gave very moderate performances; my self-esteem had gone and I knew followers were shaking their heads. I could sense the feeling. 'This fella won't make it. Indeed why is he selected at all?' With three brothers blazing the trail ahead for me, I now in retrospect, forgive supporters for perhaps thinking that 'this rose by any other name would not smell so sweet.' Physically, I was a very late developer and did not possess the teenage strength of my brothers – a factor which however, was to come good in time. This observation was contained in a follower's comment after a game, as I made my way to the dressing-room. A Wexford horsey-type prone to backward compliments, he let go the following assessment as I left the pitch. "You know young fella, if ye were all horses for sale out there, I'd have put a bid on you and if you were knocked down to me, you wouldn't see a saddle for two years!" It took me a while to comprehend its full meaning.

My career record shows that I did win a minor Wexford hurling medal. It also shows that I won a Wexford minor football medal, an honour attained in the most nefarious way.

In 1946, Ballyhogue, who had drawn in the county final, discovered that by virtue of an isolated player ruling, I was eligible to play for them in the replay. I took my place as a substitute amongst the panel for the game, which they duly won. Sometime later, I was invited to the Ballyhogue parish hall, where before a large gathering, I was handed a county minor football medal. But I still feel it took nerve and temerity to show up. Not once in support of the winning team did I kick a football in match combat or in practice.

Thirty-eight years later in my business during the course of making a sale, a rather surly-looking man turned to me with the words, 'You have a bloody medal you should never have been given.' He was astounded when I instantly said, "Ballyhogue 1946 minor football" He was the one who lost out on that occasion due to my co-option to the panel. His surly countenance changed to a broad smile as I assuaged my conscience to him over the miscarriage of justice, something which had bothered me all those years.

'What would it be like to win an All-Ireland?'

1948 saw Rathnure finally make the break through as Wexford senior hurling champions. They defeated arch rivals St Aidan's in the final. Whilst Bob Rackard had at last derived the pleasure of seeing his four sons play for the club in a county final, the previous year in 1947, it was then somewhat diminished by defeat. The title eventually came in 1948, but again this glorious breakthrough for the club did not see Bob's own personal dream materialise. He was represented by three sons on the field of action, the fourth was amongst the reserves. Strange as it may seem for someone who was deemed worthy of a place at seventeen-years of age, now a year older, I was not included in the line out. Gaelic football and hurling teams are renowned for sets of brothers, two, three and sometimes four, as in our case. Brotherly love or loyalty, let it be on the field of play, or in the committee room, can be a potent force quickly manifesting itself, but more especially on the field of play. I've seen cases where you touch one member of a family, you touch the lot, and likewise it has happened where someone won't play because his brother was not selected. When tension builds in a game and a player is injured from what appears an illegal stroke, such a happening can sometimes trigger off an ill-mannered fanatical response born out of over-zealous brotherly protection. In all the years that we Rackards played club and county hurling, not once, no matter what the infraction, did any of us see fit to leave our own section of the playing area, adopting an offensive attitude in support of a wronged brother. This is not intended as a plaudit, it was just our natural temperament. Our spirits were never inflamed with sufficient anxiety to step into battle on behalf of a brother. Conflict with an opponent was resolved without resorting to violence or feeling that turning a deaf ear or blind eye affected one's manhood. Neither were we utter pacifists. When the occasion demanded it, we were well capable of roughing it with the best or worst. When asked the question about brotherly protection, Bobby once drawled, 'Sure, those two are well capable of looking after themselves', then with a wry grin on his face 'as for me you needn't worry.'

I was still having trouble figuring out why I was only in the reserves in 1948.Why was I, having played in a senior final at such a young age, not selected when a year older and more experienced? It sounds illogical. The fact of the matter was that my brothers took the pressure off the selectors, hinting that if I were not picked, it wouldn't bother them. Rather unusual. Although I was unaware of it at the time, I now know in retrospect that they and the selectors were correct in their decision. I hadn't yet matured sufficiently to warrant a place at senior grade, as well as still being affected by the asthma resulting from my last illness. Although Wexford's senior hurlers in 1948, and again in 1949 made an early exit from the All-Ireland Championships, the spotlight was slowly swinging away from the footballers, honing in on the new breed of senior hurlers. The shrewd observers amongst the hurling fraternity were beginning to speak in awesome tones about certain players. Although Cloughbawn had yet to annex a senior title, the hurling grapevine believed that some exceptionally talented players were amongst their line out, and none more so than Tim Flood. They had never previously seen skills of the level he showed and executed at such lightening speed, all equally matched with an inherent tenacity and a ferociously competitive mind. The belief was growing that no matter what the opposition, Tim Flood would soon be impossible to handle.

In 1949, Tim was to lead his club to success, winning their first senior hurling title. My club, Rathnure, was the opposition, and this time Bob Rackard again saw his four sons in the line-out. I was selected at left half-back, but after a thrilling contest defeat was our lot once more. However, this Cloughbawn victory turned out to be the loudest rumble of the hurling volcano that existed within sight of the Blackstair mountain. Played in Enniscorthy before a packed crowd, the Cloughbawn team, backboned by two sets of Flood brothers, Pat Harrington and Billy Wickham, surprised their more fancied opponents in a game that lifted the quality of Wexford hurling to a new level. The previous county final clashes between Rathnure and St Aidan's set the stage – a strong feeling was taking root. Nickey Rackard was an established star in everyone's reckoning, but now his brother Bobby's display at club and few appearances at county level had followers looking on in amazement. Here was a tall, gangly, iron-framed young man who brought a new dimension to centre-back play. He made those around him look inferior mortals, so much so that at his best he appeared almost equal to being a one man half-back line. He manifested a casual approach towards the ball. Not given to first time striking in the air or on the ground, once he trapped it the number of opponents endeavouring to dispossess him didn't appear to matter. A quick turn with the ball in his hand seemed to easily scatter would-be dispossessors, then as casually as he had arrived on the scene, the ball was dispatched every time sixty or seventy yards. 'Why can't someone stop him?' opposition followers kept asking. Irrespective of what quality the opposition, once the ball arrived in his area, a long clearance was guaranteed. Meanwhile Wexford followers watched, excitedly perplexed. They didn't understand what they were witnessing, but had an awareness of watching an extraordinary talent, and thoughts of the future had them rubbing their hands with glee. Was there a player anywhere in Ireland to match him?

But Bobby Rackard wasn't the only Rathnure player displaying true inter-county class. The name Martin Codd was being frequently mentioned. Martin looked a real prospect, particularly at first time striking in the air. Before the end of 1949, that strong feeling was deep-rooted. Although hurling followers outside the model county were largely disinterested and inattentive to the fermenting hurling scene within, local pundits with mounting anticipation were casting their eyes about. Enniscorthy St Aidan's Padge Kehoe was another who had hurling purists of the day searching for new superlatives. A true craftsman in the best Kilkenny mould, his silken skills and accuracy were a rare sight in the purple and gold.

Enniscorthy also had two more players worthy of inclusion with the best. Eagle-eyed goalman Artie Foley and the incomparable, incorrigible man for all seasons, Sam (Wilkie) Thorpe. Not to mention the remarkable Paddy Kehoe from Gusserane. An established football star, Paddy did not have the benefit of sharpening his hurling skills at club level. It didn't matter, he was a master of both codes. The number one crowd puller, he exuded natural charisma on and off the field. Acknowledged already as a star hurler, onlookers revelled in his class touches and ball control. Without question, between those three clubs and Paddy Kehoe, Wexford had the nucleus of a top class team, but what about the missing links, could they be found? In a matter of months some of them were discovered, and the rest weren't too far off, and they were scattered about the county. Wexford followers were beginning to dream. No longer a fanciful, deep-rooted feeling. With the passing of another year the question was being asked for the first time. "What would it be like to win an All-Ireland?"

Where's there's smoke there's fire

During all this time I was still spending my weekends at Killanne, where the hurling disease had now reached epidemic proportions. In that big kitchen at Killanne, around Sunday dinnertime, you would need to be fitted with aural shin-guards. Mother smiled as she worked her way domestically through it all. Father, eager as always to enhance his hurling knowledge, kept a sharp ear out during his spasmodic appearances. The open hearth kitchen fire was still being used to boil the big black kettle. A few locals, as usual, had dropped in for a chat this Sunday. We lads, including Nickey, were all home.

"What's that burning smell?" asked mother as she crossed towards the dresser, carrying some dinner plates. Nobody heard her as hurling theories and beliefs were expounded from all sides. She asked again, but her question again went unheeded. Jimmy Houlihan, a famed Rathnure legislator, supporter and mentor, was standing arms akimbo, backside towards the open fire. A greatly loved GAA figure throughout the entire county, when it came to the subject of hurling, Jimmy usually advanced into a state of delirium, with one word tripping over the next as he endeavoured to clarify his thoughts. For years Mother dined out on the next few moments.

"Turn around Jimmy," she said "Do you know that your rear end is on fire?"

He instantly put his hand behind him, ferreting about his baggy posterior. He withdrew quickly. "Jaysus. I'm burning!" he yelled, "somebody do something!" His embarrassing predicament did not however affect the flow of his beliefs. Twisting one way and then the other in an attempt to catch a glimpse of his smouldering backside, he still managed to finish his point of view. "You wait and see", he said, "I still think we'll hurl the tar out of Cloughbawn in the County final."

The discussion had by now come to an hilarious halt. As he was turned about, a small column of smoke emitted from his rear end. Instant volunteers quickly doused the afflicted area, but nothing, not even Jimmy's wet posterior, could douse the general enthusiasm of the discussion. With a room full of such irresistible hurling fanatics, it was quickly once again on tracks. Eventually there was a lull, at which stage,Nickey stood up, walked over to the dresser, taking one of the hurleys from beside it. We watched as he tested its spring. He then tapped the heel of it against the stone floor. Nickey wasn't someone who indulged much in small talk, so consequently, whenever he spoke on hurling, we all listened carefully. He was, after all, a highly-rated experienced player and the only one of us who had really rubbed shoulders with the best in the game. He moved across the kitchen the hurley still in his hand. Not a word was said as he repeated the spring test and tap off the floor. Everyone felt he was going to say something. He then straightened up, looking at the hurley as he held it in his hand. "Do you know what?" he said. "It's going to happen not far from now, maybe in a few year's time – we will be All-Ireland champions."

Nobody spoke as everyone in that kitchen exchanged glances and slowly, then deliriously, pondered the full meaning of what he said. From my point of view, I had absorbed every word very carefully, wondering if it did happen if I would be a part of it.

Early in 1949, I had to my delight been given a run on the Wexford Senior team in a league game against Leix. I was a corner-forward and, although I scored a goal, I was not impressive. Neither did I give followers much to enthuse about in the county final against Cloughbawn, when I was given a roasting by Tim Flood, and later in the game by his cousin Gerry. My future, in the minds of more than a few, was behind me. In spite of everything I clung to my own beliefs, moderately content in the knowledge that for me there were better and brighter days ahead.

At the end of 1949, the Wexford Senior hurling team made its first visit to Croke Park. A League game against Dublin, the day was special in another sense. It commemorated Croke Park's Bloody Sunday of 1920. There were ceremonies to mark the occasion. Walking onto the Croke Park sod as a player is always special, but the first time you experience it, it's extra special. Apart from Nickey, the spectators that day hadn't a clue who the other Wexford players were. Standing to attention during the National Anthem served to heighten the Wexford team's sense of ambition. As they absorbed the atmosphere of the giant stadium, the same thought crossed many a mind. 'Would we ever return?'

Little did we know what lay ahead for us. As for the spectators, little did they know that the majority of the Wexford men they were looking at would soon be household names, and not just into the following decade, but into the following one again. At corner-back, I was once more on trial. After an undistinguished hour, I felt that I had just done enough to maintain the selectors interest in me. I also felt a bit more experienced and stronger in myself.

CHAPTER TWENTY-THREE

At the end of 1949, I was to make a second trip to the capital city, only this time to remain there. Having completed my apprenticeship in Bolgers of Enniscorthy, I now took up employment in the legendary emporium of Clery and Co., O'Connell street, Dublin, run by an equally legendary figure in the person of Denis Guiney, a Kerryman who looked like the late W.C. Fields of Hollywood fame. Was there ever a Kerryman who was not interested in Gaelic football? Denis Guiney was no exception. In spite of his dizzy position as an icon of Dublin commerce and a well-known figure in the international textile markets, he remained close to his origins. This was reflected in the people he employed. Success never altered this man. There was no fake interest in other more sophisticated cultures and when he spoke, it was rich, unminced Kerry idiom straight from the shoulder.

Denis Guiney was the man who originated the now perennial January sales, and was the first to take a full page in a national newspaper to advertise his wares. His tempting bargains stampeded the Irish housewife. They were to be found six deep, battling it out in the various departments. Many a time out of my natural habitat (the men's department) in the household department, I felt the full brunt of the onslaught. Confined to an area which was the literal coalface of the department, I pacified an insatiable stream of frantic customers in search of the old ten pence, halfpenny bargain tea towels. Commission was three pence in the pound. Left and right of me, there were articles carrying a tag of many pounds, but as house rules dictated, a new recruit had his nose in the tea towels until sick of the sight of them, and the three pence commission was hard earned. Nonetheless, I enjoyed my time at Clery's and especially the characters who worked there, and who were from all corners of Ireland. Whenever Tipperary is mentioned, it is synonymous with the name Jim Fogarty; Mick O'Callaghan with Dublin; Luke Tighe with Cavan; Molaing Guiney with Kerry, Jack Mangan with Galway and many more names and counties dovetail inexorably in my memory.

During those days, the Kickham Cup, a football competition between drapery houses in the city, was prestigious. A win in this competition meant victory in more than a sporting sense. When applying for the job at Clerys, my GAA pedigree certainly did me no harm. Neither did it harm me when, much to my surprise, and greatly boosting my ego, officials from Dublin hurling clubs arrived seeking my services. Although I was mindful that Nickey had played for Young Irelands, in the end the persuasive Tony Herbert soon had cornered my allegiance for the famed Faughs team. In a star-studded side, surprisingly, I immediately found a place. I was rubbing shoulders with men such as Harry Gray and Timmy Maher of Leix; Jim Prior of Dublin; and Tony Herbert, Mick Cashman and Tommy Boland of Galway; Johnny Callinan of Clare; and Paddy Kehoe of Wexford, his presence an influential factor in my decision to join Faughs. Every player on that team was of intercounty standard. Whilst I did not play for them in the Dublin championship, maintaining my loyalty in that area for the Wexford Championships with Rathnure, I did, however, play for the Faughs in the Boland cup competition, which we won. Mixing with these Faughs players and their fabled manager Tommy Moore was a great education hurlingwise, but my most memorable game and occasion when in Dublin was winning the inter-drapery Kickham cup.

A firm known as the Blackrock Tailoring Company off Grafton Street won through to confront Clery's in the final. This firm had already surfaced as contenders in the market place to Denis Guiney and Clery's. Challenging for their share of that market, they copycatted Clery's method of advertising and display. Their management, unlike Clery's, was not GAA orientated. Now the two firms would lock horns in a sporting contest, deciding who would be drapery or Kickham cup champions. Naturally the Blackrock's challenge to Clery's in business and the methods they used added a new dimension to this football final. It is one thing to throw down the gauntlet to a Kerryman in business, but when it comes to Gaelic football, it is an entirely different matter. Either side's desire for victory was more than merely winning a football match; it would also be a psychological commercial win.

About three o'clock on the afternoon of the game, Denis Guiney, our Managing Director was feeling the pressure. Marching between the counters, he stopped and looking at each charge hand, he uttered a few immortal words. "Ish there anyone here playing? If so let him go home, rhest and be in form to bate those hoors tonight."

Clery's team won the Kickham cup in the splendid atmosphere of Croke Park, followed by a night of rare festivity and celebration. The Blackrock company had lost in more ways than one.

"Look close, Mr Reidy. Can ou see anyone ou recognise in that photo?" As was the case, every morning *The Irish Press* was laid on Denis Guiney's desk, and as usual he slowly opened and scoured each page. A photograph of a group at a hunt ball in the Gresham Hotel had caught his attention, but to be precise, it wasn't the people in the photograph that had him scrutinising it so intensely. It was instead an intrusive face that just appeared all smiles, barely recognisable in a corner of it. Tapping the picture with his forefinger, Guiney looked up at his manager. "Do ou not recognise anyone there? Now come on Mr Reidy."

Reidy was lost. Guiney then tapped vigorously at the intrusive smiling face.

"Is that not young O'Callaghan from the curtain department? Ring the department and tell him I want him up here right away. A hunt ball in the Gresham!! How can the fucker afford that on what I'm paying him?"

Reidy put the phone down.

"I'm afraid, Mr Guiney, Mr Callaghan is not in this morning."

"Not in" roared Guiney, "no wonder the hoor is not in and he danshin all night."

Mick O'Callaghan, from a famous Dublin GAA family, was miscast working in Clery's – he should have gone to Hollywood. Rogueish-looking and gifted with a sparkling personality, apart from being a top class ballroom dancer, like all the Dublin O'Callaghans, he was an excellent hurler and Gaelic footballer. Denis Guiney had a sneaking admiration for the lad. After all, in that football final so important to the house, he showed sterling qualities in defence for Clerys. On O'Callaghan's return to work, his explanation was accepted as Guiney ordered him to go back to his department. All was forgiven, that is until Guiney one night perused the pages of the

Evening Herald. Something about ballroom dancing attracted his attention. As his eyes swept across the page, he thought he saw a familiar name. He returned his gaze for a check. Yes. The winner was Mick O'Callaghan and partner. The very next day Denis Guiney made a point of visiting the curtains department. He confronted O'Callaghan who was by nature light framed with a sallow complexion. "O'Callaghan. I see where ou are at that danshin agin. Give it up or ou'll kill urself. Just look in a mirror. Ur fucking dying-looking." And on he marched, but there was never any question of O'Callaghan losing his job. His Gaelic football potential outweighed his annoying nocturnal activities.

An exciting year

1950, was to prove an exciting year for the Wexford senior team, the Rathnure team and the Rackard family. There was a huge groundswell of interest and support in the new breed of Senior hurlers. Impassioned advocates of the game within the county no longer looked despairingly at the situation. Recent county finals had produced some players equal to the best in any county. The pick of the top three teams, now, plus Paddy Kehoe, would unquestionably make a good side, and that in spite of having to acknowledge some missing links. But what about the missing links? One by one, they came into view. Mick Hanlon from Horeswood deep in South Wexford was one. He may have looked unmethodical, as well as having a slight physical hand problem – neither altered the fact that he was a gifted hurler and, unlike most of his team mates, was an unerring uncomplicated natural first-time striker. Although always a fair opponent, those who robbed shoulders with him had reason to remember the name of Iron Mike was not a misnomer.

Another cornerstone of the fledgling champions burst on the hurling scene in spectacular fashion. Jim Morrissey from the Camross junior team, practically unknown in 1950, caught the public's imagination with a masterly display against Kilkenny in the final of that year. A player's player and a truly great centre field man. Twelve years later, Morrissey was still amongst the top midfielders in the game.

Top class players with Old Father Time not on their side, or plagued with an injury, were still around to help out with the county's rising new generation of stars; such as Tim Russell (a

Corkman domiciled in Wexford), Billy Stamp, Martin Byrne, Martin Flood, Dom Hearne and Bobby Donovan.

In the first round of the Championship of 1950, Wexford easily accounted for Offaly. Their next round opponents were Leix, the then reigning Leinster Champions. Wexford caused a big surprise by easily winning this game, a game that brought about a most unusual experience for myself. I was then in Dublin playing with Faughs, and as stated earlier, two of my Faughs team-mates, Harry Gray and Timmy Maher played for Leix. On the morning of that final, the three of us travelled down to Kilkenny in the same hackney car. I was playing at left half-back. The ball was thrown in, the game started, and who trotted down, taking up position as my immediate opponent only Timmy Maher, the man I travelled with and had been chatting to all morning.

Once in a while in sport, be it boxing, hurling or horse-racing, there comes a clash that has all the ingredients to fire the public's imagination. This 1950 Leinster hurling final between Kilkenny and Wexford was such an occasion. A stronger than usual current of optimism prevailed amongst the habitually hopeful Wexford following. They were absolutely certain that this new band of Wexford hurlers was going to be more than mere pacemakers to the title-seeking artists of the game from Kilkenny. Shrewd adherents, and they included knowledgeable Kilkenny men, felt that the black and amber would not find it easy this time, as it so proved. In dramatic circumstances Kilkenny just survived. This game at the start of the decade heralded the beginning of the end of Kilkenny's dominance in the fifties as Leinster hurling kingpins. It also saw Wexford make a prodigious leap in the rankings. It was too, the opener in what was to be a succession of Wexford-Kilkenny classics. Leinster finals that were in time to oust the much acclaimed Munster final as the pièce-de-resistance of the game. Although Wexford's lot was defeat on this occasion, the performance of this young team lit up the soul of the county. We would no longer be looked upon as a mere trial horse.

For the next twelve years, this team would be constantly in the forefront, appearing in six All-Ireland finals, almost as many National League and Oireachtas finals, with practically every individual of the team honoured in representative selections. The Wexford men's performance that day, even in defeat, was a massive statement. A new hurling power had shown its hand. Employing an untraditional style that was to become endemic to the purple and gold, this team of tall men with more than its share of personalities, was to mature into an irresistible crowd-pulling combination. Some regarded them as the glamour team of the decade. Bursting open the door of closed shop, top class hurling, they endeared themselves to neutrals and by the end of the decade, the nation had taken those sporting Wexford men to its heart.

Our successes, were attained by using a type of hurling that would not understandably meet with approval in the eye of the purist. Maybe so, but for me the greatest weapon in this unique team's armoury was their ability to treat victory and defeat in the same manner. "Meet with triumph and disaster and treat those two imposters just the same."

We were playing against Kilkenny. The year was 1950. Our goalkeeper, Art Foley, in the second-half parried a sizzling low ball. I was positioned almost on the end line just beside the goal post. As it spun on the chalk line of the goalmouth, Art lashed it clear. One umpire shouted 'Goal', the other held the opposite view. There was stalemate as an argument ensued, with the referee arriving on the scene from about forty yards away. He gave instructions to wave the green flag, which was done. During the next few moments I have an abiding memory of the referee's countenance as strong words were exchanged. I may be doing him an injustice, but his facial expression led me to believe that he did not want to referee a hurling championship game in Nowlan Park in which Wexford would defeat Kilkenny. At this stage in the game a Wexford win looked possible, and with the crowd encroaching onto the sidelines, it would be an understatement to state that the Park was a seething cauldron of over-excited fans. I am aware that Kilkenny followers are fine sportsmen, but it is my guess that survival was high on the referee's list of priorities and he strongly felt that a Wexford win would endanger that.

The long whistle sounded in desperation for both teams as a twenty-one yard Nickey Rackard free was frantically scrambled to safety, leaving the final score Kilkenny 3-11, Wexford 2-11. At right corner-back, marking Liam Reidy, it was my third championship appearance, a fact that had me thinking that the selectors at last were having confidence in me. Whilst I did nothing really wrong in that first half, I was still never happy in the corner-back position and had a feeling that I looked a bit jittery.

Sitting in the dressing room at half-time, that unwelcome thought kept invading my mind, but mine wasn't the only mind it invaded. A group of men called the selectors were of the same opinion. With a justifiable surge of apprehension I watched as they huddled in conversation. Finally the scrum dissolved and Sean Browne, our competent and popular county chairman, made tracks in my direction. I immediately sensed it. He was their hit man, and I was right. He was now standing over me with a rather doleful expression on his face, and in his renowned quavering tones he spoke as follows: "Now when you go out, would you lie down." I looked up into the sad countenance and gave three consecutive nods.

If you are not familiar with GAA rules, let me explain that in those days there was no legitimate substitution rule. In order to be substituted you had to pretend, or in the referee's eyes, appear to be injured. Groan or feign a leg injury, anything but don't display an appearance of being whole and intact. Once you've accomplished that then the substitution was carried out. Lying stretched on the ground moaning or clutching at an ankle or knee usually never failed, not that the referee really bothered anyway. Thank goodness that rule has been changed. It was total hypocracy and totally insensitive.

The second half of this game started and the foremost thought in my mind was waiting for an opportunity where in the referee's eyes I would appear to have sustained an injury. Before I could literally blink the ball landed between Reidy and myself. I pulled first time, making a good fifty-yard clearance. A little voice in my head was shouting 'lie down', but I couldn't because the sliothar was approaching again, this time dropping. I reached up, grabbed it, dodged my opponent and released a mighty clearance. Again the little voice said 'lie down.' Again I was unable to do so for here came the ball once more and I again executed a fine clearance. This time it stayed away so when the referee wasn't looking, I stretched out on the grass clutching my ankle and peering in the direction of the team sideline bench. Since their gaze was directed elsewhere, I wasn't spotted right away, but it didn't take long until I saw the rotund figure of our chairman as he shouted in my direction "Get up. You're alright." His quavering tones were glorious tidings to my ears.

1950 saw Rathnure regain the county title, and this time there were four Rackards on the winning line out. It's strange how a simple comment out of the blue and in unexpected circumstances and from someone you don't even know, can bolster your confidence and renew belief in yourself. In one of the earlier rounds of that championship, as I was leaving the grounds in the midst of a crowd, I felt a hand on my shoulder. I turned around, and a total stranger looked at me with the words, "You were the best of them today." It's natural wanting to perform well, and it is my belief that a player's mood for the rest of the evening is reflected in his performance for his team that day.

In the autumn of 1950, Wexford, got a real taste of Croke Park for the first time. It was the first of seven exciting consecutive Oireachtas final appearances and the first of some spectacular clashes with a very talented Galway team. In this, our first Oireachtas final, we lost 2-9 to 2-6. Unforced errors resulting from inexperience was a big factor in our defeat. The atmosphere and crowd at such finals in those days is only matched now by a provincial decider. Beaten by Kilkenny in the Leinster final and now by Galway in another final, our next assignment was a league clash with All-Ireland champions, Tipperary and on their home ground Thurles. The sporting scribes were not optimistic about our chances. It is my belief that sports writers are and should be a breed of non-biased, impassive, professional observers, difficult to influence and not prone to exaggeration. They place large emphasis on tradition. Starting to climb the ladder of success minus tradition is a big handicap. In our case we had no ancestral rights to it, unlike Tipperary whose name is synonymous with hurling. Similarly, being preceded with accumulated experience applies also to the people on the team bench. Lack of tradition here can also be responsible for tactical deficiency and consequent defeat. In this League game, Wexford defeated the reigning All-Ireland champions, Tipperary, on their own ground by six points. The late J.D. Hickey, a GAA reporter, who had the rare ability, where a player was concerned, to figuratively put his finger on the pulse of the situation, told me that the score line of that game was rejected three times by head office as a mistake before finally being accepted. It was after this performance that sports writers in general started to sit up and take notice. Who are these men? We would like to know more about them and is it possible that they can make the big breakthrough? That breakthrough looked possible as Wexford, for the first time in a League final, 1950-51 again confronted Galway. There was the added attraction of a trip to New York for the winners – a nerve-wracking occasion, especially for us rookies.

Lack of experience or if you wish, lack of tradition showed in a comprehensive defeat 6-7 to 3-4. A cloud of disillusionment descended as Wexford followers endeavoured to cope with defeat.

The Wexford following may have lost some heart, but not the core members of the team. We believed our day would come when we would create our own slice of sporting history. It was to be a longer hard road than expected, fraught with disappointment and ending with time running out for some of our older players.

The missing links

Early in 1951, those future hopes received a mighty boost with the appearance of two new names on this Wexford team; two soldiers of Wexford hurling destiny. As long as the game is played, they will never be forgotten. The first, a six foot-two inch blonde Viking genetically traced to the great Delaney footballers of Leix had already signalled his prowess and intentions as one of the most outstanding minors ever seen in a Wexford jersey. Fourteen years later, this midfield Titan still had the ability to bring the crowd to their feet as he lashed first time at any angle, rocketting the ball almost the length of the park. When Ned Wheeler made contact with the sliothar, onlookers' adrenalin clicked into overdrive. The second appeared unnoticed and practically unheralded as he was absorbed into the everyday community life of Enniscorthy. Word was that he had been a substitute on the Kilkenny 1947 team, just that, nothing much more.

The first time I set eyes on Nick O'Donnell I was disappointed. I was expecting an appearance of the archetypal sinewy Kilkenny hurler. Instead a rather top heavy, ungainly, langourous-looking individual, with an equally lethargic walk, strolled onto the practice ground. In that ten to twenty yard circle that is the habitat of a full-back and full-forward, Nick O'Donnell at a conceptual stage nipped ninety-per-cent of close in attacks. Irrespective of his opponents attention, his uncanny anticipation and deceptive speed always saw him in front at the vital moment. There are full-backs who have built fine reputations without ever being noticed much in the act of actually making a clearance. In the raw conflict that can exist in that confined area in front of goal, no man was ever so constantly professional. Alone, or in the throes of hard tackling, he displayed consummate skill in making room to execute clearance after clearance. Praise becomes redundant when attempting to describe O'Donnell's ability, which was justifiably hailed in later years, when the country's response made him an automatic choice for the full-back position on the team of the century. Kilkenny's loss was most certainly Wexford's gain. The dream team that the Wexford following so yearned for was slowly spiralling into place. There were four more missing links and at this stage two were battling for a place on the subs bench, whilst the other two were a little further off.

CHAPTER TWENTY-FOUR

"Don't put that in there," admonished Bobby Rackard junior, as he reached out and grabbed the bottle of Gold Label whiskey from his father's hand. His father turned and looked at his son in astonishment.

"What's the matter with you?" he asked. "Mike Mooney has just bought this and wants it in the cup right now." Bob Rackard Senior was pouring drink into the huge trophy when his son intervened.

"Look," advised his son, "those fellas have had plenty already and they'll drink like suck calves from that cup, so if you put too much whiskey in there they will be lying stoned all over the place. It will spoil the night. I tell you, it's happened already in Enniscorthy. Make it nine-tenths red lemonade and one-tenth whiskey and let 'em toast away, then there's no problem"

With a disgruntled look, Bob senior handed the bottle over to his son. When it came to drink, Bob Rackard Junior had far more sense than his father. The son boasted a pioneer pin in his lapel, an object that his father eyed with a certain degree of mistrust.

A title after forty-five years

The vicissitudes of sport! Not so very long ago, humiliated by Galway in the League final, Wexford were now Leinster hurling champions. Part of a larger dream had come true, it was Wexford's first Leinster title since 1925. Standing on the old wooden counter in Rackard's pub Killanne, was the huge Bob O'Keefe cup; a capacity of nearly four gallons, with the lid capable of holding one and a half-dozen old-fashioned size bottles of minerals. Almost twenty years now since the club was formed, enthusiasm and endeavour were bearing fruit. Grass roots men like club hurlers, Nicky Carr, Ritch O'Neill, Eddie Holohan and many more filed into the old pub to carry out close inspection of the massive gleaming trophy. Men, in whose ears, the sweetest music is the clash of the ash, were there from every corner of the parish, soaking up the Guinness and glory of the achievement.

In that Leinster final victory over Leix, Rathnure had four representatives on the team – all from the same household. Their father drank from the cup and smilingly surveyed the celebratory scene. Bob Rackard had lived to see his four sons line out in victory for the club in winning the county title. In 1950, the four were now part of the winning team that brought such honour to the county after a barren spell of decades. Did he look the proud father that night? Well, if he did, he concealed it nicely. As the night was drawing to a close, Mike Mooney, the club chairman, leaned across the counter. "Bob, you must be the proudest man alive."

Bob Rackard looked back, eyeing him silently, then after a long pause he reached out, caught Mike's lapel and pulling him close up whispered:

"There's no doubt Mike, but didn't I sire right ones?"

Only one set of jerseys

Near the end of my minor hurling career, I recall an occasion when, after leaving the pitch, a Wexford GAA official accosted me before I had reached the dressing room. Almost grabbing, he said, "Give me that jersey, the seniors are waiting to go on the field." Still walking, I pulled the jersey which was a heavy roundneck wool hand knit, no number, no collar, over my head and gave it to him. He ran and chucked it through the senior dressing room door. Yes. There was only one set of jerseys in the county. Present day counties such as Leitrim, Donegal, Clare or Derry will know what I'm driving at, when I say that once you win even a provincial title, you awaken a sleeping giant of support. It's not just the immediate followers but expatriates, men and women from all walks of life filled with pride at their county's sporting achievement, will rise up and proclaim their allegiance, pinning their colours and hopes in a money-no-object gesture to their county colours.

When we won the Leinster title, the Wexford men's association was immediately formed in Dublin. At their first meeting, these fine people wanted to do something, but what? A sage old member of the committee made a very appropriate suggestion. "I think we should buy them a set of jerseys."

Not that simple. They went shopping to discover that purple was a shade not just unavailable but in fact, unheard of in team colours, so they had to make do with the nearest which was a cotton jersey with blue and yellow bands, and was worn on our next outing against Galway in the All-Ireland semi-final. Unfortunately they were too close to the Tipperary colours for use in the subsequent final.

Our next outing, the All-Ireland semi-final against Galway was the third meeting of the teams within months. The score was 2-0 to Galway. This time we felt the odds were with us. After two consecutive wins our opponents would be vulnerable to the element of surprise, plus the fact that we found another young star called John Cummins from Horeswood in South Wexford. In a game in which some Wexford followers gambled heavily, we convincingly surprised our opponents with a final score line 3-11 to 2-9. Wexford had broken through for their first All Ireland final appearance since 1910. The question that had been so often asked, 'What would it be like to be in an All-Ireland final?' had been answered.

Now, for the first time, followers could at least savour that experience. Sitting in the dressing room before a big game, players tend to indulge in nervous banter, trying to appear nonchalant, but the fact of the matter is that underneath that jovial exterior there is a deadly seriousness. A lot of physical and mental energy has been invested in preparation for the next hour. There is a lot at stake. As a player ruminates and is perhaps assailed by doubts, nerves can take over. Will the team get the lucky breaks? Will he himself perform well? The strain shows in many ways, especially in the face. Another sign is frequent trips to the toilet or perhaps lacing and re-lacing his boots. On our team during this period there was one player who never displayed any symptom that could be remotely construed as nerves. A born joker on or off the field, he wore an enviable Satchmo Armstrong smile – and he had the teeth to match. To use racing parlance, selling plates and Derbys were all the same to him. Equally as proficient at football this hurling buccaneer also had the ability to indulge in a little on-field pantomime antics, and capable of extracting a loud laugh from the crowd. No matter what the opposition or occasion his flippancy never deserted him, always wearing that Satchmo smile. However, opponents quickly discovered that beneath the gin trap smile lay a dour, calculating competitor, who gave and asked no quarter. His name was Sam Thorpe, also known as Wilkie, a nomenclature derived from his many unauthorised safaris as a young lad into the Rev. Wilkie's rectory orchard.

"I was in that orchard more times than the Reverend was," smiled Wilkie, when asked to explain his nickname.

In this game, Thorpe was marking Galway's most dangerous forward and gentleman of the long green field, Josie Gallagher. The referee, a Mr Donohue from Limerick, a tall over-officious man wearing white tennis shoes, caught the crowd's imagination. When giving a free, he stomped on the ground, then standing motionless, he raised his arm Nazi salute style in the direction the ball should go. Then presenting the palm of his hand in a 'Wait' gesture at the free taker he bounded up field and blew his whistle. At the beginning of this game, he had threatened a 'sending off' for a deliberate foul stroke. His attitude carried that threat. A ball landed between Thorpe and Gallagher, which Thorpe grabbed, in the same motion breaking clear and swinging the stick backwards to execute a stroke. Gallagher, for whatever reason, unprotected and unlike him, moved the wrong way, in the process taking the back swing of Thorpe's stick in the face. It all happened very quickly. He fell to the ground in agony. The injury was a total accident but looked bad. The referee, who was about forty yards off, came galloping, his actions exaggerated by the white tennis shoes, but his manner and intent on arrival was plain to see. It looked like a sending off offence. I was close by but to my surprise, and certainly to the referee's, the two hurlers fell to the ground together, both men writhing in agony. Our general factotum and bottle man, Jim 'Crocks' Leary was quickly on the scene, lifting Thorpe to a sitting position and splashing water on his face. "Wilkie, are you alright? Are you alright?" he asked. As he reached for the bottle again, Thorpe fell backwards like a rag doll to the grass. 'Crocks' bent down over him again as I also did. In my innocence I was surprised to see one of Thorpe's eyes open wide and swivel about, with Leary this time spouting a different tune. Hissing from the side of his mouth he went: "Wilkie, stay down. For Christ's sake, stay down."

I straightened up and looked at the ref, who now appeared unsure. It had all happened so quickly, and with the two men on the ground showing similar injury symptoms, the conviction the referee displayed as he hurried to the scene was now well-diluted. But my conviction remained and that is Thorpe would have been dismissed, albeit unfairly. It was his quick thinking and flair for pantomime that kept him on the pitch, saving him that lonely painful walk to the sideline. Mr Donohue proved no more vigilant than the Rev. Wilkie!

Mother thumbs her beads

In the League final against Galway, an unfortunate event happened, which had an unsettling effect on our team. Our star goalkeeper, Art Foley, appeared to lose his nerve on that occasion and there were several attempts to find a suitable replacement, one being my brother Jim who played in the Leinster final. Ray Brennan, a Wexford native, was giving outstanding displays in goal for UCD around that time. He was brought in for the All-Ireland semi-final and final. Although Brennan was a fine goalkeeper, too much was expected of him, especially in the final. In retrospect, it was a mistake to drop Foley, a brilliant keeper who later proved his worth in no uncertain fashion.

In some people's eyes, sport is just a magnificent triviality. Maybe so, but it's my firm belief that the average person, certainly the average sports-minded person, feels a need to challenge energy, and focus on something other than the everyday struggle for existence. In this regard sport is surely the ideal, and when it comes to a large communal experience of that kind, capable of embracing an entire county, is there a better method of accomplishing it other than seeing your county team appearing in a hurling or football All-Ireland final? "What would it be like to get to an All-Ireland final?"

"Sure, the whole county would go mad."

This is more or less what happened in Wexford back in 1951. Sanguine in the extreme, tens of thousands rushed off to stock up on flags and county colours, which, mark you, were not their beloved purple and gold, but this time green and white of Leinster against Tipperary's blue and white of Munster. And what about tickets? Was there not a customary wrangle about them?

"Well, there you are, Tommy. Three sons playing, another a sub and not a ticket in sight. I always told you the GAA were a bad crowd."

"Ho, ho, ho! Begob Boss, that's a hard one to believe."

My father fussing about not having a ticket, was taking it out on local GAA man, Tommy Coakley. Moodily, he castigated the hapless postman. "Well, all I can say is, it's now just two weeks to the match and I haven't received a ticket yet and if I know that lot, I won't either."

He had just uttered the words, when my mother appeared from a back hallway. With a weary expression she went to Coakley's defence. "Don't put any pass on him, Tommy. He knows well enough he'll get a ticket. He's just an old fusspot looking for an excuse to knock the GAA."

Going back towards the hallway, she re-opened the door, but before closing it behind her, she told my father, with a twinkle in her eye, "Anyway, if you're stuck, you can have my ticket."

My mother had never seen her sons in action. Maybe it was because of the male-dominated scene that existed. She didn't want to see us play and wouldn't explain why. However, on this occasion, she conceded to go to the final.

"Why, Mummy?" I said. "I've heard you tell stories about your great day out in 1918 when Uncle John won that football All-Ireland with Wexford, when they defeated Kerry, so why can't you go now?"

"Oh, this is all very different," came the reply.

Nickey was the most vociferous in persuading her, and after substantial pressure, she agreed to go, but as she said, and to use her own words

"Okay, I will go this once," she said, "and it doesn't matter whether you win or lose, I will not go again – understood?"

Mrs Rackard and her husband sat in the Hogan stand watching the teams march past, their three sons leading the Wexford team; the fourth, Jim, on the subs bench. When the rousing strains of *Kelly, The Boy from Killanne* played by the Artane Boys Band came wafting across the great stadium, Bob turned to his wife. "Well Statia, aren't you proud of them – you surely must be enjoying this?"

"Yes," she replied, "I am proud of them and I am enjoying this – but I'm not so sure about the rest." What Bob Rackard did not know, nor anybody else on the Hogan stand was that whilst all the pomp and ceremony was taking place, Mrs Rackard was quietly, with her hand in her pocket, thumbing away on a rosary beads.

A Tipperary team going for its third consecutive title and probably one of the finest combinations ever to win the McCarthy cup proved too much for a still rather inexperienced Wexford side. The bulk of our players were a match for their opponents, but there were some weak links on our side which the highly observant and knowledgeable Tipperary men exploited to the full. I place myself as being one of those weak links. Two of our brightest stars were my brother Nickey and the irrepressible Thorpe. It must be stated here that in the pre-final preparation frenzy that surrounds squad training, unlike the vicar's orchard, not one visit did the intrepid Wilkie Thorpe pay to the practice field! How insouciant can you be?

This defeat by Tipperary was chastening and an unpleasant halt to our ambitions. Albeit, but the question we asked ourselves was, would we profit from the experience of appearing in Croke Park on such an important occasion as an All-Ireland final? The answer is, we did, maturing into a team that was to perform consistently at the highest level. With the advent of a few more exciting players, we were no longer to be trifled with. Our original belief was growing deeper. Nothing would alter that, but the pathway to our eventual breakthrough was strewn with disappointments and setbacks that were to test the strength of that belief in full measure.

In the autumn of 1951, our hopes received a timely and gratifying boost. After tasting defeat in three important finals, a current of pessimism was detectable amongst the followers but the dark clouds of defeat rolled away, when in the Oireachtas final of that year, Wexford, in Croke Park after a tremendous tussle, surprised the pundits and a full strength Kilkenny team to annex their first Oireachtas title with the score 4-7 to 3-7. I felt that my performance in this game would re-establish the selectors' confidence in me. Hurling followers in the County were now buoyant with optimism. Roll on 1952 and the Championship. Little did they or we know what was in store.

CHAPTER TWENTY-FIVE

The spring of 1952 saw me return permanently to my native county. It was only when I moved to Wexford town to open my gent's outfitters business in North Main Street, that I became conscious of my family's origins. I discovered to my surprise that there was a Rackardstown in Kilmore, approximately 14 miles south of Wexford town. Further research unearthed a few genealogical details. Ours is the only Rackard family in existence. Sources suggest that the name Rackard stems from medieval times, possibly derived from the christian name of one of the Butler or MacMurrough Kavanaghs.

Ramie Kelly, a lad my own age, came to work for me. Top class at his job and apart from working together, we became life-long friends. Anyone who has done so will tell you that standing behind a counter renders you a sitting duck for other people's opinions. Likewise, most players will tell you that Monday morning post-mortems are not always something to look forward to. Ramie, who was magnificently supportive in the business, was equally as expert in dealing with the Monday morning autopsies. Far better than I was in the matter. He relieved me of many a burden.

With the passing of time, I felt a strong urge to buy a horse and start hunting again. I enjoyed it so much during my adolescent years, but the appeal was more than just a day's hunting. The prospect of owning my own horse, breaking and training him, all that goes into making him an experienced hunter and then hopefully selling on at a profit, was irresistible. As the years passed, I did precisely that, always buying a young animal, keeping it until it was experienced, then selling on. Although I was a bit heavy for it, I indulged in some modest hunter trialing as well as having a go in an odd point-to-point. It was all great fun and a profitable sport. In later years I had some hunters for hire, which for me proved the thoroughly satisfying combination of being paid for the work I most enjoyed doing. Living in Wexford town, the Killinick Harriers were my local hunt. A farmer's pack, never MFH'd by an outsider, their country is the low flat basin in the corner of South Wexford. Extensively drained, it's mainly a bank country that has some stomach-tightening doubles on offer which vaunt readymade open graves at each side. Its flat heavy land, makes for excellent scenting and a lot of jumping through fields that are mainly of small acreage, a factor that places big store on a good 'leper.' If hounds really go and you want to stay in touch, you had better kick on and ask serious questions of your equine transport. If you don't, in this flatland of assorted banks, high hedges and deep trenches, it's possible that you may not see them again until the next meet. This is no country for the tremulous. If you should fancy yourself as a thruster, you had better be astride that good leper. You would also need the ability to transmit courage, down the reins to help him when he confronts those hairy doubles.

One of my favourite meets was Duncormick in the South end of the Harrier country, an area that has produced some fine horsemen, including the senior members of the Berry family so well-known in present day racing. Duncormick, a favourite meet and a favourite pub was run by Sean Sinnott and his widowed mother. For hunting people, the morning of a meet is different to all others. The adrenalin flow increases and those few liquid snorts amongst fellow followers in the local pub prior to the off, are especially embracing. A horse and a handful of leather is a great common denominator that crosses all divides, be they social, religious, political or cultural. Mrs Sinnott was a small frail little lady, slightly stooped, with her sleeves permanently rolled up past her boney-sharp elbows, which always seemed to point backward over her hips. She usually looked as if she had just taken her hands out of a deep wash tub. Gifted with sprightly charm, her honest recognition and sincere concern about you and yours was always stimulating. Whenever she appeared in the pub on hunt morning I noticed that she went straight to the counter and called over her son, Sean, always with the same question. "Are you sure Patch is locked up?" Then when she was leaving to go back to the kitchen, catching her son's attention once more, she would emphatically repeat the question. "Sean, are you absolutely sure that Patch is locked up?"

I had heard her on different occasions ask that question, but really didn't put any pass on why she was doing so. Another morning her question was answered by Dr Kevin McCarty, a Corkman, who came to reside in South Wexford. No man, ever, could have the love and knowlege of horse and hound that Kevin had. On this occasion, in rich Cork tones, he assured Mrs Sinnott, 'I came here early this morning to do precisely that Mrs Sinnott. The door is well bolted.'

About a year later, the Kilkenny Hunt under the mastership of the hospitable Major Victor Calmont and his charming wife Bonny, took over the Wexford country during a problematic lapse of mastership for the Wexford's. Looked upon as one of the finest and best bred packs in the British Isles, members of lesser hunts spoke in awe about its magnificent well-trained hounds and professional approach of the major and his whipper-ins. At boundary meets it's naturally possible for the chase to enter the neighbouring hunt's territory. This provides followers of that hunt with a franchise to attend the others meet. Whenever the fashionable Calmont hunt met near the hunt border at Wellington Bridge, the farmer lads from the neighbouring Killinick's delighted in turning out, and riding like demons across country in friendly horsey rivalry.

On one such occasion, amongst a group of about five Killinicks, I sat astride a magnificent blood mare about sixteen two-and-a-half hands high, and unusually for me, this animal whilst up to my weight, had all important speed. Belonging to a friend, Fintan Murphy, she was fit and ready. If hounds ran today, subject to staying aboard, I should be right up there, and that is just what happened. After drawing the first cover 'gone away' was quickly shouted by one of the Major's whips, and so started one of the most exciting runs across country ever seen in the area. In an almost six-mile point this splendid pack, in full song, gave chase to an ultra obliging fox. Going at abnormal pace, it turned into a veritable Grand National as loose horses were seen on all sides. Nearing the end, there were about eight riders intact including the Major and his men, and amongst the rest I was still astride the courageous mare, her sides heaving but still undaunted and giving me that glorious feeling of having plenty more in the tank. We were all glad of the check, which saw hounds for the first time that day unable to pick up the scent.

"Leave them alone," bellowed the Major at an overly industrious whipper-in. "They'll find it themselves."

But they didn't. Feathering as they moved in all directions, desperately seeking scent, the magnificent hounds slurped their floppy jowls against the stubble in a suckage sound that could be heard yards away. After a long period in a likely corner of the field, it looked a lost cause and a lost fox, but just as the Major was about to call them back we heard it. "R-R-R." Positive tongue alright. The pack looking puzzled, lifted their heads and crossed into the next field. "R-R-R." They followed the leader down the headland, feverishly sniffing. For such highly-trained canine aristocrats, they were suddenly looking baffled – someone was getting scent, but they weren't. Displaying a disinterested loose-limbed gait, they exchanged bewildered glances. The few riders followed the Master and whips, jumping into the next field. The Major went on a split-arse gallop after the pack.

"Back, back," he roared, now assisted by his whips, "It's a fool dog and he's taking them away." Not being familiar with the area, I turned to a Killinick rider and asked where we were. Wiping the sweat off his brow, he gasped, 'Oh be God. You're not too far now from Duncormick and I'll tell you something, that was some spin.'

'Duncormick,' I thought to myself and suddenly a very large penny dropped. I could almost hear Mrs Sinnott, 'Are you absolutely sure that Patch is locked up?' We were now in a large field adjoining a narrow road. There were audible sounds of engines running as all sorts of vehicles arrived at the scene, interspersed with the thunder of galloping hooves as stragglers endeavoured to get back in touch. All and sundry filtered onto the field, wondering what was going on. "Had he gone to ground?" "What is happening?"

At one side of the field, sitting in an orderly circle, marshalled by attendant, mounted whips dressed in hunting pink, were the renowned Kilkenny pack. They were staring across the field at a peculiar-looking kindred spirit. It had a face that resembled a large dirty mop with a shining dot of a nose protruding, boot button eyes peered rogueishly from beneath a ragged fringe. A lissom body was well-disguised beneath a matted coat, all of which culminated in an unfortunate kinky tail. An elderly lady dressed in autumn tweeds descended from a jeep holding an eccentric little dog in her arms, doing her best to calm his incessant yapping. As she picked her steps into the field, a weathered elderly-looking gentleman, sporting a black bowler hat kicked his horse in her direction. In Anglo-Irish vernacular she asked him, "Has he gone to earth?"

"No, my deah," he said. "We're having some trouble with a cur dog."

Standing close by, a young man with a cap perched on the side of his head looking as if it must fall of at any second, turned and in South Wexford dialect, riposted strongly: "Cur dog? You must be jokin'. More like a snob dog. Sure that's Sinnott's Patch; first he took over the beagles, then the Killinick Harriers, now he's after the McCalmont Hunt!"

But Patch hadn't shot his bolt yet. Out in front, the drama was deadlocked as Patch, with superb sangfroid continued his hairy eyeballing of the pack of hounds. Major McCalmont was the first to break. Looking in the direction of some youthful male onlookers he called, "Will someone catch that fool dog?"

Matt Roche, who was later master of the Killinick Harriers, marched across towards Patch. Centre stage and motionless, Patch sat there just staring. Roche who was now about twenty feet from him, changed his positive steps into a tentative approach and called to him. "Patch, good boy Patch, good lad Patch."

On hearing his name called out, Patch rolled over on his back, four paws in the air. Matt got closer, reached down to grab him, but Patch had other ideas. In a flash he had rolled back and in seconds topped a nearby fence disappearing from sight. There was no curtain call! For ten years Patch Sinnott, if loose, disrupted every type of hunt in the area. Why could he find scent and not the others? The answer was, he didn't. Patch imagined it all. He was merely chasing fresh air.

The hurling maestro

The Spring of 1952 saw the Wexford followers in a state of euphoria. Their team had fought its way back into a second consecutive League final in which they would meet Tipperary. En route, our most notable scalps were Dublin and Cork. The quarter-final confrontation against Cork in New Ross was, more or less, the first time for the rebel county men to rub shoulders with Wexford's new breed of hurlers. Ripened in hurling tradition, Cork people are grittingly realistic when it comes to assessing their chances and the opposition's. Using swallow analogy, in short, it takes more than a few to make a fine summer and in Barrett's Park (now Kennedy Park) New Ross, the Cork team and followers did not see enough purple and gold swallows to warrant a Wexford Hurling summer, or right then a Wexford victory.

The greatest exponent the ancient code has ever seen, the imcomparable Christy Ring, trotted to his position in the forward line. Ring was then in what I would describe as his golden period. The adage goes 'when you can run around, you can't play; when you know how to play, you can't run around.' This is not in any way applicable to the phenomenal man from Cloyne, but a player's golden period is supposed to be in-between when those two essential factors overlap. Already the winner of a huge haul of medals, including six All-Irelands, if ever a man was entitled to feel that he had seen it all and met them all, it was the Cloyne maestro.

I would not wish Cork folk to feel I'm being triumphalist or overdosing on brotherly accomplishments. Neither is the case. It's merely an account of what happened as I saw it, when Christy Ring took up position against his tall, gangly-looking opponent, who appeared slowish in his run to the ball. His name was Bobby Rackard. Wexford followers buzzed with anticipation as they watched the two men standing side by side. This was a clash they had eagerly awaited. Christy Ring, they believed, in spite of his great experience, would today meet an opponent different to any he had previously encountered. Wishful thinking. This was one of those infrequent confrontations that brings the crowd to the edge of their seats. Regarding the outcome, Wexford followers were saliently confident in their dark horse half-back. The final score of 5-11 to 4-6, whilst surprising, didn't adequately reflect Wexford's superiority. But the showdown between Ring and his marker had some sports writers looking on in sheer disbelief, and they most certainly included the Cork mentors. Holding Christy Ring scoreless is a bench mark achievement in any player's career; holding him scoreless in his prime in a serious game, and making him look mediocre, and playing a blinder yourself into the bargain, is a totally different matter.

From the very first ball, the much taller Wexford man asserted authority over his great opponent, surprising him with his non-traditional methods. Grabbing balls in the air, or trapping them on the ground, in vice-like fashion, he had his illustrious rival running around in circles, unable to gain possession or dispossess him. Rackard just didn't make simple clearances, he lashed mighty balls from a minimum of space, sixty to seventy yards upfield. The decision was taken by the Cork selectors to move Ring away from him. In the annals of Irish sporting history, justifiably the name 'Christy Ring' has a niche all to itself. With insatiable curiosity, the sporting public continue to be spell-bound by the man and his verbal dexterity. Amongst a sporting gathering the mere mention of his name brings about an anticipatory silence. It's my personal belief that he is also one of the most talked about and quoted Irish sportsman in history. How often have we heard, 'Wait till I tell you what Christy Ring said to so and so.' His magic on the field will never be forgotten, neither will his magnetism off it, which brings me to the following. A few years back at the launching of Brendan Fulham's book *The Giants of the Ash*, I had one of my most enthralling and entertaining discussions ever on the game of hurling. It was with Christy Ring's older brother, Willy John. Due to injury, his promising hurling career prematurely ended. It's more than mere conjecture, when assumed that his talent was on a par with his younger brother. What a pity, but what a relief for rival counties!

At this stage in my life, I was of the opinion that I had heard all of Christy Ring's witty aphorisms, so here was my opportunity to really find out. I hadn't, as Willy John filled me in on a few beauties, one of which I will relate here. In my opinion, Christy Ring was the greatest hurler of all time, but I also believe that the magic contained in his name is supported by other elements. His unique, attractive outspokeness is one, coupled with the ability to put a verbal finger on the pulse of a situation – harsh realism blended with wit, but never underpinned with malice. This story, given to me by his brother, explains it far better.

GAA players, certainly in my day, were not social animals. The opportunity for mixing wasn't there, neither was it sought as we went our own ways. Ten, twenty or more years could elapse after a player's retirement, and out of the blue one day, maybe on the main street of a rural town, two men would stand and stare at each other. Memories of shuddering clashes between them slowly surfacing as recognition set in. This was the scene once between Ring and that uncompromising, redoubtable Tipperary corner-back, Mickey, 'the rattler' Byrne. An ordinary stare became an extraordinary one as Ring's piercing blue eyes held Byrne's gaze, the Tip man broke cover.

"Christy," said the affable 'Rattler,' "'Tis yourself. I'm delighted to see you in the land of the living, and looking so well." Without blinking, Ring maintained his hypnotic stare. Finally he spoke. "If you, you little bastard, had your way, I wouldn't be in the land of the living at all!"

When Bobby Rackard marked Christy Ring, it was clearly evident that the big-shouldered Wexfordman had many inches in height advantage. Ring was once asked how to play Rackard. His reply was another one-liner Ring classic. "I'll tell you this boy ... you'll need no cap to keep the sun out of your eyes".

Purple and Gold

Wexford's defeat of Cork in the National League and subsequent loss in a thrilling final by a single point to Tipperary, gave them a new rating in the eyes of non-partisans. Aficionados of the game now believed that this team was here to stay, floating fans looking for value for money, made a point of being in Croker when the purple and gold brigade were in action. Now that I was in the drapery business, one of my first assignments was to try and procure a proper set of jerseys. I wrote to Sunbeam Wolsley of Cork and Balbriggan Hosiery of Balbriggan, Dublin, receiving identical replies. 'We will put gold with any colour but not with purple. The cost of dyeing purple cloth for the sake of one or two sets of jerseys is uneconomical, and since there is no demand for purple elsewhere and unlikely to be, we regret our inability to be of assistance."

I continued my onslaught, especially on Sunbeam Wolsley, honing in on one of the directors with my personal explanation and guarantee that demand for purple and gold would soon be widespread. Finally, a set of numbered purple and gold jerseys arrived, and unlike the old V-neck, they sported a white collar. With further pressure and about eighteen months later, Sunbeam Wolsley were persuaded to produce purple and gold socks to match. Nowadays, and it could be anywhere in Ireland, when I see a youngster wearing a purple and gold jersey or track suit, the memory of those persuasive letters to Sunbeam Wolsley flash through my mind.

The 1952 championship draw saw just two games between Wexford and another All-Ireland Final appearance, and in the light of recent performances, hopes had reached a new peak, but there was one snag. My brother Nickey, who had ongoing trouble with a knee cartilage, was near the end of the League final carried off in agony. He was not able to line out against Kilkenny in our first championship game in defence of our Leinster title. At any rate, in another classic, which delighted onlookers and to the unrestrained joy of Wexford followers, their team, minus Nickey Rackard, put Kilkenny out of the championship race. Nickey's replacement, John Cummins, wreaked havoc in the Kilkenny defence, the game ending with a strange looking final score, 4-7 to 5-1. Sadly due to emmigration, John Cummins was not available for the important ensuing years. This victory sent hurling followers in the county into a state of ecstacy. In the autumn, we had defeated Kilkenny in the Oireachtas final. In the League semi-final, we disposed of Cork, then lost by a single point to Tipperary in the final. Now we halted Kilkenny in the Leinster championships. Surely, with just Dublin between us and another All-Ireland final appearance, supporters were entitled to rhapsodise about our future prospects, especially knowing that Nickey had recovered to take his place. On that Sunday evening of the Leinster final between Dublin and Wexford in 1952, had the Shoemaker-Hubble comet gone off course, and ploughed through Wexford's fertile countryside, the shock could scarcely have had any more impact than the news of Wexford's defeat by Dublin.

Jack Redmond, a fanatical follower of the Wexford team, kept a few pigs on the periphery of Wexford town. He was a regular sight and one worth watching, when with two buckets dangling from the handlebars of his bicycle, he serenely and safely negotiated the traffic in Wexford's North Main Street. No matter what the traffic, Jack's balance after years of practice always kept him perpendicular. On the day after our defeat against Dublin, I went outside to peer at my shop window display and as I did so Jack and I exchanged glances as he came sailing down the street on his bicycle. The sight of me proved too much for him. The buckets swinging for the first time out of control, and Jack, like the Wexford team, crashed, ending up horizontal underneath his bike with a bucket at each side.

For me and for my club Rathnure, there was some compensation in 1952, and it came in unfamiliar guise. The club in 1950 for the first time entered a team in the Wexford Junior Football Championships. We duly won that title. Now in 1952, and it can be said almost to our own surprise, but certainly to others, hurling-crazed Rathnure became Wexford Senior football champions. The result of this was that three Rathnure players, two Rackards, Nickey and myself plus Des O'Neill, were called up for duty on the Wexford football team. Nickey and O'Neill, of course, were established inter-county footballers, particularly the latter, a member of the talented Ferns O'Neills. At this stage in my career, feverishly wanting to be seen as a decent county hurler, I now found myself representing Wexford in both codes. I was in between two extraordinary stools of mediocrity. Tolerable at hurling, but to this day followers are unaware that I represented my county in Senior Football. In fact I played at centre-forward when Wexford were narrowly beaten by Louth in the dying seconds of the Leinster Final in 1953. A Leinster Senior football medal is one I would have cherished amongst my collection.

At this stage in my life, standing almost six foot two inches, I weighed twelve stone – about one-and-a-half stone off my best weight. A late developer is an understatement. But now, finally shaking off the last vestiges of asthma and gaining in weight, my confidence and strength improved considerably. I still believed that I could and would contribute in a larger measure to Wexford's efforts in seeking that elusive title.

A Diamond for the Ring

In the autumn of 1952, the Wexford hurling team recovered some prestige and the attention of their large following when in New Ross, they saw off Tipperary's challenge in the Oireachtas semi-final. The final at Croke Park saw a truly memorable game before thirty thousand spectators. We went down gallantly to a classy, extremely talented Galway side. Mitchell Cogley in the *Irish Independent* next day wrote: "Recall the greatest hurling games you have ever seen, pick the highlights, and you have some idea of this epic contest."

The score was 3-7 to 1-10. We went into winter quarters with renewed optimism. The inter-provincial or Railway Cup competition of that period saw the best players of the provinces in action. Ferociously contested, the finals on St Patrick's day fired the public's imagination, drawing huge crowds to Croke Park. The rise of Wexford hurling naturally saw the county gain more recognition on the Leinster panel. In the St. Patrick's Day final of 1953, Leinster against Munster, five Wexford men lined out in the green of their province with one amongst the subs, Bobby Rackard, Paddy Kehoe, Ned Wheeler, Nickey Rackard and Tim Flood. The Wexford man amongst the subs was myself. Not since 1941 had Leinster defeated Munster in this competition, and there were some players on the Leinster side on this occasion who were well aware that time was not on their side. They included my brother Nickey, Mark Marnell, Paddy Kehoe and 'Diamond' Hayden. This might be their last chance at gaining that much sought after prestigious Railway Cup Medal – a final throw of the dice.

One of them, the charismatic Pat 'Diamond' Hayden of Kilkenny, was the full-back. In the second half of this game, I was brought on at right corner-back, marking Seamus Bannon of Tipperary. Alongside me stood the 'Diamond' marking Derry McCarthy of Limerick. Christy Ring, who started in the corner, was now in the half-line of attack. It was the dying seconds of the game; we were one point up. Leinster was about to halt Munster after years of tantalising defeat. Desperately hoping for the long whistle, the three of us in the full back line were literally hugging our opposite numbers when Christy Ring gained position on the forty yards mark. Racing towards us, he came with the ball on his hurley, but right on Ring's elbow with his stick already poised to interfere with the trajectory of a swing should Ring try it, was Bobby Rackard. Ring was running into a cul-de-sac, that is if the defenders in the full back line stayed close to their opponents. It proved too much for the old war horse, Hayden. After years of hurling torture and frustration at the hands of Ring, the 'Diamond' finally saw his chance to clobber him. At the last second, he abandoned his man and charged like a wounded rhino at Ring. As tight as the situation looked for the Cork wizard, with split-second timing he palmed the ball past the onrushing 'Diamond', accompanied with another split-second fade from the full backs charge. It was beginning to mist as Derry McCarthy (Limerick), a master of the ground stroke, lashed an unstoppable drop shot to the roof of the net, the mist rising from it with the impact. The ball was pucked out by the goalkeeper, Kevin Matthews of Dublin. Before it landed, the shrill long final whistle sounded, that final goal making Munster winners once more over Leinster by two points.

A mistake had been made and everyone knew it, but none more so than the man who made it. The subsequent dressing room scene was one of the most poignant I've ever witnessed. The players slumped down on the benches, staring at the floor, an odd one peeling a jersey off. Apart from the sound of shuffling feet, there was little else to be heard. Just the odd word, but no conversation. As I sat there looking at the floor between my feet, something crashed against the wall above my head. It was a hurling boot. Before I could pick it up, I was distracted by loud language coming from across the dressing room. "I don't dislike nobody – in fact I hates no one. But that fucking Ring, if I could get me hands on him right now, I'd choke the bastard."

Christy Ring's predatory genius had lured the old 'Diamond' from his lair. It was the only way that goal would have been scored and the 'Diamond' fell for the temptation offered. Now he was in the throes of gnawing remorse, combined with a score still to settle and suffering from being outwitted yet again by the Cork wizard. At this stage my brother Nickey had appeared from the shower, a towel around his waist and his hair down on his forehead. He put his hand on the Kilkenny man's shoulder, his friend-foe, and wearing a large smile he asked, "Diamond. Can I have a loan of your rack (Comb)?"

The Diamond turned around, chuntering to himself as he ferreted in a waistcoat pocket. Swivelling about, he handed Nickey a comb which had about five teeth in it. Still wearing his large smile, Nickey gazed at it, then began to straighten up his hair, all the while wearing that big grin. Not a word was spoken.

Bobby out of it

Hurling lovers in Wexford were naturally disappointed at this Leinster defeat. (Score Munster 5-7 Leinster 5-5). They had hoped to see some interprovincial medals being brought to the county. However, their disappointment was quickly forgotten, when a few days after the Railway Cup Final, what can only be described as devastating news reached the ears of Wexford followers. During that game, my brother Bobby sustained what initially appeared to be a harmless nose injury. Complications set in that necessitated a check-up which was completed at the Adelaide hospital in Dublin. A clot demanding surgery was diagnosed. He was subsequently operated on, after which he spent seven weeks there recuperating. After all this, the news was indeed grim, not just for his family, but for hurling followers everywhere. The medical advice as he left the hospital was 'You must never play hurling again.' Bobby, at this stage in the prime of his career, was seen by many, inside and outside Wexford, as the best centre-back in the game. Resurgent Wexford hurling hopes were dealt a cruel blow. Whilst history tells us that it was not to be the end of Bobby's career, it also tells us that the name R. Rackard was to be missing from the Wexford team sheets for over over a year. (Sadly, Bobby was to die in October 1996.)

During the 1953 hurling campaign, without ever gaining a permanent place, there were still some fine players on the fringes of the Wexford team such as Ted Bolger, Dominic Ahearne, Tom Dixon, Billy Wickham, Bobby Donovan, Martin Flood and Ted Morrissey. Unfortunately in the case of Wilkie Thorpe and Tim Russell, they were cruelly removed from the scene because of age. However, this was the year that three men slowly appeared from the shadows, three men who were to have a big bearing on future Wexford success.

The first, once given the opportunity, did so in a whirlwind fashion, treating onlookers to astounding performances in his first few games as, he literally overnight became a household name. For approximately eight years, Jim English stood alongside me in the half-back line. From his first game there to his last, I looked at him in amazement and admiration. Middled sized, with a light frame, if ever there was a smallish-looking family saloon with a Rolls Royce engine beneath the bonnet, it was Jim English. Once the ball reached his territory, this softly-spoken fellow Rathnure man was a veritable greyhound from the traps. With explosive energy and in a matter of seconds, it was returned deep into our forward line. Speed, stamina and lightening-quick reflexes combined with a flair and nerve for the big occasion made English one of the most exciting stick men of the fifties.

The second man, my pal on the team (the rest were all married!) was Seamus Hearne. He found it difficult to sparkle for his club and in the early fifties a perennial member on the Wexford subs bench, he was being mooted as a county corner-back. Whatever he had to offer, I strongly felt that it was not in that position and was instrumental in having him moved to midfield. A hurling enigma, he could be strangely absent-minded, and in the most unlikely circumstances. On one occasion in a championship game against Leix, much to the bafflement of his opponent who was wearing a large cap and chasing him for possession, Hearne lashed the ball on towards his own goal area. His marker completely taken by surprise at this action, suddenly thought that perhaps he had got it wrong. I can still see the puzzled Leixman standing there holding the large peak cap in a couple of fingers and scratching his hair with the others as his head swivelled, glancing to and fro about the field. The ball that Seamus hit in towards his own goal was caught and cleared by Nick O'Donnell, who shouted some acerbic comment to Hearne before returning to his full-back position. About five minutes later, Hearne standing nearby when play was upfield, still oblivious to what happened, asked, 'What's wrong with O'Donnell? He's in a very grumpy mood today?' Smallish in stature and not gifted with consummate hurling skill, Hearne was nonetheless laden with self belief. As a trier he was a role model. Hooking was his forte, a torture which he continuously inflicted on the great Joe Salmon in the 1955 final against Galway. Popular amongst fellow players, he had a wry sense of humour. Galway and Wexford played again a month later at Wexford Feis Carmain. A ball went towards the sideline. The stylish athletic Joe Salmon raced out to collect it. He was aiming a long stroke upfield when he was hooked. It was Hearne. Salmon ignored the ball which dropped at his feet and looking around he snapped: "You little fecker. You're at it again." Seamus Hearne may have been like all of us, a little absent-minded at times, but he was far from that in 1956, when his display against Cork in the Final of that year ensured for him a permanent place in the hearts of Wexford hurling followers everywhere.

When another Kilkenny man, Tom Ryan like Nick O'Donnell, made a similar move to Enniscorthy not a hurling head was turned. It was merely noted that he was from a successful county and that he played a little. No longer a spring chicken, his arrival in the Model County was minus any preconceived expectation that he would be an exciting new recruit to the fermenting Wexford hurling scene of that time. Neither were they aware that a look at his family tree indicated a close connection to a successful camán black and amber bloodline. Gradually, Ryan was to prove a refreshing surprise packet.

The first surprise came when he replaced one of the most stylish forwards on the Wexford team, Dominic Ahearne, a corner-forward whose exceptionally high work rate was unfortunately not matched with pro-rata scores. Ahearne, unfairly in many eyes, was replaced by Ryan. The two players were the very antithesis of each other. There was no 'loosen up kid and move around bit' for Ryan, who resembled a county council worker with a hurley perhaps propped against his posterior as he lurked about the end line displaying a minimum of territorial interest. Racing about in search of possession was not for him, and if he was changing habitat, his migratory instinct brought him no further than the fringe of the parallellogram. Nonetheless, he achieved surprising results, and they appeared where they counted most – on the scoreboard. What looked the minimum of effort was rewarded with maximum results, but the results weren't all scores. In addition, Ryan's particular brand of hurling chicanery had a disruptive presence around the goalmouth area, which made him a unwelcome distraction to the full backs. My brother, Nickey, at that time the cutting edge of Wexford attacks, bore the main physical attention of the defenders. In this matter Ryan was as effective as if he had scored himself, his presence allowing much needed freedom for Nickey to score.

My feelings about the year 1953 are contained in the results of finals, in all of which I took part. Wexford Senior Hurling Final – lost; Wexford Senior Football Final – lost; Leinster Senior Hurling

Final – lost; Leinster Senior Football Final – lost; Railway Cup Hurling Final – lost; Walsh Cup Hurling Final – lost; Corner-back on rest of Ireland V Universities – lost; Oireachtas Final V Clare – won.

Although losing by a mere three points to Louth in the Football Final, the loss of the hurling final to Kilkenny by just two points was the one that hurt most. The extraordinary fact about this loss was that in the course of the preceeding League competition, Wexford had trounced Kilkenny by twenty six points. What a turnabout by the Black and Amber. Our Oireachtas win over Clare 5-11 to 4-5 was another Croke Park thriller before a twenty-five thousand crowd. These finals then were laden with sense of occasion. With the pressure off, the championships behind them, the participating teams usually produced the best hurling of the year. This great Clare team spearheaded by Jimmy Smyth, gained revenge the following year after a re-played final. Those three games with Clare will always be part of Wexford's hurling folklore. From a personal point of view the '53 Oireachtas final, apart from winning, had further significance for myself. With my brother Bobby unavailable, I was given my first run at centre back. I immediately liked the feel of the position.

In 1952 Nickey had married Ailish Pierce from Tinahely. Ailish came from a similar family and business background to ourselves. My eldest sister, Sally was already married to a Limerick man, Thomas Gilhooley, whilst later in life Jimmy was to marry a Mayo girl, Mary Forde. Now in 1954 Bobby married Betty Ronan from New Ross. Betty also had a family business background, and John was married some time later to a girl also with a similar upbringing. His wife, Nuala Jordan, came from the neighbouring parish of Ballindaggin. My sister Essie's husband, Seamus Murphy-Flood from Enniscorthy is a first cousin of Tim and Martin Flood. In the early days, Seamus was a resolute defender with arch-rivals - Enniscorthy St Aidan's. One of my younger sisters, Molly, married Eamon Cullen, a prominent member of our other main rivals - Cloughbawn. At one period, Eamon was a selector on the Wexford county team. My youngest sister Rita sadly lost her first husband early in her marriage, but later found happiness with her second husband, Dr Joe Murray from Dublin.

CHAPTER TWENTY-SIX

It was the middle of August 1954 as I made my way to Killanne for the Sunday dinner. Bursts of sunshine added to my growing contentment as I settled behind the wheel of the Ford Prefect. The back road from Wexford to Killanne via Killurin is surely one of the most scenic drives in South Leinster. In the distance as the straggling hills and blue hulk of the Blackstairs came into view, thunder clouds to one side were piling up. Before I reached my destination they had released a heavy veil of rain, which at least brought much needed moisture to the grassy fields on the southern tip of Rathnure parish.

Driving around to the back yard, I noticed just one car present. My mother was expecting me, and before I reached the kitchen door, she had welcomingly opened it. We were not a tactile family or one who indulged in or exchanged pleasantries, but still I knew she was pleased to see me. I thought she looked remarkably well and healthy. She was of course many years younger than my father. My mother may have looked the same, but the old kitchen had changed dramatically. Gone was the open fire and bellows, now replaced by a smart fireplace. The advances of a modern society also showed in the new cooking facilities and fittings.

My mother was alone, but shortly her daughter-in-law Betty, the new Mrs Rackard and new to this scene, arrived. She gave me a warm welcome. After a short conversation, my mother said, 'Why don't you go talk to your father. He's by the parlour window reading the papers.'

It was a surprise to see a rug across his knees. I knew that he hadn't been well of late and, apart from the evidence of the rug, it also showed in the disinterested way he looked at me. I felt sad as he tried to bring a twinkle to his eye and say something amusing. He was nonetheless aware that the Wexford hurling team en route to the All-Ireland final of 1954 had destroyed all opposition. A good Kilkenny team were annihilated to the tune of 5-11 to 0-7. In the Leinster final, Dublin were destroyed 8-5 to 1-4. The All-Ireland semi-final against Antrim was a rout. 12-17 to 2-3, with Nickey assembling a score of 7-7 that was to put him into the Guinness Book of Records. Incidently, in the Leinster final against Dublin, he put 5-4 of the total on the score line. The county waited with bated breath for this Wexford team to take on much crowned champions Cork. Naturally the support and sympathy of the masses would be with the newcomers.

It was the first time that purple and gold flags were factory produced. One producer told me that never in their history had they known such a demand. In the weeks preceeding the game, in my shop alone, we sold approximately one hundred dozen home produced flags. There was to be a record attendance of eighty-five thousand plus.

The door in the parlour opened. "You two had better come in here." It was my mother's voice. "It's on the table." Bobby had arrived and the five of us sat down. I suppose the presence of a new bride in any household as in Killanne then, brings about, through no fault of hers, a certain amount of stilted conversation, especially at meal times. After a few uncomfortable exchanges, my father surprised me when he perked up and asked, "Well, are you going to beat Cork?"

Bobby was always a man of few words. On hearing the question, he looked across at me, exchanging glances. Before either of us could say anything, my mother intervened. "I wish to God you weren't playing in this match," she said. "I know it's over a year since it's happened. I also know you played against Kilkenny, but still the doctor in the Adelaide says you shouldn't be doing it." At this stage Betty chipped in: "I know, Mrs Rackard, but there's no use talking to him. He's made up his mind and that's it."

Suddenly, we were distracted by the noise of a car coming to a halt outside in the yard. My mother jumped up immediately, pulling back the curtains. "It's Nickey." she said "He must have been on a call somewhere nearby."

Nickey, at this stage, was a practicing vet in Bunclody about ten miles away, and regularly called in home when in the area. My mother had the kitchen door open before he was fully out of the car.

"Have you had your dinner?" she shouted.

"No," responded Nickey and "I told Ailish not to expect me."

"Men – they're impossible when it comes to meal times." My mother's pretence at irritation vanished when Nickey appeared in the doorway wearing a big grin.

"Alright then," she said. "You're just in time. Pull up a chair for yourself."

He had no sooner settled, when my father turned to him. "I've been asking these two here if you're going to beat Cork, but I can't get an answer. What do you think?" Nickey picked up a half-pint glass of milk and downed it in one go. "God, I'm thirsty, I've just dealt with a difficult calving." He dropped the empty glass hard against the table.

"Of course we will. We'll beat 'em alright, that is if we play to our known strength. You see, in a final such as this, a team with Cork's tradition will play to their full potential and exploit any weaknesses we have. The question is can we do the same? If we do, we will be too powerful for them." To my surprise, my mother entered the discussion. "I'm dead nervous – that's all. The papers are blowing you all up. Everything has been so easy up till now. I just can't help feeling something may go wrong. Anyway," she continued "you know that I'm not going and your father isn't up to it. We'll both be sitting right here in the kitchen, taking in every word from Michael O'Hehir. It's very likely we'll be on our own. I don't begrudge it but everyone seems to have a radio and a car now." At this stage, Father perked up again. "Do you know what?" he said, "the day of someone calling in, is fast disappearing in Ireland."

Epic failure 1954

At approximately 5 p.m. on the last Sunday of September 1954, thousands upon thousands of dejected Wexford hurling followers with closed faces silently trudged out of Croke Park. They had just witnessed an epic failure. If a Croke Park dressing-room was given the power of speech, it could surely submit new adjectives for describing heartbreaking defeat, it is my belief that the post-match scene in the Wexford dressing-room on that occasion would supply them. Hardened hurling warriors, with tears running down their cheeks, sat in stunned acceptance of a five-year-old, or if you wish a forty-five-year old, capsized dream. Some of them, unable to untie their bootlaces, were in a state of paralysis whilst a sympathetic friend stooped down to do it for them. This final contained all the ingredients to make it one of the most memorable of the twentieth century. Firstly a record crowd; secondly a legendary icon of the game, Christy Ring seeking a personal record; and thirdly a powerful new force with new methods backed by their huge following plus neutrals as they sought hurling's highest peak. 'Victory glosses over error; defeat leaves it bare.'

In this grim, hard-fought, finely-balanced contest, there was very little error, which a score line of 1-9 to 1-6 suggests. It also suggests dominant defences and that in spite of such scoring machines as Christy Ring and Nickey Rackard in each attack. When it was all over and the dust settled, some analysts and the bulk of the Wexford followers formed the opinion that at a crucial stage, Wexford made a defensive miscalculation which cost them the game and title. It involved moving Bobby Rackard from centre-back to full-back in place of the injured Nick O'Donnell. After this change, Rackard executed feats of defensive hurling never previously seen in a final. I am open to slight correction, but since the inception of the All-Ireland hurling competition, practically every team with a defence that contained the opposition to 1-9 ended up as champions. On the other hand, teams whose forward devision chalked up 1-6 inevitably lost. In the light of these statistics, it is quite extraordinary then to hear a thesis put forward, mainly by purple and gold supporters, claiming that the positional change in the Wexford back line was the cause of their tragic defeat. In all the agonising after-match post mortems and again bearing in mind the scoring statistics just quoted, it's surprising again that scarcely once did I hear a Wexford follower suggest that a change in the forward line might have saved the day. "Incredible," I thought. So why then did such a mass-multitude cling to the same inaccurate theory?

For a following that had never experienced the oxygen of All-Ireland success and with just one title dating back to 1910, the natural craving for this victory was more than understandable. At a vital stage in the game, victory looked on but was cruelly snatched from them. For Wexford followers, the gnawing pain of narrowly losing was further intensified by the glory of Bobby Rackard's performance, now wasted in defeat. It proved too much for them, grieviously imparing honest objective assessment, and caused delusions about a defensive error. Here are the facts – with Bobby Rackard's display in the last quarter the central issue to it all:

At a crucial stage in the game with the result hanging in the balance, Wexford's magnificent full-back Nick O'Donnell sustained a broken collar bone caused by a Ring rocket hitting him in the shoulder. Extraordinarily in this instance quite a number of Wexford followers were certain that Ring had actually hit O'Donnell with his stick. When O'Donnell went down, they were roughly twenty yards apart. Up to this, Bobby Rackard was doing well at centre-back, making many fine clearances. In O'Donnell's absence he went full-back, Ned Wheeler to centre and sub Ted Bolger coming on. Bobby Rackard's subsequent display will never be forgotten and it was this display that spawned the theory about a defensive error. With the Cork forwards swarming all over him he reached up, snatched ball after ball from between a forest of hurleys and incredibly in postage stamp space, launched clearances again and again an astonishing sixty to seventy yards upfield. Onlookers from both sides watched in admiration and awe. In spite of O'Donnell's absence, the Wexford defence remained intact, that is until the last minutes when a ground ball broke to my side at right full-back. I fatally hesitated as Johnny Clifford pulling first time, connected with a rasper. It flew past Goalie Art Foley to the net. It was all over. As long as I live, I shall never forget the misery and self-blame I felt at watching the green flag wave. In spite of defeat, a tumultous welcome awaited the returning Wexford team. I refused to climb onto any welcoming platform. The agony and self-guilt which consumed me prevented me from doing so. I empathise with any player who feels he's made a mistake that's cost his county an All-Ireland Title. Unless you have been there, the emotional torture is impossible to comprehend.

Now let's go back to the defensive theory. If Bobby Rackard had been left at centre-back, wouldn't those clearances have landed near the Wexford square, and then wouldn't we have chalked up winning scores? A simple solution, but what is forgotten in this made-to-order Wexford thesis is, had Bobby Rackard remained at centre-back, ninety per cent of the balls which he so magnificently cleared, would have passed over his head. So at full-back who was going to emulate what he achieved? There was only one man who had a hope of doing so — Nick O'Donnell, now injured and off the pitch. I put the question to Christy Ring about the feelings of Wexford followers concerning Bobby's move to full-back. His words, and I quote verbatim: "Sure if Bobeen hadn't gone full-back, we'd have wiped you off the field, maybe four more goals."

This has always been a greatly discussed issue, done so, I feel without really taking into consideration the true facts. The Wexford forward line, so brilliant in earlier games, fell flat, and they themselves are the first to acknowledge so, Nickey in particular. Prior to the game he had never in his sporting life been so uptight. After all his years of effort, and now in the winter of a career minus that senior All-Ireland medal he was, prior to this game subjected to pressure that was even new to him. At his age it looked like his last opportunity. Pressure rarely got to him, but this time it did, aided and abetted by a stupid dietary mistake. A voracious red meat eater, on the evening before one of the most important games of his illustrious career, he wrapped himself around a monstrous mixed grill and chips, which by the next day saw him still coralled into a state of nervous indigestion. He never knew this story would go into print, and it's not intended as an excuse; on the contrary as a warning to players in pre-final situations. The moral is, make sure of that feather weight feeling in your tummy. Stick to digestable food, salads or such, on the eve of a big game.

Tim Flood was another Wexford forward who naturally would not want to dwell on this final. His brilliant stick work and body swerve left Matt Fouhy flat-footed and with plenty of space he shot wide. Oh, the sin of inaccuracy! No one knows it better than Tim. Some say that he should have passed the ball to an ostensibly loose Nickey Rackard. Why should he? He had plenty of space himself, hitting lovely shots but inches wide. In fact, like the Cork forwards, the Wexford attack was throughout the game in the grip of an unyielding cagey defence. They had for three-quarters of an hour been given more than an ample supply of ball, but were unable to register winning scores. So much so that if the clearances made by Bobby Rackard had reached further upfield, it is mere conjecture to suggest that our attack was suddenly going to master their opponents. Belonging to the century that we shall shortly put behind us, this final, for many reasons, out of the hundred that took place, will always be upfront for discussion and controversy. Consequently, I want to add something very relevant to our defeat, which has never been previously examined and that something happens to concern myself.

When a player is travelling on final morning, it is only human for him to have a good squint at what the papers say, especially about himself. One analyst before this final had immediate opponents on a plus/minus assessment basis. When it came to Paddy Barry and myself, this particular writer recorded a definite plus for Cork, which was understandable. It turned out that I had one of my best ever games in the corner-back position, keeping such close tabs on this supporting star to the great Ring, that even after fifty minutes he never looked like scoring. Placing utter reliance on such a star forward as Paddy Barry, the Cork selectors hadn't bothered to look close enough. As the game progressed I'm told it was the late Jim 'Tuf' Barry, the Cork trainer, who eventually raised the matter. Contrary to the newspaper assessment, this area turned out to be a plus for Wexford. Paddy Barry was moved away in place of Johnny Clifford. It is many years since then and I hope Paddy Barry will forgive me for saying so, but as most hurlers know, some players suit your style of play. Paddy, on that occasion and subsequently, seemed to do that for me. I was always a bit insecure at corner-back, and in that position preferred my opponent in gunsight – out in front. Not so Clifford, he kept away from me, even to standing back on the end line when play was far off. It was unsettling and I lost my positive approach, resulting in that fatal delay.

Now the final piece of information in this controversial alleged fatal defensive move by the Wexford selectors. That very group did not want Bobby Rackard to change from centre-back. It was Bobby's decision, and he himself actually demanded that he be moved. Why? Prior to this match, due to a serious muscle injury, Bobby, under medical advice, kept clear of the practice field. A doubtful starter, the cure demanded an avoidance of strenuous physical activity and constant massage treatment with plenty of rest. During all this time there was one object he always carried on him, and whenever he came near a section of blank wall he chucked it at it, catching it on the rebound. I refer to the hurley ball or sliothar. His actual stick work was confined to banging a sponge ball against the old storehouse. Even travelling by car to a game, he was known to hold a hurley ball in his hand, constantly gripping and re-gripping it or if he got out, throwing it in the air and grabbing it. This is what he was curtailed to in his preparation prior to the great showdown with Cork. From previous games he carried residual fitness, but not enough to see him through the hour at centre-back. Had he not moved in and been under those dropping balls which demanded little running, he would not have been given the opportunity to put his mark on this game to such an extent. On the contrary, forced to travel for possession he would have faded, giving just an ordinary display instead of the extraordinary one, marked down by some experts as the greatest defensive play ever witnessed in an All-Ireland final.

One more question that has often been asked. When surrounded, why could Bobby Rackard, without moving, always make room for his mighty clearances? Since he was a young lad he had developed abnormal strength and grip. Stripped at around thirteen stone seven to fourteen stone, with large arms and shoulders, he had a knack of transferring the full impact of that weight to the various points of his body. Glancing off his hips, shoulders, elbows, any point as he swivelled to make room for a swing, was tantamount to receiving a blow of a lump hammer. One whiff and you moved back. It was then he made his strike, remaining pivotal and balanced. Back to that Wexford dressing-room. It's impossible to find words to describe such an atmosphere so heavy with gloom. It looked the end, especially for some of the older players. However, to quote the words of a famous leader during the last world war, it was not the end, neither was it the beginning of the end. It was, as the words go, the end of the beginning, and to quote a little Kipling: 'Can you bear to see the things you gave your life to twisted and broken – and stoop to build them up with worn out tools?' It was a bit like that. Fortunately the Wexford players in that dressing-room had it in them to rise to Kipling's noble thoughts. On the debris of that post-match despair, they built even further character. Apart from a 1955 League final defeat by Tipperary, this crowd-pulling team registered almost thirty-four straight victories. They included every honour in this wonderful game of hurling, including two consecutive All-Irelands. For loyal Wexford followers the long wait was over; the flood gates were opened as finally they knew what it would be like to win an All-Ireland. Time and time again, they drank copiously from the great fountain of success.

Champions at last

In the league final defeat of 1954-1955 by Tipperary, there were no Rackards in the Wexford line-out. Sadly my father did not live to see his three sons be part of a Wexford team that after forty-five years brought the blue riband of hurling back to the model county. On April 23rd, the week prior to the League final, Robert Rackard Senior died peacefully at his home in Killanne aged seventy-four years. The cortege contained a large number of prominent officials and players from the world of the Gaelic Athletic Association. His five sons walking behind his coffin unanimously agreed that as a quintessential sniper at the Association, he would be amused by the knowledge of such a conspicuous flavour of prominent GAA officials amidst the crowd seeing him to his final resting place.

Early in the Wexford championship during 1955, as I walked off the pitch having played with my club Rathnure against New Ross O'Hanrahans, a selector accosted me. "You weren't in great form today."

I threw him a hard look. "Neither would you be if you had to contend with that fella."

"What's his name?" he asked.

"I don't know," I replied "But I believe he's not a Wexfordman. I'm told he comes from County Carlow."

We immediately made inquiries. He was something special, of that I was certain. During that game, I had been rubbing shoulders with an unknown who turned out to be one of the most accomplished players the county had ever seen, a man who was to be the last vital link in the Wexford team of 1955. At left half-back, Mick Morrissey stood alongside me in the All-Ireland final of that year. I've never known a back so utterly reliable, no matter what situation or opposition. Around this time another player with exceptional skills also surfaced. A natural midfielder, Oliver Gough was worthy of a place on any team in the country. Due to the strength in every position of that Wexford team, a permanent place was not found for him. It was a tragedy to see a player of his talent seated on the subs bench.

The 1955 Leinster final between Kilkenny and Wexford ended in a draw, 2-7 each. The attendance was over fifty thousand. During the course of this game, Bobby at centre-back and myself at right corner-back exchanged positions. The replay, which we won 5-6 to 3-9 saw us do so again, but this time the move was permanent. Apart from a couple of occasions, I was to spend the next eight years at centre-back, confronting all the great centre-forwards of that era. Stripping now at around thirteen stone, I had at last fully developed and matured, with the necessary experience. The accumulative effect made me confident of taking on the best. As a result of this change, the Wexford defence tightened into a very formidable unit. First of all, Bobby was far more decisive at corner-back than I was, whilst on the other hand I was much more relaxed outfield, a factor which allowed whatever skills I had to fully flower. In the main, I adopted a policeman's role up and down the middle, and unlike my brother, whom I was incapable of emulating, I refrained from offensively moving upfield too much. Being back to cover off, I believed, was very important to a tight defence. The following Friday after the re-played Leinster final, I received a pleasant surprise. There are many GAA players who have experienced the same thrill, and that is opening the *Irish Independent* and seeing yourself peering out as 'Sports Star of the Week.' It made me feel that I had at last arrived. It was an honour which I was to achieve on four occasions during the rest of my career, the most notable being after the All-Ireland final of that year. But there was to be another even more prestigious honour which I will come to later.

The All-Ireland semi-final of 1955 against Limerick for a variety of reasons was a most remarkable game. Firstly, there was a record semi-final crowd of nearly sixty thousand. Secondly, it was against a team about whose personnel we knew nothing except through the press. The hurling circuit is a short one, consequently after a couple of seasons, you should know your more likely opponents' strength and idiosyncrasies, and they, yours. In this instance, it was our first time clashing with or seeing this Limerick team in action. Finally, it was our third consecutive Sunday in Croke Park. The replay of the Leinster final saw to that. In the first half, Limerick lived up to their Munster champions rating, but they were unlucky. They were unlucky to meet this great Wexford team, which on that day, I believe, gave their most competent performance ever. Irretrievably, things in the second half went wrong for the Shannonsiders, but a little could have made it a different story. I have particular memories of this game. It was the only time I marked him, and I'm glad I didn't have to do so a second time. I had never previously encountered such speed and skillful striking as displayed by this Limerick centre- forward, Dermot Kelly. From a standing position, he hit two points from literally under my nose. My stick was about half-way up in an attempt at hooking him, when the ball went sailing between the Wexford uprights. In the second half of this game I stooped on a free, which from memory was underneath the corner of the Cusack stand adjoining hill 16. I was aiming towards the Canal End. It was a very warm day with a glaring sun. Lifting the ball gently, I hit it firmly, but I thought nothing exceptional. During my swing, I can only recall dropping my left shoulder more than usual, then a sustained follow- through. The sliothar headed off into the sun. For a few moments the crowd was silent. The last thing the onlookers expected from that distance was a score. There was a delayed reaction as a mighty purple and gold fuelled roar acknowledged the white flag, which to everyone's utter surprise and certainly to mine, was being waved in the distance. Dermot Kelly immediately walked across and shook my hand. It is now a distant memory, but that sporting gesture, coupled with such a freak score will never leave my memory no matter how distant.

Boot trouble

Up to the mid fifties, a rather heavy type of boot with leather cogs, was the only playing footwear available to hurlers and footballers. The leather cogs were prone to loosen and drop off which was naturally detrimental to good gripping. Likewise the little nails which kept the cogs in position were often a source of irritation through the sole of the boot.

"You must be joking," he said.

"No, I'm not joking." I replied "I am deadly serious. He is far more essential than most people there."

It was a county board official's reaction to my suggestion that a cobbler be added to the dressing room entourage. Unlike today, players had no choice. There were no imported light-weight, indestructable designer-label boots or sports gear on offer. The boot of the day was not that reliable. A check on players' boots revealed a cog or two missing. It often was the case that a player didn't have the opportunity to have replacement cogs fitted, so, as usual, he carried on. (Incredible lack of attention to necessary detail I felt, especially by team management.) I raised the matter with our county secretary, a wonderful Corkman by the name of Liam Murphy. Through business contacts, I knew a light-weight boot could be manufactured to order. It consisted of a kid-glove upper, and the sole fitted with light-weight aluminimum cogs available in different lengths. Liam Murphy gave me the go-ahead. So prior to the All-Ireland final of 1955, I measured every player's feet! The boots arrived on schedule. I recommended they be kept specifically for match days. The result was sheer bliss and greater speed.

Igniting a Canon

"I wouldn't be absolutely sure Canon, but I'm almost certain that you could drive up there. With regard to how many tar barrels are needed, again I would not know, but what I would suggest is old car tyres. They would make an even better bonfire."

In my shop, I was merely listening and making suggestions to doddery old Canon Somers about a proper siting for a huge bonfire which he was childishly suggesting in the event of Wexford winning their second All-Ireland after a lapse of forty-five years. The Canon, now in his eighties with family roots in Rathnure, had all his lifetime payed little consequence to the game of hurling. But now that his county looked like winning their second All-Ireland title, added to which he believed that the team was backboned by men from his old parish, he was well and truly flushed out of the woodwork. The Canon, a formidable man and not just in stature, was always distinguished by the extra large wide-brimmed hat he wore. Amongst Wexford clergymen, it was his sole preserve. He was also well-known for his intransigent views on feminism, which caused him on one occasion to do a quick turnabout in the opposite direction on seeing a girl coming towards him on a bicycle wearing slacks. How he would have survived in today's religious and social climate makes for fascinating conjecture.

Now, here was the Canon in my shop, as giddy as a schoolboy, knowing something exciting was going to happen. He was suggesting that a bonfire be lit on top of Oulart Hill where it would be widely seen. With my full approval and endorsement he disappeared out the door.

When a County reaches Croke Park for the All-Ireland final day, after a big lapse of years, the impact has a shuddering effect on people in all walks of life and old Canon Somers wasn't the only one in whose bosom, parish and county pride slowly awakened. Equally as much in convents amongst holy nuns, county boundaries and battle lines were drawn. T.J. Maher, one of Tipperary's greatest sons, once said that the economy of a county is improved upon winning an All-Ireland title. Without question, in all of us, there are strong tribal feelings and urges, and one of the main release valves is through sporting achievement, when your parish or county win out in a team competition. These suppressed instincts lie dormant in a county that for years has been locked in a spiral of failure. Sporting success, be it individual, or of a team nature, can quickly light up the soul of such a county.

Prior to the All-Ireland final against Galway in 1955, the county was saturated with a strong belief that the flood gates of All-Ireland success were about to burst open. The unattainable dream was at hand. Gathered over the years, the rust of frustrating defeat and disappointment would quickly dissipate, mentally polished away by a gleaming All-Ireland victory. And so it happened.

The Great Day

The Wexford hills were alight with the crackle of bonfires and the sound of excited voices. The International Hotel in Bray was the first real rendezvous for celebration as the team were entertained to dinner. The revelry went on throughout the night. My brother Nickey, had a drink problem since his teens. His displays for years were reliant mainly on his strength and determination. Minus that drink problem plus proper adherence to training, what he would have been like, is a thought that has crossed many minds. For those few golden Wexford years, which he always predicted would happen, he gave up the drink. Naturally he wanted to be part of such success, but for that to happen, he knew that it was imperative to change. With a lifetime's intention, he became a member of the Pioneer Total Abstinence Association. On that night in Bray it must have been difficult for him. He kept his pledge and for a long time to come. But in the early celebratory hours of the next morning, he is known to have empathised with a lot of tired, thirsty Wexford fans who were outside the hotel and unable to gain access. One told me that he handed down through the dining-room window a tray containing two large whiskeys and a battery of uncapped Guinness bottles. When the fella offered the money for payment, Nickey pulled the window closed saying, "Have that on me."

Players who have been through it will never forget that feeling of waking up on the Monday morning after the final, knowing it's not just a dream, but that your county is now All-Ireland champions — and you are part of it. Down in the foyer, groups are huddled about the morning papers. It's only natural the desire to look and see if you got a mention. And the journey home! All cars, especially the lead car flag-bedecked, with the captain holding the cup aloft through the window, horns blowing. It's a memory a player will not forget, even if he lives to his nineties. As I travelled back to Wexford on that triumphant journey, many thoughts invaded my mind. I kept seeing myself as that skinny youngster, all alone banging away at an old sponge ball in Cullenstown Ball Alley all the hours I spent practicing against the old store house wall. Travelling back with the cup brings the crowds out in every village and town, even in other counties, as the cavalcade passes on its victorious return journey. Going through

Ashford, all the customers in Synnott's wonderful hostelry of the time, came out lining the road, full of admiration and good sentiment at the achievement. One old lad held aloft his bottle of Guinness.

"Up Wexford," he shouted. At that moment it was snatched from his hand by a rather liquid Wexford fan hanging out through the window of the passing car in which I was travelling.

Finally the .massive cavalcade reached the county boundary. Photos from that era highlight the fact that ninety-five per cent of the motor cars were black and predominently Morris Minors. A euphoric scene greeted us at Gorey. With bands, loudspeakers and platforms, as the cup was triumphantly carried aloft, in the midst of the ecstatic crowd. The huge cavalcade swelling even further for a similar reception at Enniscorthy and eventually the following Wednesday night to Wexford, where the volume of welcoming fans had jammed the entrance to the town. A mobile platform in the shape of an open lorry was in waiting. All aboard, complete with cup, players and officials jostled for floor space. It was tight, but it was tighter still amongst the crowd in front, as the lorry made slow progress, which ended when it came to a complete halt in Redmond Square at just the opening of the Main Street. Sean Browne, our county chairman, was a man accustomed to addressing large gatherings. Behind the cab of the lorry there was a timber lathing. It was suggested that Sean climb up and appeal for space. Gingerly, with legs spreadeagled and barely balanced, he got almost to the top rung, and with hands outstretched, started his appeal.

"People of Wexford . . ." Just then a masochistic gleam appeared in the inebriated eye of a tousled-looking Wexford player. He couldn't desist as he peered at the vulnerable chairman. Up went his hand, firmly grabbing the spreadeagled Browne in a southern but delicate part of his anatomy. Chaos reigned as the respected Chairman back-flipped head first, heels up, disappearing from sight in the belly of the lorry. Eventually the lorry wended its way down Wexford's long narrow Main Street, heading in the direction of the Talbot Hotel. Jim Morrissey, in ebullient mood, shouted across at his midfield partner: "Hey Wheeler! Take the salutes on that side just like you do the side-line cuts. I'll take over on this side." Ned Wheeler was more or less on home ground. A fan roared at him. "Why isn't Kathleen up there with you?" "Don't you worry about that," shouted Ned, "I'll be seeing her later."

Girlfriends and wives were almost a missing gender on such occasions during the fifties. Eating out and socialising was just beginning. Unlike today, wives and girlfriends of that era preferred to stay in the background. Looking down from the lorry, amongst the crowd, I spotted Jack Redmond. He looked the happiest of men and why not? The pigs were fed and the McCarthy cup was being carried aloft down his beloved Wexford's Main Street. We exchanged waves, as I did with John Rossiter, an obliging local clubman and reliable hitter when returning the ball during my unconventional method of training. Every inhabited house on the Main Street had excited faces pressed against the windows. All but one that is, old Tom Quigley, an electrician in the very winter of his business, looked befuddled at the revelry as he opened the hall door, had a quick look and banged it closed again.

"Come on Nicko – go and sign the autograph for the girl." The habitually bashful-looking Nick O'Donnell always looked lost when asked for his autograph. When it came to public relations the stars of the fifties were a shy lot. Unaccustomed to media exposure, they lacked the confidence of publicly expressing themselves as shown by present day men, and seen so often on our TV screens. To be seen, especially by team mates, in the act of signing autographs in those days was almost testimony to being swollen-headed. The Talbot Hotel, crawling with excited fans on this occasion, had the players finally overcoming the false modesty attached to declining to sign an autograph. I observed my brother Nickey as he remained sober throughout it all.

The celebrations went on for weeks as the cup visited convents, schools, pubs, public offices and private houses. Wexford followers finally knew what it was like to win an All-Ireland.

Tragically, after Nickey's retirement, he returned to his former ways and as we well know, the last fall is always the worst. Eventually, he joined Alcoholics Anonymous and in a short time had his life back on tracks, working in his veterinary practice and farming successfully, plus having notable triumphs in horse-racing. In the last year of his life, when everything seemed right, Nickey kept a dreadful secret to himself. He was in fact, condemned to death through that awful scourge cancer. By then his useful work in and for members of AA was nationally acclaimed. At fifty-three years of age, the calm dignity and courage with which he faced the inevitable, and his uncomplaining nature which won the admiration of all who nursed him, surpassed any feat of valour he ever achieved on the hurling field. You could say it was his finest hour. To quote Sister Consillo of AA: "No words can adequately explain what Nickey's memory means to all recovering alcoholics". His funeral was truly amazing, and the volume of flowers which came from every corner of Ireland, a breathtaking sight. Nickey was finally at rest.

Nickey's demise did not see the end of the dreaded cancer scourge in the Rackard family. My brother Jim, also in his fifties, after light surgery, succumbed in a matter of two months. My wife Jill, again in her fifties, was another tragic victim.

Cuchulainn's Son

A tribute to Nickey Rackard

The challenge of an ancient game
brought glory, glory to your name
though March winds blew the crowds still came
to watch you gentle hero.
In life's long march you made us proud
and many a voice from out the crowd
called out your name aloud, aloud
an echo still resounding.

And Blackstairs men who saw you then
still speak of you in awe,
on Carman's green where you had been
they tell of what they saw,
we watched you on September fields
and lightning was the drive
you were the one Cuchulainn's son in 1955.

The hand that held the stick of ash,
and the man who led with style and dash,
Oh! Carrigtwohill once felt the crash
and Bennettsbridge and Thurles.
And when in later life you beat
the devil on that lonely street
you showed us how to take defeat
with dignity and courage.

The last parade was sad and slow
the last oration spoken low
and as, on green fields long ago

the Diamond stood beside you
old friend they flanked you side by side
and the tears they shed were tears of pride
an ash tree toppled when you died
and scattered seeds at random.

Tom Williams.

Hair oil slick

After the breakthrough against Galway in the All-Ireland final of 1955, we not alone began to feel invincible but also began to prove it. In the semi-final of that year's Oireachtas we destroyed Clare in Limerick to the tune of 5-7 to 1-9, and in the Croke Park final sent Kilkenny packing 3-11 to 3-4. At this stage I had really settled into the centre-back position and delighted to be feeling free of insecurity attached to playing corner-back. In the Spring of 1956, Leinster backboned with almost two third Wexford players including myself, at centre-back destroyed Munster in the St Patrick's day Railway Cup final, winning 5-11 to 1-7. Later on we were to renew rivalry with Tipperary in the League final prior to which in the quarter-final we dismissed Cork on home ground in Wexford Park. This was quite an occasion. Cork understandably were not satisfied that we were real champions. Prior to the game, rebel county confidence was reflected in large numbers of Cork cars bumper to bumper, with flags flying and hooters blowing as they entered Wexford town. I have never since seen such a crowd or knew such an atmosphere in Wexford Park. Apart from the importance of the game to each county, this contest also had the added attraction of another Ring/Rackard confrontation, with the great Corkman again finding it difficult to circumvent his awkward opponent. The result of the game, a good win for Wexford, was merely a dress rehearsal for a much bigger occasion later in the year.

In the Autumn of 1955, a Radio Eireann morning programme sponsored by Vaseline Hair Tonic, and hosted by Michael O'Hehir, was broadcast. Its aim was to select the Sports Star of the Year 1955. It was the first such programme and requested the nomination for the sportsperson of your choice by postcard to Radio Eireann. With Wexford winning the hurling title, it was felt one of the team might be in the running and so it transpired. Nearing the end of many broadcasts, the winner was slowly emerging. It rested between three.

Firstly Pat Taffe, who had won the Grand National on *Quare Times*, the great golfer Christy O'Connor, and a Wexford hurler who turned out to be none other than myself. And so I became Sports Star, of all sports, mark you, for the year 1955. Quite a tab. The only reason I write this is to highlight the present day symbiotic nature of sponsorship compared to then. Michael O'Hehir phoned, saying he would be down to present me with the cup, which was appropriately inscribed. There was no representative from the firm Vaseline Hair Tonic nor was there even a bottle of the stuff to be seen. Michael brought me to the nearest pub, asking what I wished to drink, which was a bottle of Guinness. Then a photo was taken, ending the presentation, after which Michael shook hands with me and left and that was that. My brother Nickey was the Vaseline Hair Tonic Sports Star, the following year.

CHAPTER TWENTY-SEVEN

The first time she walked into my shop I was probably about twenty-three and she was in her late fifties. When it came to physical appearance, Mother Nature had not been kind to her. A rather masculine face and a heavy shapeless body looked out of symmetry with legs that signified lack of sufficient strength for their load. If there was ever a human being, to use a well-worn phrase, who had very little going for them, it was Nan.

She lived alone, about eight miles outside Wexford, in the very last of the little two-roomed thatched Irish cottages. Approached by what was commonly known as a blind lane (overgrown, without hardcore surface), Nan had no electricity, no running water, no immediate family, and indeed no obvious income. However, minus those debts that automatically arise from the use of modern day services, she was in the main devoid of financial committment and self-sufficient. Her self-sufficiency included remnants of firewood from a nearby plantation which kept the cottage open fire burning brightly for all purposes – in particular for the baking of her brown bread. A regular prize-winner at local shows, the sale of this prize-winning soda bread and free-range eggs to a Wexford grocer was her only source of revenue. Not exactly the trappings of a lady or a setting for happiness, that is until you engaged Nan in conversation. A natural-born lady, always exuding contentment, she spoke gently about the world and the people around her. Nan was well-informed.

When I first met her I didn't suspect it, but as time passed it became crystal clear that she had an unlikely passion for the game of hurling. Her little cottage had two framed photographs prominently positioned. One was the Pope, the second Eamon de Valera. However, as the decade of the fifties rolled by, their position of dominance was seriously challenged by another photo. Some believed the Pope was number one, more felt it must be Dev, but by the mid-fifties, quite a number of people attributed that spot to Nickey Rackard. Every Saturday, with her faithful donkey, Jack, between the shafts, Nan in her flat cart was a colourful reminder of a fading past as she made the journey into Wexford town. She never failed to call to my shop, usually bearing a gift, which was a cartwheel of her home-made bread. Again, almost every Saturday, she left a few shillings on the counter. Anything she could she purchased from me, usually cloth for a warm winter top coat (made by the now extinct local tailor). On her insistence, nothing was taken from the shop until it was fully paid for, which was done by little weekly instalments well in advance. Pointless to say that Nan was an avid supporter of the Wexford hurling team, as she was indeed of the footballers and camogie teams; but to what extent I had no idea until one day I met a neighbour of hers.

"Do you know," said the neighbour, "that poor cratur, on her own, wet or fine, trudges the eight miles into Wexford on the morning of every match to catch a train or bus, and when she returns that night, she has to walk the eight miles home again. Once in a while she might get a lift, but she's too much of a lady to look for lifts. Anyway, she is afraid that her presence in a car would trespass on the occupants' levity and enjoyment."

On hearing this I made arrangements with a close friend of mine, Jack Kirwan, to meet Nan on her return and drive her home. I also made sure that where future finals were concerned, my distribution of personal stand tickets had one earmarked for her.

These acts deepened the bond of friendship between Nan and myself. She invited me to her house for tea, a most difficult spot to find, but when I did I was enthralled by the sight. Here was a setting from the distant past. The miniature cottage was tucked in a little spinney, and kept company by little thatched out-buildings which housed the donkey and her hens. When I was leaving, Nan invited me again, but this time in her quiet way as I was saying goodbye, she asked, "Next time, why not bring a few friends?"

That invitation saw the birth of Nan's legendary hoolies. Proving herself to be a great hostess, people of many nationalities and from every walk of life were to sing for their supper in Nan's little cottage. Guests brought their own beer and music – usually an accordianist.

Once the combination of heat from the open fire and pounding feet during half sets resulted in a slight melt-down of the mud floor. For every guest of Nan's, especially foreigners, but also Wexfordians, the memory of a visit was inextinguishable. There was unanimous concensus that her abode was the ultimate in true Irish heritage, worthy of transfer in toto to the grounds of Bunratty. But there was more than that. In supreme hostess fashion, Nan kept in touch with all her guests, a fact that at Christmas time was to indirectly startle the local postman. As the twice yearly hoolies saw more and more new faces, so did it automatically see an increase in the already burgeoning load of Christmas cards delivered to the little cottage.

In the customary late autumn party at Nan's in 1956, I had a little surprise in store for her. Five of us walked up the blind lane towards the cottage, each of us with a surprise. When Nan opened the door, we marched past and laid the five objects on the little kitchen table. The look on her face is still embedded in my memory as she stared at the McCarthy Cup, the O'Keefe Cup, the Railway Cup, the National League Oireachtas Cup and the Walshe Cup. Years later, when I married and my daughter Sally-Ann was born, the usual question of godparents arose. Like all parents, Jill (who was from Somerset, England) and myself had a discussion about possible candidates. Finally names were agreed.

On the following Saturday Nan, as always, called into the shop. A social call, she usually stayed a few minutes and left. I beckoned her to one side. "Nan" I said, "I want to ask you a question. There is something I would like you to do for me." She hadn't a clue what I was driving at. With the passing years she had developed a slight stoop. I bent down and whispered in her ear. "Nan," I said "Jill and I would like you to be Sally Ann's Godmother."

She looked up at me with a long silent stare. I could see that her eyes were misting over. She was obviously completely taken aback by the unexpected request. Regaining her composure and wiping a little tear from the corner of her eye, she grabbed my hand, shaking it with the words, "Wouldn't I just love to."

From then on Nan became part of the family, always coming to us in St Helen's near Rosslare, for Christmas. Jill and all the girls saw in her the wonderful person I had been telling them about and throughout the year paid regular visits to the little cottage. I could always tell when they had been there because that unmistakable smokey aroma, derived from sitting close to an open hearth fire, lingered in their clothes. Every Christmas Nan knitted warm woolly jumpers for all my four girls. Throughout the years, their warmth and endurance was regularly commented on, plus the fact that Nan's jumpers, as they were referred to, were easily identifiable by their smell. Often I saw a jumper being pushed close to a face, with the words, "I can tell this is a Nan jumper."

Some people may have seen our relationship with Nan as mere philanthrophy. On the contrary, it was reciprocal in every way and whilst we naturally brought a lot of light into her life, so did she to ours.

Incidently, once during one of Nan's parties, a rather tactless lady asked her if she had a man in her life. In the act of hanging the kettle over the open fire, she straightened up and replied: "Actually I did have my eye on someone, but when I discovered he wasn't available, I lost interest in men."

"Anyone we know?" pursued the curious lady. "Yes," said Nan, "Clarke Gable."

As a Godmother to our child, Jill and I felt that it would be impossible to find anyone more suitable to such a committment, or more conscious of its true meaning.

Some years passed, but in spite of advancing years, Nan never faltered or appeared ill. Meanwhile my uncle, John Doran died. The night of his funeral, the family, including myself and other nephews, were assembled at his home in Moneyhore House, Enniscorthy. Looking through the window, a member of the group was heard to say 'Somebody's in trouble. There's a squad car coming down the avenue." A policeman duly knocked on the hall door.

"Is there a William Rackard here?" he asked.

My first reaction was, what had I done? I went out to him. Courteously, and in sombre tones, cap in hand, he told me his reason for coming. "In a small cottage near Ballymurrin, an old lady was found dead in her bed. She apparently lived alone, but we thought you might like to know that on her bedside cabinet was a closed letter addressed to you."

More Hurling Success

The slight reshuffle that takes place on such an established and cohesive side as the Wexford team now was, saw the emergence of just one new face, Tom Dixon from Enniscorthy St. Aidan's. Given his chance at left corner-forward, Tom did not have a long career at inter-county level, but nonetheless, he can look back in pride at his displays throughout that golden year of 1956. A skillful first time striker and a good score taker, his no-nonsense approach added even further thrust to an already potent attack.

"Well, what do you think?"

"If you want me to stay I'll stay, but to be totally honest I've had enough."

"You're right – you're dead right. I see no point in watching more of this. Let's go home."

This was the conversation between two Wexford farmers at half-time during the National Hurling League Final between Wexford and Tipperary of 1956. The language of the interval scoreboard was the catalyst for such a verbal exchange. It read Tipperary 2-10, Wexford 0-1. It was also the catalyst for one of the most galvanizing half-time pep talks ever heard in a Croke Park dressing-room – the kind of speech in a man that betokens the kind of action you will get from him. Banging his hurley against the dressing room table, Nickey Rackard's rousing tirade brought a magnificent second half response from his team mates, with his personal display and determination showing in full measure. The Wexford farmers left and went home in disgust. Even though it was Sunday, there were still chores that needed doing. One farmer brought in the cows, saw to the milking, then went into the house and had his supper. Later on that evening, slumped in a fireside chair, he called to his wife, "Switch on Sean O'Callaghan there – I might as well hear the full result." Sean Og's clear tones came across the airwaves. "Today's GAA results. First the National Hurling League Final at Croke Park between Tipperary and Wexford. The score; Wexford 5-9, Tipperary 2-14, a four point win for the model county."

Had the farmer been given a hundred volt shock of electricity, he would scarcely have jumped any quicker from his chair. To this day he hasn't forgiven either himself or his friend. This was indeed a remarkable game. Bursts of warm April sunshine deceivingly soothed the strength of a gale-force wind. Playing against it in the first half, I recall hitting a ball with all my might. It should have travelled sixty to seventy yards. It curled up to within twenty yards of me. Since then, for Wexford followers who have sadly had to exist on more or less scraps of success, this is a victory, during hurling conversation that is inexorably trotted out, especially if there is a Tipperary man or woman in the vicinity. Of course the phenomena of hauling back such an interval lead would not exist to the same extent had it not been spiced with the pedigree of such victims as renowned Tipperary.

After this great victory, Wexford, now in search of another All-Ireland title had the inevitable confrontation with Kilkenny looming up. The Leinster Final against them in 1956 was a bruising battle between two fit teams, played before a record crowd of over fifty thousand spectators. In gaining their third Leinster title in a row, Wexford, as champions, had to dig deep to chisel the narrowest of victories, the score 4-8 to 3-10, a mere point win. My immediate opponent in this nerve-wracking encounter was Sean Clohessy. A couple of years previously, I had watched from the sideline as Clohessy, in a Railway Cup final, made star Munster hurlers look like third-raters. For me that memory lingered on. This man wasn't just a hurler, he was a magician with a stick in his hand and now he was my responsibility to mark. He was Kilkenny's most dangerous forward. In the week before that game, it is no exaggeration to say that my nerves were raw and my hands were shaking at the prospect. I knew I hadn't a hope of matching his skills. After a lot of thought, I decided on negative obstructionist tactics. If I don't hit a ball, but in the process neither does he, that will be a good day's work for my team. In a sense it worked, with Sean staying practically scoreless. I must say that in this confrontation, had the boot been on the other foot, I would have found it difficult to be as stoically sporting and tolerant of such inelegant tactics as Sean was.

Corner-back on the Wexford team on this occasion was Ted Morrissey, a brother of midfielder Jim. Ted, a top-class player was like Oliver Gough, worthy but unlucky, through the in-depth team strength not to command a permanent place. In the subsequent All-Ireland semi-final dismissal of Galway by 5-13 to 1-8, a game in which Nickey Rackard scored an incredible five goals and three points, the full potential power and thrust of this Wexford team was amply demonstrated. Now the final was a showdown with Cork. Apart from having a score to settle with the rebel county men, it was in almost every way a repeat of 1954, with Christy Ring again looking for a record medal. As Nickey had said two years previously in the kitchen back in Killanne, "If we play to near our full potential, Victory will be ours."

And that is more or less what transpired. Before over eighty thousand spectators, this game had all the right ingredients and drama, including a crucial save at a crucial moment by our goalkeeper, Art Foley. That save from Christy Ring is destined to be talked about as long as the Ancient Code is played. This final caught the imagination of the *Irish Independent* sports writer, Mitchell Cogley to such an extent that he labelled it the greatest final of the century. He had seen most of the earlier finals and his assessment was made years after 1956. Quite an accolade! Mitchell Cogley also labelled Art Foley's save from Christy Ring – 'The save of the century.' Sorry Art, and Mitchell, but I disagree with that, I will explain later.

In this game, defending the Railway End, I was at centre-back marking Josie Hartnett. Behind and to my right my brother Bobby was in charge of the inimitable Christy Ring. The first fifteen minutes of this game saw fearsome pressure coming our way, but it came at a suitable angle – from out of the sky! I'm probably correct in saying that we Wexford men originated it, especially Bobby and myself, and I feel I'm also probably correct in saying that we didn't do the game of hurling any favours in doing so. In that All-Ireland final it was still relatively new, and without a proven antidote it took the overhead striker by surprise. I refer to reaching up at the last second in the midst of hurleys, and coming away with the ball.

In that first half, with Nick O'Donnell doing similar behind me, I think I reached up and grabbed four from on high. All were well cleared, but one was a complete fluke. Josie Hartnett made the mistake of staying too close to me, resulting in no impetus to his swing as the ball dropped. On this occasion he more or less bulldozed me sideways, my free left hand going up and back around to the right of my head. I kept my eye on the ball and fluke of flukes, in that position, I caught it in the left hand. It was all split-second stuff. Josie didn't realise that the ball was in my hand and moved away just enough. I then lashed a mighty clearance upfield. During those few seconds, Christy Ring had dashed out on the prowl to my rear. I was very aware of his predatorial presence. He appeared taken by surprise with what happened and I have a vivid memory of Christy's fury, as he chillingly and briefly let fly with his feelings which were directed towards Hartnett and myself. "That isn't f . . . hurling, it shouldn't be f . . . allowed, etc. etc."

Endowed with only moderate ability to play an overhead ball in the traditional fashion, a fleeting acknowledgement of his point of view crossed my mind, but just then was no place for discussion! Nearing the end of this dramatic final, watching and listening Wexford supporters were horror-stricken as they detected an emerging pattern of the 1954 defeat. Their team had been setting the pace and in front, but now at the make or break stage, they were a point in arrears. But they needn't have worried, as the mighty purple and gold machine opened full throttle, with our forwards this time making no mistakes and with every man on the team rising to the challenge, we went away to a glorious six points win. The score 2-14 to 2-8. A very important factor in this score was without question Art Foley's magnificent save from Ring, and it was magnificent. But to rate it the save of the century is, I think, stretching the imagination. I feel that for a save to remotely enter that category, it should result from the keeper stopping his most unfavoured shot and from a most unfavoured angle. This was not the case. At eye level, in a standing position, as it came at him Art grabbed the ball – a favourite shot for any keeper, especially Foley. Also Ring was being tailed and in fear of being hooked. I believe the circumstances surrounding this save are what make it so memorable. A great moment in a great game involving a great player, thwarting him of a record. This battle for hurling supremacy proved to be the final All- Ireland curtain for the immortal man from Cloyne, who, in a sporting farewell, was lifted shoulder high by two Wexford players, Nick O'Donnell and Bobby Rackard. For the second year running the hills of Wexford were alight with bonfires as the McCarthy Cup came to rest once more by the banks of the Slaney. Ecstatic followers again savoured the fruits of a great win. There is no substitute for Victory.

More than a hundred years of competitive hurling has spawned some great artists of the game. The sporting century is peppered with the names of magnificent players. From Tylor Mackey to D.J. Carey, they spring from the pages of hurling history: the sound of each legendary name, almost like re-opening the pages of a favourite book, triggering a compulsion to continue reading and resavouring their great deeds and displays. Followers of the Ancient Code are nurtured and delighted by reflection on such names, memories, moments and displays. When it comes to selecting the greatest exponent the game has ever seen, measured opinion sees one name out of reach – above all others. That name as stated is Christy Ring of Cork. The nearest challenger is seen to be Mick Mackay of Limerick. For almost two decades Ring's artistry brought warm sunshine to the hearts of hurling purists, but to be labelled the greatest, other factors had to be present and in equal abundance. Amongst many, an unquenchable competitive spirit wedded to a fiendish desire for victory are just two, but the one that stands out most in my mind was his balance. Again and again, with dancer's aplomb, he first timed chillingly accurate passes to team mates, points between the uprights and with lethal selectivity, rockets to the back of the rigging. I watched once, when with two defenders tail-gating him, he chased a disobliging ball right to the corner flag. His back to the goal posts, he took his opponents by surprise. Without checking, he swivelled and with complete fluidity of movement, he pulled again first time, curling the sliothar between the uprights. An impossible shot belonging only to a genius. Yes – none can compare.

Usually when preparing for games, I trained on my own or with a few others. However, I always joined the panel in the get-together prior to an important match. When alone, I engaged a good striker to hit balls to each side, overhead and in front, as I stood in the centre-back position. Playing an imaginary game, I returned these balls up field as if the result of a great final depended on them. This meant with a lot of proper speedy ball practice and backed up with sprints and lapping, I could tell exactly how my fitness was progressing. Costly, well-intended squad training with twenty or more players in the Park, whilst it is a PR factor in supporter re-assurance and may satisfy management and public neurosis, it is also, I believe, at times prone to being harmful. I am aware that we now live in a different society but even so, I still suspect, that the elongated process and in some cases long-distance travel demanded of such a continued get together can be damaging. First of all squad training, by its nature, does not allow sufficient space in the park for proper ball practice, plus the possibility that the long drawnout process involved is liable to cause unwanted player mental fatigue. When it comes to fitness, individual player initiative looks to be a thing of the past.

"Don't tell me where you're going to hit it – just make sure I must run after it." I was shouting at Pat Doyle, a farmer's son from outside Wexford, who was employed in Wexford town. He was a great help to me when training. An engaging, wild youth and a great striker of a ball, for Pat at that time there was only one sport in this world worth playing or watching, and needless to say that sport was hurling. When it came to selecting the number one Rackard, I very rarely got, or expected, such a vote, but I had a strong feeling that where Pat was concerned, I could be sure of a first preference. Usually Pat travelled with me to matches, as he did to the 1956 Final.

We parked the car in Kildare Street, and took a taxi to Croke Park. When it was all over, we left the Stadium bubbling with excitement over such a wonderful victory, and with Pat emphatic on how I had outshone my older brothers. We made our way across the city. Benefiting from a lift, we finally walked up Kildare street to the car. Halfway up I heard my name being called out. I looked across the street and recognised a middle-aged woman who had worked in Clery's during my time there. We crossed over. "Billy," she said. "I'm delighted for you. You must feel very proud."

We shook hands as I acknowledged her sentiments, after which we parted, continuing in opposite directions. I had taken about two strides when I heard my name once more. We turned about. It was the woman from Clery's again. "I needn't ask, were you at the match? Surely with the brothers playing you must have been at least in the Hogan Stand." And off she went walking down Kildare Street. Pat stood open-mouthed with disbelief, as he gazed after her.

Near the end of September, a Wexford team minus some regulars, annihilated Limerick in the Oireachtas semi-final, played in Wexford Park. The score was 8-7 to 1-5. The final against old rivals Kilkenny was scheduled for later in the year.

The list on the following page compiled by the *Free Press* Wexford, shows the names of all players who appeared on the Wexford inter-county team from 1950 to 1956 inclusive. It also shows each individual's number of appearances:

CHAPTER TWENTY-SEVEN

Wexford Intercounty Team 1950 – '56

W. Rackard	91	M. Flood	18	B. O'Leary	2
T. Flood	87	R. Donovan	18	P. Harrington	2
N. Rackard	86	T. Russell	17	M. Hennessy	1
Padge Kehoe	85	W. Wickham	11	J. Rackard	1
J. Morrissey	84	H. O'Connor	9	D. O'Neill	1
R. Rackard	81	P. Shannon	6	P. Kelly	1
M. Hanlon	76	J. Quinn	5	S. Power	1
A. Foley	75	S. Flood	5	D. Sinnott	1
N. Wheeler	74	C. Casey	5	J. Wall	11
N. O'Donnell	71	T. Lenihan	4	J. O'Brien	1
Paddy Kehoe	60	R. Brennan	4	J. Kehoe	1
J. English	52	J. Deegan	4	S. Lambert	1
S. Hearne	51	J. Mitchell	4	F. Millar	1
D. Ahearne	51	W. Murphy	3	P. Nolan	1
M. Codd	45	W. Stamp	3	T. Leahy	1
T. Ryan	41	T. Hayden	3	J.J. Kennedy	1
S. Thorpe	35	S. Cleary	3	J. Lambert	1
T. Dixon	33	W. Bradley	3	W. Barron	1
J. Cummins	30	M. Walsh	2	C. Gough	1
M. Morrissey	30	R. Sleator	2	J. Murphy	1
T. Bolger	28	J. McBride	2	J. Kerins	1
M. Byrne	25	W. Harris	2	Pat Kehoe	1
O. Gough	20	P. Barron	2	S. O'Brien	1
T. Morrissey	19	F. Morris	2	S. Somers	1

CHAPTER TWENTY-EIGHT

It was the autumn of 1956. I was seated in the departure lounge at Dublin airport awaiting a flight that would take me to London. Journeying with me was a man called Bill Ryan. Older Wexford folk will remember him as one half of that well-known insurance business which flourished for many years in Enniscorthy and Wexford, known as Creane and Ryan Insurance Brokers. Bill was an enthusiastic follower of all sports, in particular the Wexford hurling team. He was on friendly terms with every member of the team, and was affectionately known to one and all as 'Billta.' He was a most jovial character and an excellent travelling companion. On our arrival in London we travelled by train to Dover – from there by boat to Ostend, from where we went again by train across the lowlands of Belgium through Germany, and via the Brenner Pass (where Hitler and Mussolini had their tête-à-tête) down into lovely Innsbruck in Austria. From Innsbruck we travelled by bus down through the breath-taking scenery of the Dolomite Mountains into the Northern Po valley of Italy and across to Venice, where we naturally visited St. Mark's Square plus the obligatory trip down the famed Grand canal of that astonishing city of waterways.

From Venice we travelled down to the eternal city of Rome – four days there absorbing its ancient architecture – where we were lucky enough to join a large gathering who were granted an audience with the then Pope Pius XII at his summer residence in Castel Gondolfo. From Rome we headed further South to Naples. The Bay of Naples is such a breathtaking vista, that the adage 'see Naples and die' becomes understandable. From Naples we went further down the coast, paying a visit to the excavated city of Pompeii, before going eventually by boat to the idyllic island of Capri, famous for its blue grotto. Capri was where we u-turned for home, the highlight of this part of our journey being a visit to the wondrous city of Florence, home of the aristocratic Medici family. No city in the world compares with Florence.

Bill and I were contemplating the delightful prospect of the journey to come, when I opened the *Irish Independent*. I went to the sports section, and there right across the top of the page was emblazoned the words, 'Wexford and Cork to renew All-Ireland final rivalry in New York Polo Grounds next June.' Savouring the excitement of my immediate holiday and now the additional anticipation of travelling to New York the following June was indeed an intoxicating moment. However, there was something of more immediate interest on that sports page. It said 'Kilkenny and Wexford for Oireachtas final in Croke Park', stating the date which was eighteen days later – this turned out to be the exact date of the last leg of our journey from London back to Dublin. That evening on the return flight as the announcement to fasten safety belts came across on the plane, Bill turned to me.

"You are not going to renege on that promise you made me?"

I looked him in the eye.

"You needn't worry."

After landing we just had about enough time for something to eat and head for Croke Park, where we encountered some of the Wexford players heading towards the turnstiles. As I edged through, I felt I had lost weight. I also felt tired. No doubt that eighteen day, two thousand five hundred mile almost non-stop journey, plus the change of diet, had taken its toll. However, I wasn't worried because I was not going to play – this was my promise to 'Billta', who felt a certain responsibility; he being the instigator, but not realising when booking that the date of our holidays would turn out to be so unfortunate. I went into the dressing-room with the other players. 'Billta' was with us. I moved across the room, chatting to some of the lads. As I looked down, staring at the floor between my feet, I felt a strange mix of emotions. There was probably about thirty-five thousand outside judging by the noise that came through the tunnel door when someone opened it. I was suddenly jerked from my lethargic mood by the sound of my bag hitting the floor between my feet. It made a very definite thud, and before I could look up a hurley was sprawled across it. I looked up and there with a very firm gaze on his face was my brother Nickey, pronouncing:

"Get togged off!"

"But Nickey . . ." I tried to protest.

"Get togged off!"

For the next few minutes I sat silently with a grinding struggle going on in my mind. I weighed up the situation in every direction. Finally, Nickey's command to get togged off and the strong possibility of winning my fourth Oireachtas medal in a Croke Park final was too much. It was a classical case of look before you leap. I bent down to untie my shoe laces, and as I did I caught Billta's glare from across the dressing-room. It went from all smiles to a look of horror. He came straight across. "What the hell do you think you are doing? You bloody promised me – you know I am going to get the blame for all this," he continued. I hadn't the courage to look him in the eye. I just kept on at what I was doing.

Wexford beat Kilkenny in that final, and the following Friday in the *Irish Independent,* the Sports Star of the week was shared by two hurlers. One was Ollie Walsh (Kilkenny), and the other Billy Rackard (Wexford). As we streamed out from behind the Cusack stand after the victory, I got a tap on the shoulder, turned around and there was my old friend 'Billta.' A fruity grin spread across his face.

"Sure I knew you had it in you all the time."

Some present day teams, let them be labelled champions or not, still feel, that after a heavy campaign, they are entitled to a holiday abroad. This is a creeping new ethos, now more or less accepted and taken for granted. Funded mainly from the coffers of supporters clubs, I think I'm correct in saying that having opted out of any financial assistance for such trips, the GAA just dispassionately observe. It's not my intention to get involved here in the politics of such a perk, but I can understand the Association's fear of establishing ugly precedents. Back in the fifties, National League winners sometimes had the then dazzling prize of a trip to New York as a bonus with the title. However, that criteria did not apply to the Cork and Wexford hurlers. It was by public demand coming from both sides of the Atlantic, that brought about this re-match of the 1956 Final in the famous Polo Grounds, New York. Incidentally, today's trips abroad are very different in content. Now with wives and girlfriends and with no match commitment, they are of a more hedonistic nature with guaranteed sun a must. Anyway, prior to the All-Ireland championships of 1957, the Wexford and Cork contingents along with champion Irish handballer John Ryan (also invited through public acclaim) met at Shannon Airport, travelling on the same plane for the flight to New York.

The Big Apple

Before we travelled, we were subjected to the obligatory smallpox injection. In our case, a supposedly minimum dose was administered by the team doctor, the late P.J. Daly. The majority of players were not affected, but a few were and I was one of them and I shall never forget it. Approximately a week later, I went down with a raging fever. It lasted about three days and if during that period someone had whispered in my ear "I can stop this fever, but if I do, you will not then travel to New York", my reply would have been "Put an end to this torture and to hell with New York." The pain was that horrible.

Finally, when travel arrangements were sorted out, the team was given a big send-off, particularly at New Ross where a huge midday crowd turned out. Suppose that a present day team had taken part in the last three All-Ireland finals, unluckily beaten in the first – in the process creating an attendance record, then won the next two and are now heading off for a repeat of one of them to a world famous stadium in far away New York. I say to their followers 'try and imagine that' and then you will have some idea of the euphoria engendered by that trip. I was also saddled with the distracting burden of having to write an account of it for *The Wexford People* a report which I have just looked up and see that I described my situation as a schoolboy who went to the circus, knowing well that next day the teacher would spoil it all by asking me to write an essay on it. Only now the situation was worse because I had to do my work right at the circus.

The flight, which was one of the last propeller ones to cross the Atlantic, took approximately fifteen hours, which included a one hour stop-over at Gander, Newfoundland. Prior to boarding the aircraft, which we did around midnight, the Wexford team, along with the Cork team, attended Mass, said specially for us by the late Canon Hamilton, in the airport chapel. During that Mass I detected a strong surge of spirituality. If the Good Lord was keeping a close grasp on the situation, he must have been a bit baffled at such an unexpected torrent of devotion. It was a first time long-distance Atlantic flight for some, and you must know that fatalistic feeling of being airborn for the first time when you wonder if you might meet your maker sooner than expected.

Once we landed, apart from a big sigh of relief, there was also a distinct wane on the spiritual front. The zeal displayed in the chapel was only surpassed by the rush to attain a different kind of spirit and it resided not in the church, but in the duty-free shop which we were seeing for the first time. Just imagine Hennesy 15/-, Power's Whiskey 12/6- or 62.5p today. During that flight we were served at least three meals. This Herculean task was accomplished by a solitary air-hostess. I only saw the one. Her charm and capability won the hearts of all, igniting fantasies, especially amongst the bachelor hurlers. You know the romantic Irish ethos? Wouldn't she be just the job in front of the kitchen sink back home! She survived at least one marriage proposal before landing in New York.

On arrival at Idlewild airport (now Kennedy Airport) we were submerged in a tidal wave of welcoming ecstatic Wexford and Cork supporters, from the airport to our accomodation which was The Henry Hudson Hotel, West 57th Street. It was quite luxurious, especially in comparison to what we would have known back here at that time, and approximately thirty-five stories high.

One morning I was talking to Ned Wheeler in his room, which was on one of the top stories, when there was a loud knocking on the door.

"Come in," shouted Ned.,

The door opened and there stood an enormous black man. He had a wide leather belt hanging down from his right hip and just at the base of his stomach, hung a large pouch with cloths dangling from it.

"Clean you windows man," he announced in a gravely voice.

"Sure, man," retorted Wheeler. Whereupon the big black fellow strode across the room towards the windows, and as he did, his eyes were inexorably drawn to Wheeler's display of Shannon duty-free whiskey.

"Care for a drink, man?" voiced the observant Ned with a rascally grin spreading across his face, and instantly pouring out the biggest dollop of Gold Label, I have ever seen into a nearby glass and depositing it in the welcoming paw of the big fella. He threw it all down in one go. Almost instantly he gave a loud gasp.

"Man, that shoo is mighty strong liquor," he proclaimed.

I felt he had every reason to say so, and gasp, as I considered the amount of undiluted Gold Label that had just beaten a fiery trail past his tonsils down into his innards. The next instant he jerked up one of the windows and hooked the large strap at each side and then flopped backways out over the thirty or so stories.

"My God," I thought, "he's a goner!"

Minutes later, I could hear him humming and whistling as he cleaned that window. I went over and had a close look out at him, and the happy look on his big face was eloquent testimony to the effect the Gold Label was having as it washed about the walls of his stomach. Man, he shoo was enjoying the cleaning of Massa Wheeler's windows.

This Wexford team had been on the go for the past six years, and had seen everything and was now a very tight combination, accustomed to absorbing pressure. Yet this game was different. For the first time, we were going on display before an Irish-American audience of approximately thirty-seven thousand in a hallowed stadium. Most of the spectators were of Wexford origin, and the majority had never seen the team in action, just savouring our sensational success from word of mouth and through the medium of newspapers. Now this was it – they were going to see the live article. We were apprehensive, naturally wondering would things go right. The stadium was different and the heat was horrendous – it said it was 80° in the shade. The final score was Wexford 7-15 to Cork 5-5, a resounding victory, and incredibly one of our best performances. Cork were no match.

The scenes after that great win were highly charged with emotion, as Irish-American supporters streamed onto the pitch embracing the Wexford players, some of those supporters with tears of joy running unashamedly down their cheeks. They had heard and read so much about that team. Now they had seen for themselves. Wexford subsequently played a New York selection in Gaelic Park – a game which Wexford won easily. Anyone who takes part in sport, in order to get to the top, must be endowed with the necessary talent for that sport, then you should be reasonably successful. However, in some cases you may see an individual who is fanatically fit with only the minimum talent, yet achieving excellent results. The ideal combination is naturally super-fitness coupled with superb talent. If you can absorb that philosophy, then how do you equate a man, who can boast of (at a guess) eighteen All-Ireland titles, and in the process of all these wins, always had his preparation, so to speak, on the back burner. What sort of phenomenon would he be? He would have to be a genius at the game. Well, he was and his name is John Ryan, our legendary handballer from Bridgetown, Co. Wexford, now living in Ballymurn. John travelled with the team, again by virtue of public demand. He was to play the New York champion Harry Hyde, and the match was fixed at 10.30 a.m., the next morning after our celebratory victory night over Cork. Rotten luck, but Ryan was not one to pass up a good night's celebration no matter what was taking place the next day. Did he get any sleep at all that night? The question remains unanswered. The scene in the futuristic covered-in ball alley next morning was equivalent to one from a *Rocky* film, as the supreme athletic bronzed figure of Hyde came bouncing into the arena, resplendent in garish attire to confront the glowering sloping-shouldered, long-armed Irishman in his modest garb. In that packed alley, Ryan's followers, who were aware of his nocturnal activities, had every reason to be apprehensive. The man himself looked totally unconcerned. The result was a massacre. Scarcely moving from the one position, he destroyed Hyde in three straight sets. I would like to know the ratio of talent as opposed to fitness that lurked in the frame of one John Ryan on that historic occasion.

At the end of two weeks, John Ryan and the Wexford team returned to Ireland except for two, namely Seamus Hearne and myself. Overland flights were extremely cheap and I wanted to see what was described as the world's most incredible strip of land, namely Miami Beach and its surrounding area, which is about two thousand miles from New York. Seamus was agreeable to travelling with me and I remember the culture shock it was for some of our party when they heard that news. What a change! Just look where some Irish are holidaying at present. We also exchanged the return half of our flight tickets for a return trip by liner. Just imagine, instead of being cooped up in an aircraft for that long journey home, we were given, at no extra charge, a nine-day return voyage on a big luxury liner. Those nine days, six of them going through the lovely warm conditions of the Gulf Stream, were in fact the best part of the whole adventure.

During our stay in The Henry Hudson, a lot of well-wishers showed up offering members of the team trips here and trips there. It was difficult selecting who to travel with, but there was one man who will never be forgotten. The whole Wexford team eventually ended up referring to him affectionately as 'Uncle Mylie.' He was born in Temperance Row, Wexford. Mylie Kavanagh was his name and he went to St Mullins in Carlow at a very young age, from where in his teens he emigrated to America. He was now in his late sixties, a wealthy man, with his family grown up, but he always had a mental block about returning to the country of his origin because, to use his own words, 'Who the God damn is going to know me back there now.' Mylie, who resembled a Runyonesque character from *Guys and Dolls*, was a big hit with all the lads and also a big spender. Little did he know that his generosity and hospitality were to be returned and with interest. Apart from entertaining the team at his lovely house on Long Beach, plus boat trips around New York harbour, Mylie also brought most of them in two large automobiles all the way to the Canadian border to see the beautiful waterfalls of Niagara. After all this, Mylie had changed in himself, especially in his attitude about travelling back again to Ireland. He had, by now, built up a strong rapport with every member of that team. He turned to me one day and said in his typical American vernacular: "You know, when you God damn assholes go back to Ireland, I'm gonna have to cross that God damn pond to see you all."

Mylie's emotional block about travelling to the land of his birth gradually disappeared. It finally happened. He made his first return visit. It was a huge success and was followed by many more. He usually based himself in Wexford's Talbot Hotel, where we would call on him. He also visited the homes of most of the team, particularly my late brother Nickey's and Ned Wheeler's. All the lads had memorable evenings with him, as well as some chauffering him around the countryside. He was a very generous man, a delightful character and the friendship with the members of that team was truly reciprocal. It was a new life for him as he made many happy return visits to see us all, but sadly he is long since passed on.

There are many stories about New York and especially about my trip with Seamus Hearne down to lovely Florida and on the liner back home, but one is more than enough. It's the story known as 'The Shirt.'

Hearne gets shirty

Firstly let me explain that Seamus was short of a light-weight suit so necessary in such a tropical climate as Miami in June. Dress was very conservative compared to now, jacket and tie being the norm. A shortage of funds gave us only one option but to borrow. We would not only have to find the right man, but he would also have to be the right size. However, I felt that I had already spotted our man knocking about the hotel chatting enthusiastically to some of our party. I checked his name. He was known as Axle Cahill. I waited my chance and sidled up to him and with all the charm, I could muster. "Axle" I said, "I have a problem and maybe you could help." Little did I know. Axle a flambuoyant character (claimed his antecedents came from Blackwater, Co. Wexford), had worked all over the world and was indeed the right man. If asked he would have togged out the whole team. "Come with me this minute," he insisted. Seamus and I followed him onto the street where he opened the doors of a monstrous automobile.

"Get in," he ordered. In about twenty minutes we arrived at his plush apartment. Looking through his wardrobe, which was vast indeed, he offered Seamus a lovely off-white lightweight suit. It was just the job. As we were leaving his bedroom he put his hand in a drawer, pulling out a shirt. "Take that too," he called as he chucked it towards Seamus. I have seen some gaily coloured shirts in my time, but never anything like this one. It was covered with cowboys riding bucking broncos, pine trees and wild west scenes plastered all over. Seamus put it in the bag with the suit.

One morning, in the Shore Club, in Miami where we were staying, I was seated in the dining-room waiting for breakfast and also for Seamus who was due down from his room. I could see the lifts through the big glass doors of the dining room and watch the hotel guests. The doors opened back on this lift; it had only one passenger. It was Hearne and he was wearing the shirt, hanging down on full display over the top of his trousers. He loped towards the open doors of the dining room where the head waiter was standing side on, with a menu tucked under his armpit. I couldn't take my eyes off Hearne as he approached, clad in the awful shirt. He went past the headwaiter, who remained motionless, but about three strides on Hearne abruptly halted, quickly turned about and gave a long hard stare at the headwaiter. I couldn't figure out why. Seamus arrived at the table swearing under his breath.

"What's the matter?" I enquired.

"I wouldn't mind belting that fellow one – the smart alec," he grumbled.

As Seamus passed by, the headwaiter said out of the side of his mouth, 'Howdy cowboy,' a remark Hearne didn't take kindly to, and which was the sole reason for his annoyance.

"Well, well, well, so that's it," I said to him. 'Just take a look at yourself. You haven't exactly the straightest pair of legs in the world, and as for that shirt . . . and furthermore, are you aware that a whole bus load of cowboys actually just booked into the hotel? Can you honestly blame the man?' I argued.

"I still think he's a smart alec," he retorted, "and I still feel like sticking one on him."

CHAPTER TWENTY-NINE

Prior to our journey to Florida, Seamus and I returned to Gaelic Park, and we were paid to do so. It may also come as a surprise to know that those badly needed funds were given to us, not for hurling, but for our Gaelic football services! Continuing the surprise element, the name of the football team was none other than Kilkenny, in which jerseys we have a much treasured photo. Now more than a month later, after nine glorious relaxing days at sea, some of them spent in the rapturous climate of the Gulf Stream, we looked from the deck of the great Cunard liner towards Cobh's noble harbour. In 1849, Cobh was changed to Queenstown, because of Queen Victoria's visit to Ireland. It was also the place where vast numbers of Irish emigrants waved goodbye to their homeland.

With no news from home since we left, Seamus and myself, along with other passengers, made our descent down the gangway. Everyone waited for a few men who were ascending. One of them, stopped, greeting me by name, after which he shook me by the hand and said:

"I was very sorry to hear about your brother," he said.

His gesture, coupled with those words instantly evoked a shattering implication. Realising my obvious lack of information, he swiftly explained. "Your brother Bobby has had a serious farming accident, but he will be alright." The incident, which became a national news item, was a common enough mowing-bar farming accident, resulting in serious damage to the ligaments and tendons at the back of his ankle.

"He will recover – but not sufficently to ever play hurling again" was the medical prognosis.

Approximately two years on he did play again, and later again playing at full-forward, he was a member of the Rathnure team that in 1961, regained the County senior title. Although only thirty-two and looking his old self, he still, for a variety of reasons, was not the same. The main factor, his loss of appetite or interest in the game was compounded by family and work commitment. The Polo Grounds and Gaelic Park were destined to be his last two appearances in the county colours. Minus Bobby, but with much the same personnel as in previous years, Wexford looking for a fourth consecutive Leinster title, once again locked horns with their great rivals, Kilkenny.

Sport is strangely enigmatic. Ostensibly all the ingredients which have borne previous success are still there, like the committment to training or the well-honed skills, and the insatiable hunger for more titles. That's how it appears, but beneath the surface there is an imperceptable, intangible, unidentifiable slippage, for which there is no cure. That slippage has a label attached, and that label reads 'defeat.' Maybe what's wrong is the lack of that mysterious element called 'rising sap', and if that is the case, ours was certainly not upwardly mobile on this occasion, as an eager Kilkenny team literally wiped us off Croke Park to the tune of 6-9 to 1-5. In the first few minutes of this game, Ned Wheeler received an accidental blow, which resulted in his removal in an unconscious state to the Mater Hospital. After the game, Seamus Hearne and I called to see him. As the popular Ned lay there still unconscious and unaware of our humiliating defeat, I looked out of the ward window. The heavens had opened. That very moment for me was the nadir of the fifties. After this defeat, my brother Nickey, now approaching his thirty-sixth birthday, decided to retire from inter-county hurling. He did, however, line out for individual appearances with his club in the forthcoming local championships.

I mark Christy Ring

I said earlier that sport was enigmatic. Well, that element was further borne out when in late September, Wexford emphatically reversed the Leinster Final defeat by Kilkenny, now All-Ireland champions. Looked upon as an aged team, this Wexford victory 3-10 to 4-4 on Kilkenny's home ground surprised hurling pundits, and prompted some experts to support a notion that there was life in the old dogs yet, and indeed there was. On our winning way to the League Final, we disposed of Cork in New Ross by one point, 5-4 to 5-3. The only reason I mention this game is because on that occasion I had the honour of marking Christy Ring. After that game I could claim that I held the great man scoreless, but in all honesty he was only a shadow of his former self. In what J.D. Hickey of the *Irish Independent* newspaper reported as the greatest hurling game ever played, Wexford defeated Limerick in the subsequent League final. This was a truly amazing contest. From the throw-in, it was non-stop action in a see-saw struggle, with the final score 5-7 to 4-8. On the Wexford team, three new faces appeared amongst the old-timers. John Redmond, Martin Lyng and Harry O'Connor. Whilst this was the only major success for Martin Lyng and Harry O'Connor, they both hold an exceptionally high rating amongst critics of the game. Model sportsmen, their artistry was on a par with the best. The record book tells us that this Wexford team, backboned by half of the men who started out in 1950, would again oust great rivals Kilkenny in another Leinster Final classic. These Leinster Final clashes between the almost neighbouring counties had by now, in very knowledgeable minds, ousted the Tipperary/Cork Munster Final as the classic of the hurling world. The year was 1960. It was another thriller, and by a mere two points, with a score of 3-10 to 2-11, Wexford were through to their fifth All-Ireland final of the decade. In this dour win over the sporting black and amber men, I was judged by onlookers to have given the best display of my career. There were two non-Wexford players without whom this victory could not have been achieved. Seamus Quaid from Limerick and Sean Power of Waterford.

The subsequent final before over seventy-seven thousand spectators saw a Tipperary team that was rampant in Munster, now red hot favourites to take the title. In one of the biggest upsets in Final history, a Wexford team of old and new brushed them aside by almost double scores, 2-15 to 0-11. Every single one of the old timers played to his known ability, but none more so than greying veteran Padge Kehoe, whose hurling brain – and co-ordination with the younger team members – was mainly responsible for engineering Tipp's downfall. Amongst the younger players, John Mitchell's performance in the back line was the very epitome of top-class corner back defending. Behind him in goal, Pat Nolan, the most reliable keeper ever produced in the county, dealt efficiently with anything that came his way. The new Wexford full-forward, Jack Harding, made full use of the great occasion to gloriously carve his name in the annals of Wexford gaeldom. Of the other newcomers, Jimmy O'Brien and Tom Neville can also look back in pride. However, their contribution wasn't just confined to 1960. Two of the most tenacious, talented men of their era, they were the backbone of future Wexford title seeking attempts, culminating in another All-Ireland win in 1968. Finally, I come to John Nolan, the goalie's brother, who played alongside me in the half-back line and another forward known as Oliver 'Hopper' McGrath. By whatever criterion you wish to apply, Nolan's performance in this game was truly remarkable. Just imagine, to begin it was his first Senior Championships hurling game and his opponent was Jimmy Doyle, then acknowledged and subsequently selected as one of the best six forwards of the century. Add to that, the fact that Nolan's club hurling experience was mainly in junior grade. Consider his state of mind prior to walking on to Croke Park. He asked me for advice. "John," I said "You are going out to play on Jimmy Doyle, a gentleman and a true hurling artist who won't lay a finger on you. You've been playing intermediate and junior hurling, so what's going to happen between you and Doyle won't be anything as physical."

He seemed greatly relieved. Frankly I didn't know much about Nolan prior to this, and was in fact opposed to his selection. His subsequent display truly astounded me. A skinny-legged individual, cool and unperturbable as if he were strolling about a hay field back on his farm, masterly in his timing and clean striking, he uncannily outwitted his classy opponent. Once perhaps in a decade or even longer in most sports there comes along a talent that has not been seen previously. This happened in Wexford when a smallish lad by the name of Oliver 'Hopper' McGrath, appeared on the scene. A brilliant minor, overnight he was a sensation in senior ranks. Marking him was like trying to catch a butterfly with one hand, as in Maradonna fashion, he jinked his way through even the tightest defence. If I were making an educational film about the art and repertoire of hurling strokes, I would have this fella standing by the camera. I often studied him in training. Affected by problematic legs, he did very little running, keeping that for match day. In a game that demands such bodily contact, he lacked the necessary physique to compete in such manner, but his body swerve and natural artistry, which was mainly in his wrists, compensated handsomely. Like a professional golfer demonstrating the art of chipping, McGrath had such sensitivity, judgement and accuracy in his arms and wrists that from a short distance he was capable of stroking a succession of hurling balls into a bucket.

The Battle of New Ross

In the semi-final of the Oireachtas competition of 1960, Wexford and Cork clashed in New Ross. Clashed is the operative word. A hurling game between two counties that, for all the wrong reasons has been given a high vantage point in Irish folklore. Down the decades there has been many a hurling game punch-up and many a hurling game called off and all quickly forgotten about, but for whatever reasons of morbid curiosity, a couple of our national newspapers, having chewed the subject of this one, relentlessly pursued it. Even a year later, there were articles and poems about the infamous happenings. So much so that there is hardly a person of the era who doesn't know about 'The Battle of New Ross.'

From the start, an eager, tense Cork team adopted very belligerent tactics. On at least two occasions in the first half, with a calm approach, I endeavoured to reason with my opposite number, Eamon Goulding, about the methods he was using. It would be a euphemism to say he was pulling hard. I kept my cool, managing to ignore it. During the progress of the game, I was running back to cover as full-back Nick O'Donnell came out to make a clearance. His stroke was blocked and in the subsequent tackling, he sustained a head injury, groaning as he fell down. This injury looked purely accidental. Looking at O'Donnell lying injured upset me. I was standing about with the other players just watching, when I received a blow in my rib cage. In all my time playing I had never been stabbed with the handle of a hurley in such a manner, or known such darting pain. My subsequent action was purely reflex as I instantly turned about, releasing my left closed fist, making contact with the jaw of my marker, Eamon Goulding, who was standing behind me. The referee immediately came across and justifiably ordered me off. It was the only time I suffered such a fate and I must say that my march to the sideline, brought about a hitherto unknown feeling of shame. Much to my surprise, Goulding was also ordered off, so the referee obviously witnessed what happened just prior to my retaliation.

Walking up the sideline with Goulding beside me, my foremost thought was to get dressed and get out of the place. Walking along silently, he was putting conversation my way. I looked left at him.

Oozing confidence, I was really surprised to hear him say, "If it's fighting you're after, I will give all you want."

I remember saying in a subsequent letter to Central Council that I was issued a challenge that I could not ignore. Deep down, I've always seen myself as a bit of a coward with self-preservation high on my list of priorities. Consequently, I was more than surprised at my fortitude and calmness.

After a dozen steps or so, I turned to him. "That's a deal. You're on."

The watching crowd did not suspect what was going to take place. They kept their eyes on the game as we made for the exit from the sideline, ostensibly heading for respective dressing-rooms. Just as we approached the exit, I turned and said to him, 'Let's go somewhere private and how about a witness?' He agreed. I pointed to a man wearing a brown hat. I assured Goulding that this man, George Ryan, from Enniscorthy, would see fair play. Ryan came with us and we all agreed that behind the toilet block was the most suitable and private place. We did not want a mob around. All three of us calmly strolled behind the toilets. Eamon and I dropped our hurleys. "Right then," I said. "Are you ready?"

He adopted a boxing stance. Going any further with this is purely egotistical, but the fact remains that Goulding never suspected that I was as proficient with my fists as I turned out to be. Neither did he suspect my true strength. In a matter of seconds, he was practically out as he staggered helplessly about from straight punches. He went down. Getting up, he looked a sorry sight. The next few minutes were terrifying. Part of the crowd on top of an embankment, who spotted what was happening, came running. The fight was over at this stage, but a rather big bossy individual suggested we go elsewhere and continue. I gave Goulding an inquiring look. "I think you have had enough," I said. He nodded. Trying to get him out of there safely was a frightening experience. At one stage I had to put my arms around him, screaming at the crowd to disperse. It was a manly fight, with the result naturally making it a pleasant memory for me. Years later Goulding and I met socially and had a good laugh about it all.

In the second half, Oliver 'Hopper' McGrath, one of our forwards and an out and out ball player was, when going through, cruelly chopped down by his Cork marker O'Riordan. It appears that this particular incident infuriated a small portion of the mainly Wexford crowd, causing a slight encroachment, which the referee was unable to stem, as followers from both sides, strolled onto the pitch. Eventually the game was called off and Cork, being in front, were subsequently declared winners. There is no doubt that there was questionable behaviour amongst both sets of followers with apparently an odd punch being thrown, but no real battle as such, as far as I know. Players from both sides still on the pitch remained on the periphery of would be violence. There was also mutual goading by rival supporters, which continued later on in the town of New Ross. For example, a county jersey was tied behind a motor car and dragged through the town. Another jersey was tantalizingly waved for a period through a hotel upper window. Such calculated goading, with the atmosphere in the town as it was, was a down payment on further violence. Fortunately, nothing more occurred.

Most of what had happened on the field is possible in team games and therefore, to an extent, can be understood, but there is something which to this day, I just cannot understand. Maybe I'm naive in believing so, but the Wexford team of that era was looked upon as a fine lot of sportsmen who played the game and ninety per cent of the time were never involved in unsporting incidents. Every player on the team throughout his career was devoid of rough play censure by his own county board or from a higher level. I believe it fair to say that this yardstick would not apply to the Cork team that took part in that ill-fated ignominious game. I pose the question: Why was there such a sustained effort to blacken the name of such a fine sporting team as Wexford? A subsequent hearing in Croke Park exonerated them. I again ask the question: Why was such an unnecessary theme pursued so relentlessly by newspapers? The Battle of New Ross, as we all know, was really fought in 1798.

CHAPTER THIRTY

"Look Ramie," I said, "I just cannot get any smell."

"Okay," he replied, "but come over here and try again. Now can you get it?"

"No, I can't," I repeated "Anyway I'm not like you. My nose has been broken twice playing hurling, so my faculty of smell is not what it should be."

"Well, even so, it's still amazing that you cannot get a whiff of that. It's rank balldoon piss you know, and it's coming through that skylight from the valley where those cats hang out. It's very difficult to work with and I think you should have a word with Mrs Donovan about her cats."

Ramie Kelly, who along with an apprentice and myself, ran the shop, was a fastidious young man but a shrewd judge in everything he said and did. In a flat with a separate entrance over the rear of the premises lived Jimmy Donovan and his wife. A childless couple, Jimmy was a janitor in a local bank and known as 'Sir Gordon' because of his likeness to the great jockey, Gordon Richards, and also his love of having a little flutter on the nags. Mrs Donovan may have been a small, insignificant looking lady, but she was one person whose respect I would like to think I had. She always looked at you with humourous friendly eyes, behind which there was plenty of moral fibre. Never did I witness a frown on her face. Now as her landlord, I was faced with the distasteful task of bringing up the subject of her smelly cats. Climbing the backstairs to knock on her door, I was unable to conquer a gut feeling that those same cats meant a lot to her.

The door opened and there stood the diminutive Mrs Donovan. An engaging smile accompanied a first name greeting.

"Do come in," she said.

"No, Mrs Donovan," I said. "Thank you very much but I just wanted to have a word about your cats."

At the sound of the word 'cat', her facial sunshine instantly shuttered over. It struck fear in my heart. I quickly did a u-turn. After a couple of light coughs as I desperately searched for a way out, I clicked my fingers and mumbled: "Are you sure they are all there? I just thought I saw one on the street." She speedily turned about, went and looked through the window, after which the bright smile returned. "Thank you Billy – they are fine. I can see them all out there." I retreated in full knowledge that when it came to her cats, she was one woman that I was not prepared to do battle with. I went back to the shop and informed Kelly. If he wanted to take up the issue with her, he was welcome to do so.

About a month later, around the beginning of November, I went to my local for a pint. Now a yuppie watering hole, known as the 'Centenary Stores', it has reverted to traditional decor. Then its clientele reflected the personality of its popular owner, Joe Ahearne. I'm sure well-known county footballers and hurlers will empathise with me when I say that the moment you walk into such a pub your presence immediately instigates a discussion on the game you play. You are expected by some to give a little performance, involving cogent analysis mixed with a spattering of humour. There are times, depending on your mood, when this can be enjoyable, and as we all know, there are also times when you just want to be on your own. On this particular night, for whatever reason I cannot recall, but my socialising gears were not meshing. In spite of the ball being literally hopped in front of me, not once but several times, I still maintained an obdurate silence. Of course at that time with Wexford on top in the hurling world, the subject of the game wasn't difficult to set in motion. Anyway, after a few large mouthfuls of Arthur G's mood-altering substance, I perked up and went on the attack.

"You know," I said, "you fellas astound me. I doubt if there is another sport in the world you are capable of discussing other than hurling."

"Frankly, right now," I continued, "I would prefer to discuss anything other than that, even . . ."

I searched for some eccentric indulgence. "Even cock-fighting."

I am afraid I was not good company and my last comment more or less halted any budding conversation on the subject of hurling. About half-an-hour later, that wild youth and agent provocateur, Pat Doyle, who was involved in a dart game, sidled up to me.

"I noticed," he grinned, "that you mentioned cock-fighting earlier on. Well, you know that I could arrange a cock-fight right now ."

With dismissive, acerbic nods, I said, "Sure you could Pat. I know you. You're the type who could arrange anything."

"Honest to God, I could" he asserted. "If you are prepared to give me a little help. It can be done, I promise. I'll need a car for one thing."

With as much teasing cruelty as I could muster I countered:

"At ten o'clock on a November night, just like that, you can arrange a cock-fight!"

It had no effect. Disposing of an enthusiast can be difficult, but opposing an irresistible fanatic is another matter. With unbridled belief in what I thought was a ludicrous idea, he continued to make his case, which proved to have an interesting appeal to the foolish side of my nature. Anyway, he went on, "Our farmyard cock, a big black fella, is at war with a neighbour, Bernie Murphy's farm yard cock. They're always at it. Bernie and the missus live alone and will have been to the Mission in Castlebridge. They visit relations afterwards and don't come home till all hours. I know Bernie's set-up well and he doesn't lock the fowl house door. No bother either with our fella. I'll just have to spend five minutes in the kitchen with me mudder, and on the way out I'll get him."

The ludicrous idea, which by now, had permeated bar conversation, was gathering momentum. The prospect of a cock-fight, hitherto unheard of in Wexford, seemed to increase liquid intake, and it wasn't long before all imaginations were inflamed sufficiently for the idea to receive a resounding majority approval.

Pat and myself, with a borrowed flash lamp, set off. Nearing Bernie Murphy's cottage, I slowly began to identify him as a very highly respected customer in my shop. I could feel my toes curling up in shame at the thought of this man finding out, or worse still, catching me redhanded raiding his hen house. With positive assurances from Pat that this couldn't happen, I remained silent.

"Now, when I open the door, you'll see him sitting on the roost, centre, with the hens all round him. Never mind the hens – just keep the light on the cock. Dazzle him, make sure he blinks and I'll do the rest."

Bernie Murphy's cottage and little outhouses were models of proper upkeep and arrangement. Here was this magnificent big Red Island cockerel living in an idyllic set-up, surrounded by his harem. I was unable to suppress a tinge of envy. In a state of slumber, the hens who were also dazzled by the flash light, began to make disapproving censurous clucks. It was all over in seconds as Pat, from beneath and behind the slanting roost, appeared with the cock upside down and held by both legs.

I was very glad to get out of there and shed the criminal feeling that had enveloped me as I stood at the hen house door, holding the flash light. The rest was easy. Right on time, Pat re-appeared from his home farmyard, holding another fine big black cockerel upside down.

"We'll put this fella in the boot" he shouted "These two hate each other so much, we don't want them to start in the car."

On arrival back at the pub our *fait accompli* announcement was greeted with intense anticipation. The thought of two lords of rival dung heaps in such close proximity and about to engage in gladiatorial battle, added a sharp edge to everyone's thirst. After consuming what I felt, was a well-deserved pint, something crossed my mind. Where were we going to hold this cock-fight? The barman immediately squashed the idea of having it on the premises, but the irrepressible Pat quickly had alternative plans. "Why not in your shop? In at the back," was his suggestion. The pub almost emptied as all and sundry carrying the two cocks, marched the hundred yards or so up the street, and into my menswear shop, in the process giving an affectionate greeting to the now extinct pedestrian Garda. The neon lights were switched on, the cocks were held for a short while to make sure they had properly identified each other. After about thirty seconds, with everyone now unobtrusively backed off to the side, they were released. We watched with thumping hearts. They marched straight towards one another, but continued on as if the other didn't exist. They then stood blinking and disorientated, and almost in unison dropped large ploppers on the floor. They were caught and repositioned, but again they totally ignored each other's presence, and again dropped more ploppers. Pat, by now mystified and apologetic at the lack of aggression between such known archenemies, suggested catching them once more and forcing them to rub beaks. This was done – but luckily, in hindsight, to no avail. It was all much ado about nothing. Having thoroughly cleaned up, we immediately returned them both to their respective roosts and the matter was written off and forgotten.

That is until I entered the shop next day. My mind was elsewhere, when I noticed Kelly standing in a corner going 'sniff sniff'. He then moved elsewhere and again began another series of sniffs. Remaining silent, I just observed him. Eventually he came to me. "You know," he said, "I hate raising such a subject again, but I am beginning to think there is something the matter with my nose, because right now I could swear that I smell hen shite."

"Well, there you are Ramie," I said with a smile, "your nostrils could also be playing tricks as in the case of Mrs Donovan's cats."

Advancing years

1961 is a year that Wexford hurling followers will want to forget. The reigning All-Ireland champions were well beaten by six points by Dublin in the Leinster final. A lot of people saw history repeating itself here with the memory of our shock defeat of 1952 by Dublin. This, however, was not quite the case. With the benefit of hindsight, followers in general acclaimed this fine, exceptionally talented Dublin team, who were unlucky to be narrowly defeated by Tipperary in the subsequent All-Ireland final. On a personal note, during 1961 there were still some bright moments ahead. Now at the ripe old age of thirty-one, they were to be of great help in maintaining my interest in the game and more importantly still, my appetite for training.

When a player passes the thirty mark, his sporting life can become difficult. In his prime as an established star, a poor display is quickly forgiven and sometimes blithely referred to as 'an off day.' Once over thirty, a similar poor performance can be looked upon in a totally different light. Most times it's attributed to being past it, a fact that can be disheartening to someone who still feels he has more to offer. At the top of the heap in any sport, a small slip is quickly noticed and quickly exploited. When over thirty, if he wants to maintain his rating and form, a player has to make more than accustomed unwanted sacrifices and contend with the contradictory elements involved. Briefly, he now needs more training but has less appetite for it. However, if he is the type who loves the game and is lucky enough to keep an undiminished competitive stalwartnesss, this shouldn't be too difficult. The worst enemy in a lot of cases is not advancing years, but instead, advancing weight. More training and less desire for it is one problem, but if you're unlucky to have the sort of metabolism that automatically sees extra poundage added to your frame, irrespective of all precaution, then you are faced with an uphill battle. This means an inescapable loss of speed, and over thirty, only a player with true talent will survive at the top in such circumstances. Finally for a player to carry on in his thirties, the most essential factor of all is one of incentive and desire. Something is driving him on. In most cases that something is the prospect of a first title. In others, it's the attraction of yet more honours.

After our Leinster final defeat by Dublin in 1961, I took a personal audit and was surprised to find that my appetite for hurling was as keen as ever. Also my lanky frame was well-capable of absorbing the little extra poundage which is natural with ageing, and thus keeping me outside of the avoirdupois disadvantage. When Rathnure regained the Wexford senior hurling championship, I found myself named as captain of the Rathnure and Wexford teams, the latter a team which went within a whisker of pulling off a major upset later in 1961. In spite of advancing years, which applied to the majority of the panel, this now battle-worn purple and gold brigade pulled out all the stops to draw with All-Ireland champions, Tipperary, in a thrilling Croke Park Oireachtas final. We may have lost the replay, but in those two games, we regained a lot of respect and issued a warning that when ready and in the proper frame of mind, this Wexford team of old and new were still a formidable combination.

Those particular games with Tipperary evoke special memories for myself. My opponent was the same man whom I confronted in the 1960 All-Ireland final, and on another occasion when I was picked on the Rest of Ireland selection against champions, Tipperary. One of the best centre-forwards of his era, Liam Devaney, apart from his own scoring potential, was the truly skilled professional, masterly in his distribution of intelligent passes on the ground or other wise, to his two incisive wingmen, usually Jimmy Doyle and Domie Nealon. The late hurling correspondent, John D. Hickey, rated that Tipperary half-forward line the best he ever saw. The scoring power of this trio had wiped out formidable defences. I always believed if you could curtail Devaney's defence opening 'lay offs', then you seriously hampered the thrust of the entire Tipperary forward division. I would like to think that in the 1960 final, without being seen to play what is termed a good game, I did nonetheless prevent Liam from achieving his distributive ball destructiveness. Devaney's display throughout the Championships, and especially in the All-Ireland final of 1961, had him an automatic choice for the title 'Hurler of the Year.' In the drawn Oireachtas game against Tipperary, I took Liam by surprise. Before it, I had prepared assiduously and felt confident. Liam was not his usual self and as the likely winner of the 'Hurler of the Year Award', my performance against him as acclaimed by the press, seriously undermined his position in that regard. The return contest in the replay is one I will not easily forget. He was a different opponent. Like a coiled spring, he quickly subjected me to previously unexperienced but legitimate pulling. During the interim between the final and the replay, Liam had obviously changed. I too was even fitter for the replay, in which again I was credited with outplaying him. Around this time a certain press man phoned me to say that after those two displays I was running very close to supplanting Liam Devaney for the title 'Hurler of the Year.' Justice, however, was done and Liam Devaney, one of the truly gifted natural centre-forwards and a fine sportsman, was subsequently named 'Hurler of the Year' of 1961. The following further underlines this man's unique talent. He holds the incredible distinction of playing in fourteen different positions for his native Tipperary.

Walking up the steps of the Hogan stand to collect any sort of cup is a guaranteed memory of a lifetime for even the worst amnesiac. After the Leinster hurling final of 1962, in which Wexford defeated Kilkenny 3-9 to 2-10, my moment of such glory arrived. Within roughly a period of a decade, the mighty Bob O'Keefe team, champions of Leinster cup, was paying its sixth visit to the banks of the lovely Slaney. There was great rejoicing, and Wexford followers were in an up mood at the prospect of yet another show-down with old foes, Tipperary, who were seeking two titles in a row. There are some finals, not memorable as great contests, but due to perhaps, freak incidents or an unforgettable individual performance, that are destined to remain sporting voyages of the mind. There are others, far more classical and far more qualified as pulsating combatative struggles, that are somehow consigned to the shadows of sporting memory. For me, I shall always see the 1962 Wexford-Tipperary hurling final in the latter category, but still one of the greatest ever played. For me also, it is one game, that for the strongest personal reasons, I would like to push into oblivion. I'm sure anyone who has ever trained for a serious final will identify with my words when I say that a big mental and physical investment in training, resulting in the expected general increase in fitness quotient, gives a player a secure confident feeling. This is vital as the match day of reckoning approaches. On the other hand, if that big effort is not rewarded, and for some inexplicable reason, instead of sharpening your fitness edge, all that effort in training seems to be worsening your position, then you have a player who is not looking forward to the big day.

As captain of the Wexford team prior to the 1962 final against Tipperary, that is exactly how I felt and was. It's a horrible feeling leading your team on to Croke Park to do battle for the highest honours, knowing in your heart that you, the captain, are not up to the required fitness level, and that it's something, in spite of all effort, you could not put right. Your corpuscles just refuse to bounce. As I led my team-mates during the pre-match parade, my only contingency plan was a forlorn hope that I would be lucky and that I would get the breaks, and figuratively speaking, that's what happened, only not the sort that I had dreamed and hoped for. After just five minutes, during a mêlée, as I went hurtling to the ground, a hurley connected with the base of my thumb, causing a multiple fragment fracture. It necessitated a plaster of paris for eight months and took years to properly mend.

This game had a bizarre beginning. Almost before we or our followers had time to settle, the sharp-shooting Tipperary forwards had planted the ball twice in the Wexford net, then the game settled into the customary battle. During the second half, Wexford with the help of three enduring new stars, Phil Wilson, Paul Lynch and Ned Colfer, in a welter of frenzied excitement, levelled and, I believe, went one point in front. One of these scores I registered from a seventy. Bearing in mind my disability, I still wonder at the achievement. You're thinking 'Why was I left on the field?' At half time I requested to be substituted. This was ruled out, added to which our medical dressing-room observer astonishingly dismissed my hand injury, which was not acknowledged until the following week. In the dying minutes, with Wexford a point up, that Tip flyer, blonde Tom Ryan rounded me. I watched helplessly and lead-footed as he headed for the square. During those few moments, as he went careering in with goal written all over him, I just fought off an impulse to let go my hurley stick, boomerang fashion, at his shoulders. But I didn't.

By not doing so, I missed out on the chance to be a possible Wexford hero or an unforgettable villian in the eyes of Tipperary followers. 'Titanic struggle' is a description I use guardedly, but this game was most certainly that. A humdinger, it never abated, ending in a just about deserved Tipperary victory 3-9 to 2-10. Had I been substituted at half-time it's possible that we may have won. That sporting ponderable and the hurtful recall of my own display, are now just distant memories, that on certain occasions return to haunt me. During the immediate aftermath of that final, my physical wound was indeed severe. Nonetheless it in no way compared to the severity of the emotional wound caused by such a narrow defeat and my own inadequate display. Any man who has captained his county in an All-Ireland final defeat and performed poorly, will know what I'm driving at. The pain is now a long time gone and forgotten, but on the Monday immediately after that game it was indeed severe.

CHAPTER THIRTY-ONE

At this stage in my business life, I had opened a second premises, a furniture shop also on Wexford's main street. The shops were about one hundred and fifty yards apart, and I was a familiar sight as I walked from one to the other. On the Monday after the final, consumed with sporting anguish and mental torture, my mind in a shambolic state, I walked from one premises to the other. In short, I was in a black mood. The sound of my name being called out was a welcome distraction. Without looking, I knew who it was. The accent had a familiar Scottish, Northern Ireland ring, a relic of where the owner had spent his youth.

"Wallie, hey Wallie. How are yi gettin on?"

Standing in his delapidated electrical shop door was Tom Quigley, an aged hulk of a man, now holding forth in the last bastion of what was once a large thriving business. A veritable frontiersman in the fledgling days of urban and rural electrification, Tom had made a fortune and spent it. Now with no family interested in continuing the business and with just a threadbare stock on the shelves, he sat behind the counter, a small electric fire between his feet. A character right out of a Dickens page, always wearing that soiled waistcoat, in his slippers he made an occasional foray to the shop door. Standing with hands clasped behind his back, he would peer up and down the street. His sagging lower lip had a little red channel in the centre, the very spot where Tom had sucked from hundreds of capless Baby Powers. Now, having shut himself out from the world, he was more or less a recluse, whose escapism was through his tipple. He acknowledged very few people. I can boast of being one of them. We were bonded because of a mutual love of driving horses and carts. Tom had a lovely trap and cob whilst I boasted a trap and a 'back to back'. The mere mention of a good trotting cob and a fanatical light flickered in Tom's hoary old countenance. Crossing over the street to him, he asked me,

"Well Wallie, where did yi go for the wakeend?"

"I was in Dublin, Tom," I replied.

"Aye, and what were yi duin there?"

"I was playing a hurling match."

"Aye thin, and did yi wan?"

"No Tom," I replied "We didn't."

"Aye and who were yi playin?"

"Tipperary"

"Tapperary. Aye, 'aye be God, I hear tell them Tapperary men are good at the hurlin' – and I'm told they practice a lot."

"Indeed they do, indeed they do Tom," I replied and marched on.

Jet lag lesson

In 1963, after yet another classic battle with Kilkenny, Wexford went out early in the race for provincial honours. This narrow defeat marked up my fourteenth year in championship hurling. Even though I say so myself, I produced as good a performance as I ever did for my native purple and gold. At thirty-three years of age, a player is usually contemplating retirement, but there is nothing better suited to keeping such thoughts from his mind as retaining the ability to perform successfully at the highest level. This I felt I was doing. Also in the Spring of 1964, my enthusiasm in that area received a further boost with the announcement that I was one of six nominated to play in the Kennedy games in New York. We were slotted on to different teams in the New York equivalent of our National League finals. Amongst the six were footballers; Sean Murphy (Kerry), Joe Lennon (Down) and Des Foley (Dublin).

The idea behind all this was that guest star players, on opposite sides in final games, would swell attendance figures. You must also bear in mind the high emotional content involved. In the aftermath of President Kennedy's assassination the Irish-Americans still suffering from the shock were on an irresistible high to raise funds for the erection of an appropriate memorial to the late President back in the country and county of his ancestry. In order to draw the crowds, guest players got a big publicity. Fine, but they were also expected to perform, and according to their status. When I got my ego-boosting invitation I decided to get myself ready. I took the invitation and my personal fitness very seriously, leaving no stone unturned. Wexford were already doing well in the National League and due to meet Cork in the semi-final. Having trained seriously, I carried my fastidious approach a stage further, asking to get out there well in advance for climatisation purposes. After settling into The Henry Hudson Hotel, I actually took the subway to Central Park, and in tracksuit I went jogging. There was nothing to go wrong, at least that's what I thought at the time. On the Thursday evening, before the game, this fine-looking athlete heading in my direction, crossed the foyer of the hotel. Recognising him, I stood up. We indulged in a warm handshake. I was delighted to make the acquaintance of that greatest of Kerry footballers, star half-back Sean Murphy.

"We know you're here," he said "and I've been asked by the Kerrymen's Association to invite you to the function in my honour tonight."

"I'd love to Sean," I said, "but I'm taking things seriously and at a time like this would wish to pass on late nights."

After some incombatable Kerry persuasion, I agreed to go along. After all, I told myself, I had two more nights to catch up on sleep. At 3 a.m. I hit the sack. On Friday evening, in the same foyer, who crossed over in my direction only another footballing great, Joe Lennon of Down. Down won an All-Ireland in 1960 and so did Wexford, he pointed out.

"You're pencilled in as a Celeb at the dinner in my honour tonight."

Sometime later, about 3.30 a.m. I was comforting myself that at least on Saturday night I would freak out in the land of Nod and catch up on all lost hours of sleep, which I seem to need more than the average person. About 5 p.m. on Saturday evening I heard my name coming over the hotel public address system. It was two excited, but two of the most hospitable and generous men I had ever met. Namely Jack Hearne (brother of Seamus) and Mylie Doran, both of the Wexford men's New York Association. Guess what? They had something to tell me. The function in my honour had to be brought forward, for reasons outside their control, to that night.

Dare I mention that old chestnut about 'beggars not being choosers.' At approximately 4 a.m. on the morning of the game, bleary-eyed and mentally deranged, I flung myself into bed, clinging frantically, but insecurely to the notion that I would remain in bed until about an hour-and-a-half before the game, which was scheduled for 4.30 p.m. By then, I told myself, my batteries would be sufficiently recharged. After this I would take a taxi to the Gaelic Park. Yes. That would put me right, or so I thought. I was in bed for about four hours, wafting along serenely in a relaxing slumber, when I was awakened by heavy pounding on the bedroom door. With a thick paste of sleep holding my eyelashes together, I stumbled towards the door and opened it. Two enthusiastic members of the newly formed Wexford hurling club burst into the room. They had fantastic news. I listened with stultifying dismay and disbelief as they informed me about their exciting last minute discovery. The New York Wexford hurling team was having its first outing that very morning, and guess what? It was discovered that I was eligible to play for them. This would be fantastic for the lads they gleefully chorused. Games on Sunday in Gaelic Park went from early morning throughout the day. By leaving right now we would be in time. My chin dropped to my chest as I stood there gazing at them with eyes resembling piss holes in the snow. They didn't seem to care or notice my plight as I repeated.

'. . . and this will be fantastic for the lads . . .'

Togged off for this junior game, mentally drained, in the midst of a very excited group of hurlers, I stumbled on to the rough surface of Gaelic Park. There were just a few people there, the bulk of which during the game marched up and down the side line yelling non-stop. My old team-mate, Seamus Hearne, now working in New York, and playing at midfield was the ringleader and principal motivator amongst the Wexford players. He was expecting a big performance from his old pal. The ball was thrown in and the game was on. My opponent came running and took up his position alongside me. After five minutes or so I began to feel like something out of a zoo as I realised he was continually eyeing me up and down. Running about like a lost labrador and unable to concentrate, my feeble performance was quickly targeted. First it was my old pal, Seamus Hearne.

"What the f . . . hell is the matter with you. You're a f . . . dead loss." Finally a bloke with a rich New York accent opened up at me from the sideline. "And that son of a bitch is supposed to play in the big game come afternoon." That did it. I had had enough of this exploitation. I just walked off the pitch, went to the locker room and put my clothes back on. Complete with my gear, I reappeared on the pitch. It was now about ten o'clock in the morning and a lovely warm day. I called over one of the Wexford New York officials.

"Look" I said "Sorry about that, but I can't concentrate. Now, do you see that grassy mound there in the very far corner? I'm going up there to lie down. If I'm not back here by four o'clock, come and rouse me."

He agreed. When I went up, it was just what I had hoped for. Nicely secluded with a good matting of fresh grass, I was soon stretched out and fast asleep. At 4.30 p.m., the New York Gaelic Park, owned and promoted by the legendary John Kerry O'Donnell, was packed to capacity. Clare and Cork were about to take to the field for the New York version of a League final. In the dressing room, togged off, I was fiercely reclaiming all my concentration and indulging in knee-bending, muscle-alerting exercises. Whilst doing all this with No. 6 on my back, I was wearing the Cork jersey. The following Sunday I was due back at Croke Park, centre-back for Wexford against Cork in the National League semi-final. Victory in the League that year carried a prize of a trip to New York. Bearing this in mind, the Wexford New York officials prudently insisted that in the game about to start, they would prefer that I played with Cork not against them. Miraculously later in the week the Irish New York papers, such as *The New York Echo* in its coverage of those games rated one W. Rackard, centre-back for Cork in the hurling final as man of the match!

The next Saturday morning, I arrived back at Dublin airport feeling dreadfully tired. I went straight to my youngest sister's house, Rita, now married to Doctor Joe Murray, who lived in Clontarf. In retrospect making a big mistake, I went straight to bed. Foolishly unaware of jet lag and changing time zones, I slept soundly. The next day standing at centre-back in the middle of Croke Park, just as the game was about to begin, I was overwhelmed with a desire to creep into bed and go to sleep, and for all I contributed to Wexford's win over Cork, I might as well have done so. Arriving back on the day prior to this game was utter stupidity. In fact, I shouldn't have been allowed to play. In the subsequent League final, Tipperary trounced Wexford 5-12 to 1-4.

The final whistle

This comprehensive defeat had hurling cognoscenti marinating the belief that it was time for some of the older players to retire. My display in the League final most certainly put me amongst them.

Although some had retired by the 1963 Championships, the annual confrontation with Kilkenny of 1964 saw the final fade out of nearly all of the pioneering players of the fifties. In a hurling maelstrom, the old rivals produced yet another classic with Kilkenny eventually getting through 5-9 to 4-8, this was my fifteenth year to play championship hurling. Contrary to my display in the league final, I had an excellent game and felt that I had reclaimed my old form. Thoughts of retirement didn't even enter my head. In 1964, my club Rathnure was also defeated in the Wexford championships. Soon the telephone was ringing, with calls from GAA correspondents, and all asking the same question, "Was I retiring?" and what were my thoughts on the matter. "I don't feel like it right now," was my answer, "and I have no idea of how or when I will come to such a decision." In the autumn of 1964 on a Sunday evening I headed in the direction of the old homestead in Killanne. My mother during the week, had asked me to come up in time for my supper.

On this journey back to the parish and village of my birth, my usual desire to enjoy the beautiful scenery was peculiarly absent. Instead, I found myself in a very introspective mood. Parking my car at the kitchen door, my mother was quickly on the scene. In no time I had an enormous plate of delicious cold roast placed in front of me. Having completely satisfied my appetite, we chatted for about half-an-hour. Then I stood up

"Mammy," I said "That was great. Thank you. I'll just go up and see who's in the bar. I'll be back in to say goodbye."

Several regulars were drinking at the bar. The conversation inevitably turned to hurling. I slipped away as soon as I politely could and stood uncertainly on the doorstep to the back yard. There was something different which had never before struck me. For a moment I couldn't identify it, then I realised, it was the silence.

Walking past the kitchen towards the old dairy, something made me open the door. Inside, instead of the milk churns and big wooden tables laden with large bowls for the cream to rise in, there was a big ugly furnace with piles of wood surrounding it. This fed the central heating system in the house. I hurriedly closed the door and moved round the yard. No Shep to greet me, tail wagging and eyes alight with welcome – just a disinterested collie-cross scratching himself in a corner. I looked in the hen house. No signs of life, merely a musty smell and dust where once there had been a bustling, cackling feathered community. On to the cowshed – again emptiness. The pig house told the same story. The stables evoked even more memories.

Not a horse in sight. I decided not to climb into the loft overhead where John Kelly's and Nickey's initials were graven into the wall for posterity. Instead, I wandered sadly in the direction of the haggard. Here was the six span hayshed, now redundant. Instead of sweet-smelling hay, it housed a variety of lorries and tractors. At the back on fresh ground, new farming methods were winning out in the shape of silage pits and baled hay.

As I stood alone in the emptiness of the haggard, I felt I was being watched, and turning round, met the doleful gaze of Bill, the chestnut cob, as he stood old and alone in the adjoining paddock. He had grown very heavy and developed what's known as a 'cresty' neck. "Poor old man," I soothed, as we walked towards each other, at least you're still here." He snickered and managed a short trot to the fence and we stood for a few moments in refound companionship.

"See you, Bill," I said, and walked away towards the road. For no reason I can explain, I felt a heavy weight in the region of my solar plexis as, standing at the old storehouse wall, I gazed down the road. It seemed I was at some turning point in my life and in my mind's eye, ghosts from the past came walking up and down the road towards me. Auld Tommy, looking content and jaunty as I remembered him before his first wife's death; Lydia, stepping out with her pail, short skirts swinging about her shapely legs; Fred Crabbe with his white enamel bucket hanging from his shoulder, the inevitable jaw-warmer pipe glued to the corner of his mouth; a bicycle with the familiar ballooning coat of Pat Lynch, and Coakley with his cows.

I returned to the parlour. My mother was alone, knitting socks for her grandchildren by the fireside.

"I'll be off Mummy." I said. "Will you be alright?'

"Don't worry about me, Bobby and Betty should be back soon. Meanwhile, take these jackets back to your shop" she instructed, "Bobby is keeping one." I picked up the brown parcel and with a final "See you again soon." I went out to the car. When I opened the boot, there were two hurls and a ball staring up at me. I dropped in the parcel and picked up a hurley and the ball. Tapping the ball on the stick and seeing the dairy door from the corner of my eye, the old temptation returned. It was still an irresistible target. As I threw the ball in the air, with the intention of striking it at the door, a voice resounded through my head.

"No hurling at the dairy door. Do you understand? No hurling at the dairy door."

Suddenly I was a guilty small boy again and at that moment something clicked in my mind as I dropped in the ball and the hurley and slammed the car boot. I had made my decision. I had played my last senior hurling game for Wexford.

Driving around onto the road, as I approached the cross, I slowed right down. Once again my mind started playing tricks with me. In the time warp I had become caught up in, I was shocked at my surroundings. Stopping the car, I just sat and looked around. The Crabbes had long since left and their once dapper little cottage, the venue of so many delightful tea parties, was now a derelict ruin – as was the cottage next to it. Opposite, the Garda barracks was also empty. The era of the squad car had taken over. Bike-pushing policemen were just a memory. Johnny Neill, the famed village ploughman, had also gone, his cottage and little out-buildings on the other side of the cross levelled to the ground, the site was purchased by the National Telephone Company. I turned the key in the ignition.

Going left, and eventually passing Caim church, I could see the lights of Enniscorthy twinkling ahead – the paternal bulk of the cathedral lurking in the shadows. I drove through the narrow streets and over the bridge, heading right towards Wexford. As my car gathered speed, so did my mind. Like a drowning man, my life flashed past me. My hurling career had lasted almost twenty years since I first togged off in the Wexford colours as a raw lad of fifteen or sixteen for the minor team. Oylegate loomed up ahead. Careering on, I was soon on a hill above beautiful Ferrycarrig, with the lights of Wexford beckoning ahead.

My feelings? A mixture of pride, regret, sadness and, yes, relief. That monkey on my back called 'committment to training' was gone forever. My world would never be the same again. This chapter of my life had ended and I felt whatever was to come could never be as totally satisfying. How wrong I was . . .

INDEX